IRISH SOLDIERS
IN EUROPE
17th-19th Century

For the patrons of the
Newberry Library
Best wishes

George B. Clark

DATE DUE

JAN 14 2014			
FEB 0 1 2014			
the card is lost			

MERCIER PRESS

Cork

www.mercierpress.ie

Trade enquiries to CMD BookSource,
55a Spruce Avenue, Stillorgan Industrial Park,
Blackrock, County Dublin

© George B. Clark, 2010

ISBN: 978 1 85635 662 6

10 9 8 7 6 5 4 3 2 1

A CIP record for this title is available from the British Library

Printed and bound in the EU.

This book is dedicated to my beloved wife of many years,
Jeanne J.D. Clark
and my friend of many years,
James T. McIlwain, MD

CONTENTS

… then Kelly said:
'When Michael, the Irish Archangel, stands,
The Angel with the sword,
And the battle-dead from a hundred lands
Are ranged in one big horde,
Our line, that for Gabriel's trumpet waits,
Will stretch three deep that day,
From Jehoshaphat to the Golden Gates –
Kelly and Burke and Shea.'
'Well, here's thanks God for the race and the sod!'
Said Kelly and Burke and Shea.

Joseph I.C. Clarke (1900?)

PREFACE

The idea for this book originated many years ago. I decided to include only those individuals whose success in a continental European country was far beyond what they might have accomplished if they had remained in Ireland. Additionally I decided the book would be limited to those who have not been widely written about before. Therefore none of the Dillons or Lally of France, nor even the great Max Browne of Austria are included.

One factor of great significance was how to decide who was Irish. Mostly those included, or their progeny, were born in Ireland. A few grandchildren and great-grandchildren have been mentioned if they attained a strong legendary place in their adopted or native land. I have not included those Irish who served in the United States nor those who went to Great Britain. I have included only those on the European continent and in a few colonies. While religion has not been a criterion for selection or omission, most were Roman Catholic.

One term that could create some confusion is *Scot* or a variant like *Scoti Ibernic*. Historically almost every nation in the western world identified the Irish as 'Scots'. This came from the fact that the Romans named the Irish who raided the British coast *Scoti*. Later Scotland took its name from a group of these raiders who settled in the northern portion of the land of the Picts soon after the Romans left the British Isles, establishing the powerful Dal Riata kingdom. In the dark ages the Irish, still known as *Scoti*, established abbeys and universities in almost every country on the continent.

Enlisted Irishmen ventured as far afield as officers, but they usually didn't do as well for themselves. They were the men whose stories were not recorded, a great horde of mostly unnamed individuals who served in Spain and France. In two brigades they fought on nearly every European battlefield of consequence from the late seventeenth to the early nineteenth centuries. Their defeats were few and their conquests many, but their individual stories remain untold.

The timeframe of this book is from approximately 1689 to the late nineteenth century and it provides information about those Irish who were forced to look far afield to make their way in life.

For many years following the defeat of the Irish army of King James II during the Jacobite War of 1689–1691, Irishmen followed their kinsmen to France and Spain. They boarded French or Spanish ships surreptitiously from Irish ports. The 'cargo' were called 'wild geese' to forestall interference from port authorities who looked very unkindly upon Irishmen who joined the armies of France or Spain, the countries which England was most frequently at war.

Beginning in the latter part of the sixteenth century, Spain was the earliest beneficiary of Irish soldiers, both leaders and followers, primarily for the Spanish-Dutch 'Eighty Years' War'. Another large body of Irish went to France, a kindred nation. The Irish in the army of Spanish Flanders were soon facing their countrymen in the army of the French Artois. Spain allowed the Irish immigrants to integrate fully into Spanish society, most notably in the ranks of the Spanish armies, but also into civilian positions, where they often attained the highest ranks. As early as 1680 a royal decree, confirmed in 1701 and again in

1792, established that Irishmen settling in Spain enjoyed the same rights and privileges as native Spaniards. All offices and employment were open to them without restriction. Irishmen or their descendants served in Spain as recently as the Civil War of 1936–1939. Groups and individuals left Ireland and many other nations to serve as volunteers and there were descendants of the Irish on both sides, but the majority were with Franco.

France also welcomed Irish soldiers from early periods but most notably from the mid-seventeenth century onward. Later, after the Treaty of Limerick, numerous Irish soldiers accompanied Sarsfield to France to join the dethroned King James II's army. When the Peace of Ryswick was signed in 1697, France's King Louis XIV was forced to disavow support for the Stuarts. The Stuart 'army' was technically disbanded, but a portion of the Irish regiments continued as part of the French army until nearly a hundred years later when they were disbanded during the French Revolution. Irish names have appeared regularly in French military and naval history ever since, up to and including service in the Second World War, although most are now Irish in name only.[1]

While many served in France and Spain, Irish soldiers had also served in Swedish and Danish armies in the Thirty Years' War and were part of the military forces of various German states. From the same period, individuals served the Holy Roman Emperor and the Austrian crown with great distinction and their descendants, such as Gottfried von Banfield, earned accolades during the First World War. Czarist Russia's army was home to the Lacys, O'Reillys and O'Rourkes, among others. Italy's various states accepted many Irish soldiers as did Catholic Bavaria. While the Roman Catholic states tended to attract most of the exiled Irish others served in Protestant countries, such as Prussia, with equal distinction. On the continent the Irish demonstrated a military success that they failed to reproduce at home. That is what this story is all about.

A complex work like this could only be produced using many fine historians' earlier accomplishments. Those to whom I am especially indebted include Dr Christopher Duffy, who made available so much about eighteenth-century Austria and its Irish soldiers, and Dr Micheline Kerney Walsh, without whom little could have been written about the Irish in Spain. I recommend the works of Richard Hayes, John de Courcy Ireland, William S. Murphy, Rupert S. Ó Cochlain and Francois W. van Brock. Of a more recent date, let me express my appreciation to the editor of *The Irish Sword*, Kenneth Ferguson, LLB, PhD, and to my friend Colonel Patrick G. Kirby, USMC. Whenever I needed assistance one of them was there. All of the aforementioned have contributed to *The Irish Sword*, the publication of the Irish Military History Society. Without it, this book would never have been completed.

One more friend who has been with me throughout my journey is James Tyrell McIlwain, MD. Jim, one of those *Scoti et Ibernia*, has encouraged me to keep going when I was prepared to throw out the whole manuscript. His help in several important translations aided me immensely, so for that and many other reasons I am dedicating this book to him and also, as always, to my beloved wife Jeanne who has borne up under the severe strain of being married to me. I trust that her reward is in heaven; she certainly deserves it.

George B. Clark

CHAPTER 1

THE REASON WHY

This introductory chapter provides a brief chronology of Irish history and the events that led to the exodus of the Irish from their native land in the sixteenth to eighteenth centuries. Although the intent is to be as unbiased as possible it will become obvious that during this period England was the main source of the problems of the Irish in Ireland.

Henry VIII modified the religious climate of Great Britain and to a limited extent, Ireland. He and his successors' efforts to force the various sects of his kingdom to conform to the new state religion were the beginning of nearly three centuries of cruelty, bloodshed and repression against non-conformers.[1] Ireland, for the most part, continued to worship under the standards set by the popes in Rome. The English worked overtime with fire and sword but failed to convert the majority of the Irish people to the state religion. However, the Irish people continued to suffer because of those efforts.

After a brief respite for Catholics during the reign of Mary I, her successor Elizabeth I, insisted that the Irish people must be converted to the new faith or face the consequences. So began a lengthy period of war in Elizabethan Ireland which was frequently as unpleasant for the Queen's armies as it was for the Irish. They lost about as often as they won. And even when they defeated Irish armies, the English were often too physically debilitated to press their advantage, losing whatever gains they had made.

During this period there were a number of Irish rebellions with much of the trouble stemming from the old Gaelic families in Ulster. Even though the English government sent many Scots and English to settle the lands they conquered, the Gaelic families managed to retain some of their land and maintain control over their followers. Earl O'Neill and Earl O'Donnell were the most dangerous to the English government, particularly as they had Spanish backing. The Nine Years' War, 1594–1603, was a give-and-take kind of struggle in which both sides failed to gain the final victory. With the accession of King James I, peace was achieved. In 1607 the Ulster earls and their closest followers sailed to Spain to try to gain Spanish support for a renewed rebellion, but failed. They ended their days in relative comfort as honoured guests of the Spanish King or the pope. Unfortunately for those who remained behind, the English crown quickly initiated the planting of additional territory and drove many more Irish off their land and into poverty.

The plantation of Scots and English settlers on Irish soil, started by Elizabeth I, set the tone for future relations with England. Land was taken from Irish people, and a new class of people was created in the northernmost section of Ireland – a landless class. It also created a new group of people who owed the crown their support and services. The 'mere Irish', the original owners, were not only dispossessed but mistreated as well. The cruelty imposed upon the landless class was sufficient to develop the hatred felt by the Irish for the English to a much greater extent than existed before.

Elizabeth's successor, King James I (James VI of Scotland), was famous for many things, but for the Irish he will always be remembered for taking the plantation system to an extreme. By dispossessing the 'mere Irish' and driving them off their land each English monarch created a large group of malcontents. Some of the dispossessed were sent by the English to foreign rulers to serve in the continual wars on the continent, which was one way of removing them as a threat to English rule in Ireland. Most of those exiles never returned.

In each period of medieval Irish history there were efforts by the English monarchs to assert their control over Ireland, but none exerted as much effort to that end as Oliver Cromwell. His impact upon the Irish was cruel and inhuman, and the effect of his policies there endured for centuries. Cromwell's followers were granted the majority of the most valuable property in Ireland, and even though they were the enemies of the English crown (they had aided and abetted in the execution of Charles I), after the restoration of Charles II (Stuart) in 1660 they were allowed to retain their ill-gotten gains.

In 1685 Charles II died without issue and his brother James II became King of England, Scotland and Ireland. Charles had left behind a very divided nation, whose unsolved problems soon raised their ugly heads. The most divisive of these problems was to do with religion. James Stuart had earned an enviable reputation while serving in Europe as a soldier and sailor for England during the third Dutch war. He was married for a second time to Mary of Modena, a practising Roman Catholic. James was a convert and like most converts was more Catholic than the Catholics. That troubled the English nobility, but they expected James to die without further issue and be succeeded by one of his grown married daughters, who were Protestant. Besides, only a member of the state religion could occupy the throne. Should any child be born of this second marriage he or she would have to be confirmed in the acceptable faith. But the unexpected infant, James, was baptised illegally soon after birth as a Roman Catholic.

Some English gentlemen then invited William of Orange, who was married to James' daughter Mary, to come to England from the Netherlands and usurp his father-in-law's throne. William did just that and succeeded almost without firing a shot. The Glorious Revolution was over in half an hour. James and Mary of Modena fled with their infant son and were soon in France, being consoled by Louis XIV who was very magnanimous to the Stuart family.

Meanwhile an Irish army began forming in Ireland. It was guided by Richard Talbot, Duke of Tyrconnell, a Catholic lord lieutenant appointed by James II. The land-owning Roman Catholic Irish quickly assumed roles of leadership and created an army of substantial numbers. Unfortunately numbers didn't count for much since few if any muskets were available to them and no artillery or military stores of any kind. They had very little training and suffered greatly because of it. In the meantime James II was invited to return and take command of his 'army', which he soon did. However, James and Talbot quickly managed to alienate most of the volunteer officers who had taken up the Stuart cause, as it quickly became obvious that they were simply using the Irish soldiers because they were useful and James had no interest in declaring Ireland an independent kingdom.

James arranged to borrow 6,000 trained French soldiers from Louis but at the cost of nearly the same number of veteran Irish soldiers for Louis' use on the continent. James mistakenly believed that the professional French soldiers would provide him with a superior force to the Irish. However, they didn't and the trained Irish soldiers, who were the backbone of the Jacobite army, were lost forever. The French soldiers were lacklustre in the few engagements in which they participated. It was a very bad trade for James and for the Irish people. Several engagements were fought during the next few months. Having survived a major defeat at the River Boyne, James rapidly found his way back to France. In the following months the Irish Jacobite army lost all their battles. By the end of August 1691 the Irish forces were besieged in Limerick. A month later Patrick Sarsfield, the town's commander, agreed to very fair terms which gave the option to the Jacobite soldiers of either leaving to serve in France, serving in William of Orange's armies or to return home. Sarsfield himself headed for France.

Many of the Irish soldiers in Sarsfield's army who sailed with him and landed in France were established by the French government as 'King James' Irish Army'. The Irish who remained at home paid for their error. The English government soon enacted the Penal Laws which were intended to convert all Roman Catholics to the state religion. If they refused, those who had retained anything of value soon lost it. The laws were numerous (over 130) and designed to keep Irish Catholics in subjugation. The harshest of the laws debarred Catholics and their successors from ownership of property. Others included debarment from education, attendance at church services (other than the state religion), membership in professions, and commissions in the army, navy or any governmental post.[2] These Penal Laws were not revoked until the nineteenth century, and as a result provided a steady stream of Irish men and women to the lands beyond the sea for nearly 200 years.

Chapter 2

Synopsis of major wars (1566–1815)

The wars in the Netherlands (1566–1609)

Spanish misrule in the Lowlands resulted in a series of wars involving most of the modern Netherlands, Belgium, Luxembourg and the French provinces of Flanders and Artois. Spain was powerful during the period and the wars were bloody and fraught with hardships for the residents. In the beginning the Irish presence was very limited. However, the Irish association with Spain brought Irish soldiers into Spanish service and they developed a continental reputation for ferocity which made them desirable mercenaries. Spain worked overtime to continue the allegiance, recruiting in Ireland itself, and was frequently assisted by the English government. The Tudors were anxious to eliminate as many potential troublemakers as possible.

The Thirty Years' War (1618–1648)

This war was fought between the Roman Catholics of Europe led by the Holy Roman Emperor, Ferdinand, and the Protestants led by their own electors, princes and dukes. Later the Swedish King Gustavus Adolphus (1630–1632) assumed command of the Protestant side. Upon his death at Lützen the command briefly fell to Swedish military leaders and finally to a coalition of German Protestants. The Irish were scattered throughout the war on both sides, primarily as individual combatants. Most served the Emperor though there were a few in the various German Protestant states' armies and later in the French and even a few in the Swedish army. The Wallis, Butler and Taaffe families were well represented in the Holy Roman Empire and continued that affiliation for centuries. The English government tried get rid of their Irish troops by sending them to the Emperor, but that did not work out very well for either party, as there were logistical problems in getting the soldiers to the Empire and in many cases they ended up fighting against the English armies.

THE WAR BETWEEN FRANCE AND SPAIN (1635–1659)

Cardinal Richelieu had pursued a policy of enlarging France at the expense of every nation surrounding her. Most of the expansion was into Lorraine and Alsace which lay within German states. Spain's attempts to support her troops in the Lowlands via the Spanish Road, which ran through Alsace and connected the port of Genoa with the Netherlands, became more difficult.

Both nations enlisted Irish soldiers in regiments and as individuals. Spain, with her superior military system, won most of the battles, but France eventually won the war. In 1659 France, which had previously made limited progress in Flanders, was now able to push Spanish armies aside.

As usual the Irish were primarily fighting for Spain, although France made some progress in hiring them. Both the Hamilton and MacCarthy families began a long association with France, which included the formation of semi-permanent regiments in the French army. The Irish fought for both France and Spain in the War of the Devolution, 1667–1668. France did not win this war but retained a series of fortresses on the Flanders frontier with the Spanish Netherlands.

THE WAR OF THE LEAGUE OF AUGSBURG (1688–1697)

When Louis XIV revoked the Edict of Nantes in 1686, William of Orange, later King of England, found it easy to establish an anti-French coalition.[1] The always-aggressive Louis grabbed the Palatinate (a historical territory of the Holy Roman Empire) in 1688. Consequently, the coalition went to war with France, a war which became known as the Nine Years' War. Meanwhile, King James II had been driven from the English throne and fought a war in Ireland, which was lost in 1690, resulting in a large number of Irish troops arriving in France. This was the first war on the continent in which Irish soldiers were heavily engaged.

THE WAR OF THE SPANISH SUCCESSION (1701–1714)

There was little rest in Europe as long as Louis XIV sat on the throne of France. In 1700 clouds were darkening over western Europe once again. The question of who would wear the crown of Spain after Carlos II died led to the War of the Spanish Succession. On 13 March 1700, Philip d'Anjou, grandson of Louis XIV, was declared heir to the Spanish throne and when Carlos II died on 1 November, d'Anjou was proclaimed Philip V and ascended the throne of Spain, but not without opposition. Leopold I, Holy Roman Emperor and a Habsburg, appointed his son, Archduke Charles of Austria, as the new ruler of Spain.

Both sides had a legitimate claim to the throne, but perhaps because of various prior agreements made before Carlos declared

Philip his heir, Leopold's was actually more valid. Austria, England, the Dutch and Portugal lined up as an alliance with Leopold against France and over half the population of Spain. England had soldiers (including some Irish) in the ensuing peninsula campaign and used her naval fleet to great advantage, surrounding Spain. Later Bavaria, always at odds with Austria, came into the war on the side of France and Spain. Its position allowed it to interfere with Austria's involvement in the war in the Low Countries. Some of the Italian states had been conquered by both sides and to a certain degree participated on both sides.

The war lasted until 1714 and was fought in several parts of Europe, with the main theatre in the Low Countries. The English General Marlborough and Eugène of Savoy, with their English, Dutch and Austrian troops, were active there. They predominantly fought the French and were frequently successful because (except for the Duc de Villars) Marlborough and Eugène were the best generals of the day. In the early days of the war France and Austria fought each other in Italy with mixed results. France was also fighting along the Rhine, as well as in Italy and in Spain.

Even though the war would continue for seven more years, the Battle of Almansa in 1707, was the decisive encounter in the fight for the Spanish throne. As a result of this battle the Franco-Spanish armies gained control over practically all of Spain, effectively cementing Philip V's position as King of Spain. The Habsburgs were out and the Bourbon French were in. This completed the conquest, making France the dominant power of the continent.

Throughout the war the Irish were heavily engaged on both sides, as individuals and in Irish units. Individual Irishmen served Leopold but Irish regiments fought for Spain and France.

The War of the Quadruple Alliance (1718–1720)

Louis XIV, grandfather of Philip V of Spain, died in 1715. Philip was barely secure on his Spanish throne when he began to usurp his nephew, the recently installed French King Louis XV. Additionally, Elizabeth Farnese of Parma, Philip's second wife, wanted sections of Italy for her children. Spain had been negotiated out of Italy at the end of the War of the Spanish Succession, but Philip desperately wanted to regain land there. Charles VI, the new Holy Roman Emperor and former aspirant to the throne of Spain, wanted him kept out. Charles was at war with the Ottoman Empire and wasn't able to put up much of a fight against Spain. Then on 4 January 1717, England, France and Holland entered into an alliance to oppose the ambitions of Spain in Italy and France.

Austria had been awarded Sardinia at the Treaty of Utrecht (1713), and this decision was reinforced at Rastatt (1714). Regardless of this, in 1717 the Spaniards landed a force in Sardinia to recapture the island. Then in July 1718, Spain landed troops in Sicily which had been awarded to the kingdom of Savoy in the same treaties. A month later Austria, which had settled her problems with the Turks, joined England, France and Holland to form the Quadruple Alliance.

During 1717–1718 the Spanish Irish Brigade was heavily engaged in Sicily fighting against the Austrians and in April 1719 France invaded Spain with 30,000 men. Their forces were led by the Marshal Duke of Berwick, the illegitimate son of James II and the pretender James III's half-brother. Meanwhile the English were primarily attacking along various shorelines or engaging in fleet actions in the Mediterranean.

Philip finally realised that the losses of the Spanish forces were going to continue, and signed the Treaty of the Hague on

17 February 1720. In it, Philip abandoned all his Italian claims including those of his wife. In a reversal of the original order Sicily was ceded to Austria and Sardinia to Savoy.

The War of the Polish Succession (1733–1738)

This was a war to determine who would sit on the Polish throne: Stanislas Leszczynski, the father-in-law of Louis XV and the former King of Poland, or Augustus III of Saxony, son of Augustus II, the most recent King. The former was supported by France, Spain and Sardinia, and Augustus was supported by Austria and Russia. The actual fighting in Poland was between Polish adherents of Stanislas, who had been popularly re-elected to his former throne, and the Russians led by Generals Burkhardt C. Münnich and Peter Lacy who was Irish, fighting for Augustus. There being no Polish army as such to defend his position Stanislas fled to the city of Danzig. The French made a half-hearted attempt (2,200 men) to help, but the Russians and Saxons easily took the city, while Stanislas escaped to Prussia.

In 1734, the French continued the campaign and in the Rhine River valley successfully besieged Philippsburg, having overrun Lorraine. Soon thereafter peace negotiations commenced. Prince Eugène of Austria died and the Duke of Berwick, Marshal of France, was killed at the taking of Philippsburg. Operations in Italy were fought mainly at the Battle of Parma and at the bloody field of Luzzara. Austria had the slight advantage at Parma and France at the latter. The Franco-Irish Brigade was in the forefront at Luzzara.

Stanislas unsuccessfully tried to restore his fortunes in Poland during 1734–1735. In November 1738 Stanislas abdicated his rights to the throne of Poland and the coronation of Augustus III was fully recognised. Stanislas became Duke of Lorraine, and

Carlos, the son of Philip V of Spain, became King Charles of the Two Sicilies (Sicily and Naples).

THE AUSTRO-RUSSIAN-TURKISH WAR (1736–1739)

For centuries France had used the Ottoman Empire to keep Austria busy, but Turkey's primary enemy was Russia. In 1736 Russian Marshal Peter Lacy was once again very busy and successful against the Turks, but his losses, and those of Marshal Münnich, were so heavy they were both forced to abandon their conquests and retire, Lacy from the Crimea, Münnich from the Ukraine.

The Russian fight against the Turks continued during 1736–1737 and though Lacy was successful in his advance, his flank support from Münnich fell apart. Both were again forced to withdraw from the Black Sea area.

Austria declared war against Turkey in January 1737 and sent an army into the Balkans. At first they were successful but were later forced out of the areas they had conquered. The two allies, Russia and Austria, did not co-ordinate their efforts and gave the Turks too many valuable opportunities, of which they took full advantage.

In 1738 the fighting between Austria and the Turks was once again inconclusive. Lacy proved himself to be a competent tactician by delivering various hard blows against the Tartars and Turks in the Crimea. Nevertheless Münnich was unable to breach Turkish lines in the Ukraine and was once again defeated.

In 1739 an Austrian army led by General Georg von Wallis was compelled to fight a superior Turkish force and was beaten at the Battle of Kroszka.[2] His only hope for survival was to gain the walls of Belgrade and then to withstand a siege. Austria's dismal performance in this war forced her to make peace thus freeing up two armies of Turks which then turned on Münnich in Moldavia. The Treaty of Belgrade, which brought peace between these two enemies was signed on 18 September.

Russia then decided that peace at almost any price was essential. On 3 October the Treaty of Nissa was signed. At the cost of numerous lives the only success was that Russia gained was the expansion of their Ukrainian frontiers towards the Black Sea by fifty miles.

The War of the Austrian Succession (1740–1748)

The war of the Austrian Succession was made up of a number of smaller campaigns. On 20 October 1740 Emperor Charles died and Maria Theresa inherited the Habsburg throne in accordance with the terms of the Pragmatic Sanction, which allowed for the legitimacy of a Maria Theresa inheriting her father's kingdom. Frederick II of Prussia immediately demanded the region of Silesia for his support against several other claimants for the throne. Maria Theresa refused his demand and on 16 December 1740 Frederick invaded Silesia. In the summer of 1741 Bavaria joined the war against Austria and invaded Bohemia. Soon afterwards, Bavaria's ally France also joined the war on the Prussian side. This was the First Silesian War, 1740–1742.

On 9 October 1741, the Austrians and Prussians entered into a secret treaty (Klein Schnellendorf) in which the Empress approved Prussia's conquest of Silesia. Then both countries gathered their scattered armies to take on the Franco-Bavarian invaders in Bohemia. One Austrian army invaded Bavaria and quickly conquered it. Another led by Prince Charles of Lorraine marched towards Prague, but that city had in the meantime fallen to the Franco-Bavarian forces. Charles Albert of Bavaria was quickly crowned King of Bohemia and later Holy Roman Emperor.

In December 1741, the Austrians made moves to recover Silesia and Frederick tried to join with the allies at Prague in early 1742. Before long, on 11 June 1742, Maria Theresa once again made peace with Frederick, ceding Silesia anew but personally hoping that a fortuitous future might allow her to recover the province. From 1742 to 1743 military operations in Bohemia and south Germany were mostly between Austria and France.

The Second Silesian War (1744–1745) began in August when Frederick re-entered the war by invading Bohemia. The Austrians collected together several new armies, converged on Bohemia and took Bavaria. Maximilian Joseph, the quasi-elector of Bavaria, conceded the throne of emperor to Francis Stephen, Maria Theresa's consort, and Bavaria was restored to Maximilian.

A major battle was fought during 1745 at Fontenoy in Flanders. The French army included most of the Irish Brigade and on 10 May they met the British army with their Hanoverian, Austrian and Dutch allies and defeated them. However, despite the outcome of the battle, it had little effect on the war.

From that time forward, 1746–1748, most battles were fought in the Netherlands and northern Italy. During this period Marshal Count Maximilian von Browne, arguably the most important Austrian officer of Irish parentage, was heavily engaged in Italy.

The war that the invasion of Silesia had triggered, ended with the Treaty of Aix-la-Chapelle on 18 October 1748. Frederick, now 'the Great', was still in possession of his ill-gotten gains.

The Seven Years' War (1756–1763)

This could easily be called the war that England won, as every other nation involved sustained crippling losses. England was heavily engaged in colonial wars with France and because France was fighting Prussia, England became Prussia's ally. The members of the coalition against Prussia (and England) were France, the Holy Roman Empire (Austria and various German states), Russia, Sweden and Saxony.

By this time the numbers of Irish in French regiments were beginning to thin and Irish recruits were scarce. The Irish had been in the forefront of various wars since their arrival on the continent, in Spain as well as in France and Austria. Many Irish had died and by the later eighteenth century not many were choosing the soldier's trade.

Frederick the Great of Prussia took Dresden, the capital of Saxony, on 10 September 1756. Austrian armies tried to reverse the situation but Frederick moved rapidly and defeated the Austrians at nearby Pirna. Frederick had an army of 175,000 men, Austria about the same.

Frederick invaded Bohemia with the bulk of his army and on 6 May 1757 again defeated the Austrians outside Prague in a short but bloody battle and proceeded to lay siege to the city. In the battle the losses on both sides were almost equal, but Marshal Maximilian von Browne of the Austrian army was mortally wounded by a shell, and the Prussian commander, Marshal Kurt von Schwerin, was killed while leading an assault.

In the meantime the Austrian Marshal Leopold von Daun moved to relieve Prague. Frederick attacked von Daun at his camp near Kolin in Bohemia but was repulsed with 12,000 casualties and was forced to lift the siege of Prague. That summer France invaded Hanover with two armies and another Austrian force led by Charles of Lorraine moved on Prussia. The Duke of Cumberland was badly beaten by a French army under Marshal d'Estrées and forced to evacuate Hanover.[3] That same year Frederick fought major battles at Rossbach and Leuthen and was triumphant, but was facing enemy armies on all sides.

In August 1758, the Russians were defeated by Frederick at Zorndorf. Then on 14 October Frederick was defeated by the Austrians at Hochkirch, but was able to withdraw in good order.

In July and August 1759 the Austrians and Russians once again invaded Prussia and decisively defeated Frederick, forcing him back at all points. However, he regrouped and managed to drive the Russians back behind their frontier. Then he sent General Finck with 12,000 men to meet von Daun's army of nearly 100,000. At Maxen, Franz Lacy (see Chapter 10), with a small portion of von Daun's force, caught Finck in a trap and captured most of his forces.

The year 1760 was also less than satisfactory for Frederick. By a clever manoeuvre in August at the Battle of Liegnitz he once again managed to escape his enemies. But he couldn't continue to fight on the field and protect his home base. Berlin was occupied by a joint Austro-Russian force on 9 October. The Austrian leader was General Franz Lacy. At Torgau on 3 November Frederick, because of bad luck on the part of the Austrians, managed to 'win', but with losses exceeding those of the Austrians.

By 1761 Frederick had barely 100,000 soldiers and his Austrian and Russian enemies could put three times that number in the field against him. In December the English were going to pull out and Frederick was down to 60,000 available men.[4] He was in serious difficulties, but as always when times were bad he somehow found a rescuer. This time it was the new Czar Peter III, an admirer of Frederick, who withdrew all Russian forces and began peace negotiations.[5] Peter even went so far as to loan an army corps to Frederick.

The following May, Frederick entered into a treaty with Sweden and this left him to face just the Austrians, while Ferdinand, Duke of Brunswick-Wolfenbüttel, held off the French with his Prussian army. The year 1762 was not a good time for either side but Frederick managed to hold his own and in November the aggrieved and thoroughly exhausted parties agreed to an armistice. The following February the Treaty of Hubertusburg acknowledged Frederick's hold on Silesia. In other words, they reverted to the *status quo*, except England, which gained enormous tracts in India and North America from France.

OTHER WARS (1765–1815)

Individual Irish soldiers continued to serve in the armies of most of the nations of Europe. They participated in the Franco-British War in India, the American Revolution (both in Spanish and French formations but this time fighting on the same side), various smaller wars and during the French Revolution. Many continued into the new century fighting for and against Napoleon; they even formed a unit within Napoleon's army called the Irish Legion. But by this date most of the Irish who wanted to fight were joining the British army and navy. The Irish on the continent were primarily descendants of the original immigrants of the seventeenth and eighteenth centuries, and were by now fully-fledged citizens of their new homelands. Those Irish who decided to leave home and didn't join the British forces went to the New World.

Chapter 3

The Irish in Spanish Service

Irish men and women served Spain for many centuries. The main connection and attraction was the prevailing religion of both nations. The Irish there were treated well in Spain and prospered. Consequently most Irish who went into exile there remained in Spain and their descendants are still numerous.

Initially the largest influx of Irish to Spain was from Ulster. The arrival of the O'Neills and O'Donnells in the early seventeenth century set the pace; later many other families including the Antrim MacDonnells arrived. However, Irish soldiers had been serving Spain in their fight to maintain control of Flanders at least as early as 1582. Spain required manpower for her armies especially during her eighty-year war with the Dutch. At this stage the Irish did not provide the numbers of men that Spain required; in fact Geoffrey Parker listed them as 'British' and their numbers were insignificant compared to German and Netherlands formations.[1]

The first regiment given the name Irish, seems to have been a conglomerate of officers and men raised partly in Ireland in 1586 by Colonel William Stanley, an Englishman. Although Stanley's regiment was organised by the English government and was sent to serve the Dutch, fighting at Dixmunde and later at the Battle of Zutphen, its service to England ceased on 19 January 1587 when Stanley changed his allegiance and went over to the service of Spain. On the list of officers there is only one name that could be said to be truly Irish: Ensign Patrick Dillon; all the others appear to have been English or perhaps Scottish. The English hadn't paid the regiment, and the same problem was to occur in Spain. In 1594 a large number of Stanley's men refused to serve him because he was English and that, along with a mutiny of Italians in his command, finished Stanley's Regiment.

At that time a number of unattached companies were being formed under the command of Irish notables such as Edward Fitzgerald for Spanish service in the Flanders campaigns. He attracted eighty Irishmen who had been occupying the castle of Granloy in Belgium, but by June 1602 he in turn was replaced by Captain George Barnewall. The commanders of these companies seem to have been replaced regularly and there is rarely a record of what they had done or why they were replaced.

As early as 1607 documents from Spanish archives list the names of Irishmen selected as Spanish knights. The earliest recorded was a Don Daniel O Sulivan de Bearhaben en Yrlanda. Many other Irish followed him.

The formation of an Irish regiment by Colonel Henry O'Neill in 1605 seems to have provided some consistency for the Irish serving in the Spanish army. A number of the regiment's officers had, despite altered spelling, Irish antecedents. The list included names such as Preston, Hagen, Maconel, Barri, Art Oneill, Eugenio Oneill, Geraldin, Bernaval, Barret, Carti, Driscol, Quelli and Desmond, among others.

Henry O'Neill was the second son of Hugh O'Neill, Earl of Tyrone by his second wife Siobhán, the sister of Hugh Roe O'Donnell, Earl of Tyrconnell. As a youth Henry had been sent to Spain as a hostage for Spanish military support in Ireland and had been educated in Spain. In 1605 Henry requested that he be allowed to form a regiment from Irishmen already in Flanders and for those he might recruit from Ireland to fight for Spain, which was approved by the Spanish crown. He served as colonel of this regiment until his death on 25 August 1610.

The English crown was at this stage beginning to recognise that the Irish serving in foreign military formations abroad could potentially be a serious threat to English rule in Ireland, especially those who served in Flanders, such a short distance from English shores. Henry promised the English representatives in Flanders that he would abide by agreements his father and Tyrconnell had made with James I, to abandon recruitment of Irishmen in Ireland for Spanish armies.

Upon Henry's demise the regiment continued in service until 1628 as the Regiment of Colonel John O'Neill. John, the youngest son of Hugh by Catherine Magennis, had arrived in Spain at the time of the Flight of the Earls in 1607. Because John was still a child in 1610 the actual command went to Major Edward Geraldin until John was old enough to take over in 1625.

Owen Roe O'Neill was born in Ireland in the 1580s, fathered by Art McBaron, known to the English as the 'base-born' brother of Hugh. His mother may have been the daughter of Sir Brian McPhelim O'Neill or the daughter of Sir Turlough Luineach O'Neill. He became one of the finest soldiers of the period. Young and unseasoned, he probably served under his uncles and brothers during the Nine Years' War, learning the soldier's art. He served Spain in 1605, where he was known as Don Eugenio (Spanish for Owen). On 23 February 1606 he and his brother Art Oge received Spanish commissions as captains and command of companies in the Irish Regiment of O'Neill. During that summer the regiment fought at Brabant against the rebellious Dutch. Later they fought at the sieges of Grol and Rheinberg where Owen and his company were cited for their bravery. The successes of the Irish in Spanish service began to seriously bother the English and impacted negatively upon the O'Neill's and O'Donnell's relationships with the crown. It was at this time that they left Ireland and went to Spain for the last time.

Meanwhile, mainly to placate the English, Hugh O'Neill's regiment was cut by five companies. When Henry died Owen expected, as did many other officers, that he would be named to the command. But Hugh appointed his ten-year-old son, John, as the colonel commanding. Owen was out of a job and out of money and he assumed a lesser position in the regiment as sergeant-major. This put him directly under the acting commanding officer and responsible for training and, in effect, all operations. Meanwhile Owen married a twenty-year-old widow and, in 1633, with the assistance of Isabella, Infanta of Spain, was awarded a regiment which was named after him.

In 1640, during the Thirty Years' War then devastating the continent, Owen became governor of Arras, an important Spanish town in Flanders. Owen made defensive arrangements but by the third week in June the French forces, totalling about 70,000, had completely cut off the city from any possible aid. His 1,500 Irish did their best and for several months refused the entreaties of the French Marshal Meilleraye to surrender the town. Finally he received new orders from Don Ferdinand, governor of the Spanish Netherlands, and on 9 August surrendered Arras.

During most of this period Owen was making appeals to Thomas Wentworth, the English governor of Ireland, to return to Ireland. In spite of the efforts of Wentworth to keep Catholic Irish people away from their homeland, Owen eventually managed to return.

The Irish continued to arrive in Spanish Flanders and Spain. Hiberno-Spanish regiments existed with colonels named

O'Donnell, Fitzgerald, O'Sullivan, Morphy, Moledy, Costelloe, Dillon, Grace, Dempsey, O'Meara, Taaffe and O'Byrne. Unfortunately records seldom recorded the names of the ordinary soldiers.

When the Thirty Years' War began, Marquis Ambrose Spinola, the supreme commander of Spanish forces in Flanders, brought 20,000 men to support Emperor Rudolf in retaining the Bohemian lands. Included was a company commanded by Sorley MacDonnell, the only officer from Colonel John O'Neill's Regiment to go on to achieve that position. His men were joined by numerous deserters from various Protestant armies in central Europe, mainly Irish Catholics who wouldn't fight for Protestants against Roman Catholics. This substantial group participated in the first major battle of the war on 8 November 1620 at White Mountain in Bohemia.

A single Irish regiment with various commanders continued serving Spain as late as 1686. Individual Irishmen were employed as officers in other non-Irish units until 1659 and some served with Francis, Duke of Lorraine. When these officers were paid, which wasn't all the time, they were paid quite well. Anglo-Irishman Thomas Preston ranked as major-general on 1 April 1651 with a salary of 300 crowns monthly. In contrast, an Irish private could sometimes (infrequently) expect four crowns a month.

Though the English government did everything possible to intercept the movement of soldiers, Irishmen continued to be recruited in Ireland, usually in bands, and transported to Spanish Flanders. Following the overthrow of the Stuart family in England many more left Ireland, usually to go to France. Major changes occurred after the Peace of Ryswick in 1697 which ended the Nine Years' War. Louis XIV was forced to discontinue his support for James II and the Stuart cause, and the so-called Irish Army of James Stuart was technically disbanded with the numerous Irish

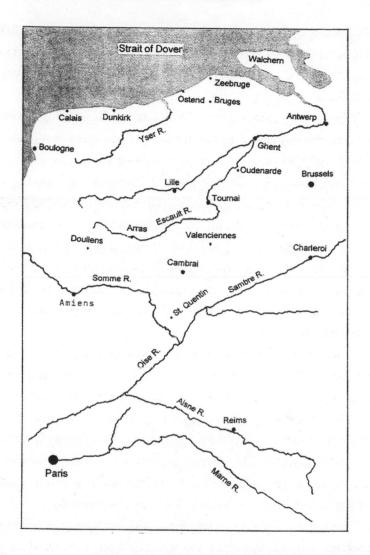

France and the Low Countries

regiments becoming casualties of this peace. But not all of the regiments were disbanded. Some were absorbed into the French army while others were sent to support Louis' grandson, King Philip V of Spain.[2]

After the Treaty of Limerick many of the MacDonnells of

Antrim left their native land. Daniel MacDonnell had two sons, Alexander and Randall. Randall's sons were Daniel and Reynaldo. Initially they went to France, but having served with his father in the French wars Randall then went south to Spain and soon became an officer in Hibernia, an infantry regiment in the newly created Irish Brigade of Spain, which was made up of a number of different dragoon and infantry regiments. As lieutenant-colonel, Randall MacDonnell was in effect in command, although under Spanish law the colonel commanding had to be Spanish.[3] Hibernia went into battle for the first time in 1710, serving under Berwick in Catalonia and then at the siege of Barcelona. Although his older brother, Alexander, took part in the Stuart enterprise known as the '15', where they made a number of attempts to foment rebellion in Scotland, Randall does not appear to have left the service of Spain.

King Philip's Italian wife, Elizabeth Farnese, kept Spain busy for many years in her efforts to provide her sons with Italian principalities, which had been signed away in 1714 with the Treaty of Utrecht. This drain on Spanish resources, along with the Eighty Years' Dutch War and the wrecking by England of Spain's hold on their wealthy American colonies, led to the nation's ultimate decline. Nonetheless, the Irish in Spain, like those in the Habsburg Empire, stayed as long as possible.

Randall was strongly involved in the Spanish success in taking Sardinia from Savoy in 1717 and during the following summer led Hibernia as part of the Irish Brigade's retaking of Sicily, which had been ceded to Savoy during the Spanish War of Succession. By now he was a brigadier and commanded the Irish regiment Irlanda while Alexander assumed command of Hibernia. However, although the army was successful in taking Sicily, in 1718 France invaded Spain and in 1720 Philip made peace with his enemies. The Treaty of the Hague saw all of Elizabeth's schemes go awry, as Spain was forced to relinquish Sicily to the Austrians and Sardinia to Savoy. Late in 1720 Randall, Alexander and the rest of the army had to return to Barcelona.

In 1721, by enactment of a law in Spain, Irishmen who were serving the Spanish crown were granted the right to become Spanish citizens. But Randall was dissatisfied, as he believed he was due more than he had been given by the Spanish and decided to look elsewhere for promotion. He attempted to obtain a position at the court of James III in Rome, but when this failed and nothing else came his way, he was forced to remain as a soldier of Spain.

In the War of the Polish Succession, Spain was engaged with France and Savoy against Austria and Russia. Spain's main theatre of war in this conflict was Italy and they soon conquered Naples. But as their campaign in Sicily dragged on, Randall complained about his position in letters to various people, including James III who was in exile in Rome, without much response other than condolences.

In November 1735 Randall returned to Spain. He settled his family in Barcelona in 1737 and continued serving in the army during the War of Jenkin's Ear between Spain and England in 1739, then during the War of the Austrian Succession which broke out in 1740, when he was once again in Italy. On 8 February 1743, as part of this war, one of the bloodiest battles of the century was fought.

Twenty miles north-west of Bologna the Spaniards were on the north bank of the Panaro River and the Austrians on the south. Leading Spain's forces was a transplanted Walloon named John de Gages, who was attempting to surprise General Otto von Traun's Austrian army. When the Battle of Camposanto was fought, the Spanish right took most of the punishment and this included the Irish Brigade under Randall's command. Especially battered was the Hibernia regiment, whereas Irlanda regiment's losses were moderate in comparison. This was a most important battle for Spain, and since the Austrians retreated it has been claimed as a Spanish victory.[4] Randall and his two sons Daniel and Reynaldo were severely wounded, but they all survived. Daniel was later killed at the Battle of Velletri in 1744.

In May 1745 Randall senior died and his son Reynaldo assumed command of the Irlanda regiment, although he was not entirely recovered from his Camposanto wounds. Reynaldo, whose career began with the Sicilian campaign in 1718 and the Italian campaigns, received many military awards in his lifetime. He was made Knight Commander of the Military Order of Santiago in 1736. Like his father he continued to beg for James III's permission to serve his son Charles Stuart in his missions to retake the British throne for his father.

Spain began to suffer major reverses in the war. The Austro-Irish General Maximilian von Browne decisively defeated Spanish General John de Gages at Piacenza in Italy and drove Spanish forces from that peninsula in 1746. Reynaldo, now a brigadier-general, had remained in Savoy and later Provence during that period. Philip V died in 1746 and the new ruler, Ferdinand VI, wisely pursued a policy of neutrality. Consequently the army, including the Irish regiments, were left with only dull routine in daily life for some years.

In August 1748 Reynaldo married a young woman from a distinguished French family, Gerónima de Gondé. Enrique Reynaldo, the oldest child of this union, was born in 1753 in Pontevedra. Following his father's death in 1762 the eleven-year-old second lieutenant was transferred from Irlanda to Ultonia, the third regiment in the Irish Brigade. At eighteen Enrique became a full lieutenant and at twenty-two a captain. His association with the naval base at Ceuta, both in the army and later the Spanish navy, continued off and on for many years. He left there in 1768 when half his regiment sailed for the Americas.

In May 1776 Enrique took the unusual action of applying for a commission in the Spanish navy. By this time the Irish brigades were no longer all Irish; only the officers were Irishmen, the ranks being solidly Spanish. Meanwhile Carlos III was making great efforts to rebuild the navy. After a brief period of training as a sub-lieutenant, Enrique joined his first ship on 1 July 1776.

Having done battle with several Algerian ships, 'because of excellent behaviour', he was promoted to lieutenant. When France and Spain went to war with England to assist the American colonies his ship, the *Pilar*, went to the West Indies where she engaged a larger British ship. Enrique was wounded but distinguished himself and two months later assumed command of the gunboat *Andaluz* which was attached to a convoy transporting the regiment of Hibernia to the West Indies. At General Galvez's siege of Pensacola, Enrique volunteered for duty and in command of Spanish marines, went ashore in April 1781. With the subsequent victory over the British he was promoted to commander.

As the British were taking possession of the coastal portions of Nicaragua and Honduras, Enrique was to find and destroy them. Success brought him a captaincy and command of a corvette, the *Diligencia*. On his return voyage to Spain, while just north of Bermuda, he and his ship met a well-armed British privateer and following a fierce action, he sank her. This was after peace had been signed, unknown to those on the high seas. His position in the Spanish navy seemed secure; in six years he had risen from sub-lieutenant to captain.

Enrique's next command was of the 74-gun *San Domingo*. However, during the next few years Enrique became a major nuisance to his seniors and the navy administration in general, as he only obeyed orders he liked and engaged in common brawls. He was restored to duty after a hearing about his participation in one such brawl held before General Alexander O'Reilly. Made captain of the port at Cadiz, the dullness of the job eventually induced him to seek service with the Swedes against the Russians.

In May 1789 he was granted leave and made his way northward to Stockholm, where he was immediately given command of the xebec *Odin*.[5] In his first fleet engagement, his ship fought against at least seven Russian ships. Fighting on until he was wounded, and with more than a third of his crew dead or dying, he was forced to surrender. He was brought to St Petersburg as an honoured guest, but was soon released and reported back to Sweden. Having given his word to his Spanish commanders not to fight for Sweden again, Enrique was forced to refuse the Swedish King Gustav III's offer of the command of a flotilla of thirty-two ships and a force of 22,000 men. Gustav asked Charles IV of Spain to allow MacDonnell to be released from his promise, but Charles refused. Nevertheless, Enrique gave the Swedes valuable advice for their next engagement.

Back in Spanish service he was again in battle with Algerians, but complained continually over the next few years about the quality of the ships he commanded and that he was being passed over for important assignments while younger men received the rewards. He was relegated to less desirable assignments, then given no duties and less (if any) pay. But then came the Franco-Spanish battles with the British fleet off Cape Trafalgar during the Napoleonic Wars. Enrique's command, the one-hundred-gun *Rayo*, was one of those ordered to fall back to Cadiz on 21 October 1805. Nelson's ships cut the Franco-Spanish line in half and the Allied commander Dumanoir was later blamed for not fighting against the prevailing winds to come to the aid of the overwhelmed Franco-Spanish ships. Despite the withdrawal, Enrique's *Rayo* suffered eighteen casualties.

Two days later he and four others agreed to participate in a daring plan to retake captured ships. In this sortie his ship lost all three masts in a gale and her steering gear was crippled. Drifting between two British ships and being pounded to pieces, Enrique was forced to surrender. However, the British crew was unable to handle the *Rayo* and she drifted ashore at Torre Carbonera. Technically a British prisoner, Enrique was instead free in Spain. He insisted upon a court-martial to investigate the correctness of his actions in the battle, he was acquitted of any wrong-doing and promoted to rear admiral on 9 November 1805.

The next few years found him unemployed and fighting for a renewal of Spain's naval power. Godoy, the Prime Minister in power, instead favoured the reduction of the Spanish navy and what was once the most powerful fleet in the world soon became nearly the weakest. Over the following years Enrique held various land commands including captain of the port of Cadiz, where during Spain's uprising against Napoleon, he led the operations that captured the French fleet based at Cadiz. Literally begging his superiors for a command at sea, he even offered to take a reduction in rank from rear admiral to commander, but nothing came of it. In 1813 he was promoted once more, this time to vice-admiral, but the promotion was then delayed for about three years because of his constant carping about the 'do-nothing' government. As the years went by he volunteered to lead a battered fleet against the Simon Bolivar rebels in Venezuela but was turned down. In 1820 he played a part in suppressing a mutiny at Cadiz.

Having suffered years of sickness Enrique MacDonnell died alone in a Cadiz hospital on 23 November 1823. His funeral was paid for at public expense. Sixty years later Admiral Pavía noted that if a medal had been made listing his services to Spain on one side, it would have been 'necessary to inscribe the single word *INGRATITUDE* on the reverse' about Spain's attitude to him.

Marshal Leopoldo O'Donnell y Joris, Conde de Lucena, Duque de Tetuan, commonly known as either O'Donnell or Tetuan, was a descendant of Joseph O'Donnell, one of two brothers from Oughty, County Mayo, who left Ireland for service in Europe. Joseph's brother, Henry, entered Austrian service while Joseph selected Spain, both around 1750.

Joseph married a daughter of Chevalier François d'Annethan, Marie Anne Marguerite, by whom he had six sons and two daughters. His sons all followed him into the army; all became distinguished and one was elevated to the peerage as Count Abisbal. His second son, Carlos, was popularly known as 'The General'. He died on 7 February 1830, but his wife survived him. She had held a position in the household of Queen Amalia, third wife of King Ferdinand VII.

Ferdinand's fourth wife, Cristina, delivered an infant daughter named the Infanta Maria Isobel Louisa in 1830. Contrary to Salic Law, which forbade women from inheriting land, Ferdinand discovered a decree allowing him to name his infant daughter the heir to Spain's throne. In line for the throne, his brother Don Carlos refused to take an oath of allegiance to baby Maria and was granted permission to leave Spain. Following Ferdinand's death Don Carlos campaigned for a revolt and soon had many adherents. At Marie Anne Marguerite's urging, among the many Carlists were all but one son of herself and 'The General'. Her third son, Leopoldo, instead supported the infant Queen.

Leopoldo was born at Santa Cruz de Tenerif on 12 January 1809 and at age ten entered the Imperial Alexander Regiment of infantry. He was a captain during the civil war that broke out over the succession and became a colonel before the age of twenty-five. For his victory at Unza he was promoted to brigadier and the dislodgement of the Carlists from Galarreta in May 1836 earned him the Cross of San Fernando. During that action he received a bayonet wound which laid him up for a period of time. He attained the rank of major-general by June 1837 and at thirty years of age he was made captain-general of Aragon, Valencia and Murcia. He was acknowledged as the man who prevented Valencia and its environs from falling to the Carlists by his victory at Lucerna. For this he was raised to the rank of lieutenant-general and made Count of Lucerna.

Peace was signed on 20 August 1839, but the turmoil in Spain continued. Cristina, the Queen regent, did not get along with her Prime Minister Baldomera Espartero, who was unofficially trying to rule Spain in her stead. Asking O'Donnell's advice on how to get rid of Espartero he suggested: 'It is very simple – send for a file of soldiers and tell them to shoot him.' Cristina didn't act upon his suggestion and the situation deteriorated. She eventually left Spain for Paris in 1854.

Espartero became regent in May 1841 and remained as such until 1843 when O'Donnell played a serious part in his overthrow. O'Donnell was then involved in the government that dissolved the regency and induced the Spanish Cortes (government) to declare Isabella of age at thirteen years. O'Donnell was awarded the governor-generalship of Cuba, a position that was considered a prize. The story is that he, like so many others, reaped a modest fortune in the four years he ruled there.

Back in Spain to enter the senate and accept the post of inspector-general of cavalry, O'Donnell became involved in a political mess and was banished to the Canary Islands in 1853, but he ignored the order and remained in the slums of Madrid, emerging in July 1854 to help overthrow the existing government. A new cabinet was formed with Espartero heading the government and O'Donnell holding the position of Minister of War. A Carlist uprising broke out in Aragon which he put down, but this rebellion spread to Catalonia and grew. Soon it was successful and the party in power, including O'Donnell, was ousted.

On 1 July 1858 Queen Isabella was back in power and O'Donnell became Prime Minister. He had plans to keep his party in power and unite Spain after years of civil warfare by waging war with Morocco. Spain already had two bases in that country, at Melilla since 1470 and at Ceuta since 1688. The latter had been laid under siege several times by Moroccans, once for twenty-six years. O'Donnell demanded that the Moroccans return some recently taken prisoners and cease harassing Ceuta. The negotiations were carried out during 1858–1859, at which time the British became involved in the situation, demanding that Spain cease and desist. Britain didn't want the Spanish in a strong position at the entrance to the Mediterranean opposite Gibraltar.

War was proclaimed in October 1859. Preparations were made in Spain for a military force of fifty-six battalions of infantry,

Leopoldo O'Donnell y Joris

eleven squadrons of cavalry, eighty pieces of artillery, half of which were rifles, and a siege train. The Moroccans could muster at least 100,000 men, many mounted. Spain's major difficulty was to obtain a fleet of ships to carry the invading army across the sea. She hired practically every available merchant ship in the area, including many British ships.

Marshal O'Donnell was made commander-in-chief of the invading force and one of his subordinates was his brother, Lieutenant-General Henry O'Donnell, who commanded a division. The troops were landed at Ceuta and Colonel Thomas O'Ryan, a veteran of the Sebastopol campaign in the Crimea with the French army, was put in charge of military engineering.

Of two points selected for attack by O'Donnell one was Tetuan, located about twenty-seven miles to the south, and the seaport of Tangiers about the same distance to the west. O'Donnell decided to move against Tetuan first, on 1 January 1860. This was an exceptionally successful campaign, with the Spaniards winning a well-planned battle on 6 February 1860 and raising the national emblem over the fortress. When news reached Madrid, O'Donnell was created Duke of Tetuan and raised to the rank of Grandee of Spain thereby granting him the ground over which the battle had been fought. The chief of all the tribes that participated in that defeat were subsequently decapitated for their failure by Moroccan Crown Prince Muley Abbas.

Tangiers was the next target and the march forward with approximately 22,000 men began on 23 March 1860. A short distance later, with the Moroccans holding all the best positions, the Spaniards were near the Pass of Fordach when they were attacked. At around 4 p.m. the Spaniards had come to within six miles of the pass, but that was the end of the fighting. The next afternoon envoys from Muley Abbas approached O'Donnell's headquarters asking to negotiate. The terms agreed upon were mainly beneficial to Spain and were soon agreed by the *Cortes*. Casualties on the Spanish side, including wounded, totalled 9,034 officers and men, about half of whom died of cholera or wounds.

Now a national hero, Marshal O'Donnell returned to Spanish politics until he had a difference of opinion with Queen Isabella and retired to Biarritz, France, in the summer of 1866. Suffering from typhus, he died there on 5 November 1867 at age fifty-eight. His remains were returned to Madrid where he was buried at the Church of the Salesian Fathers, with a monument erected in his memory. Though married to Doña Emmanuelle Barges in Barcelona on 23 November 1837, no children were born of this union and his nephew, Carlos O'Donnell, soon to be a lieutenant-general, became his heir.

CHAPTER FOUR

LIEUTENANT-GENERAL COUNT DANIEL O'MAHONEY

'Taken by a miracle – lost by a still greater one'
Prince Eugène, on the loss of Cremona

Daniel O'Mahoney was born in Dromore, County Kerry, to John O'Mahoney, son of Cornelius O'Mahoney and Catherine FitzGerald, and Mary Joan Moriarity, the daughter of Thady Moriarity and Julia Hussey.[1] He was a captain of the Royal Irish Foot Guards during the Williamite war in 1691 and a major upon his arrival in France with Sarsfield's army in 1692. His brother Dermod also fought for James II and distinguished himself at the Boyne, Aughrim and Limerick. Upon arrival in France, Daniel transferred into, and then out of, the Regiment of Limerick. In 1701 he was in Italy as a subordinate of Villeroi in the Irish regiment of Dillon, set up by Theobald Dillon in 1688.

While still in France he married Cecilia Weld, daughter of a well-connected Jacobite English Catholic family of Dorsetshire. After her death he married again, this time the eldest daughter of Henry Bulkeley, a Jacobite family of substance in Ireland. She was

Charlotte, the widow of Charles O'Brien, Fifth Viscount Clare. This marriage made Daniel the brother-in-law of the French marshal, the Duke of Berwick, which certainly didn't hamper his career. At first a relatively junior foreign officer, O'Mahoney rose rapidly to positions of command within the Irish regiments fighting for France, and finally into the minor nobility of Spain. Eventually he became a lieutenant-general, developed a European reputation during the War of the Spanish Succession.

The War of the Spanish Succession broke out in 1701. The fighting was widespread: the main theatres were Belgium, the Netherlands, parts of Germany as well as Italy and Spain. Bavaria joined France but other German states joined Spain and her allies. The overall ramifications of the war were felt by most Europeans for many years after the actual fighting was over. Irish swordsmen and other displaced soldiers were among the beneficiaries of this war. They gained employment for a number of years and many individuals as well as regiments formed lasting relationships all over the continent.

In the spring of 1701 Prince Eugène of Austria, in a secret march along little-used roads, by-passed the French commander Catinat, and in May reached Vicenza, Italy. Eugène had rather easily out-manoeuvred his French opponent, and Catinat was soon recalled to Paris where he was replaced by the aging Duke de Villeroi. In September the French attacked Eugène and his fortified position at Chiari with much larger forces but were soundly beaten and Villeroi subsequently retired to Cremona, where he took up winter quarters. In the meantime Eugène selected Mantua, the pro-French Italian province, to be his winter quarters.

Because Eugène's master, the Holy Roman Emperor Leopold I, hadn't bothered to provide money or sustenance for his army, he was forced to live off the country. With a minimal force he was reduced to fighting the French in Northern Italy, but could not carry out any serious actions against them. Despite this on the night of 31 January–1 February 1702 Prince Eugène attempted to take Cremona, during the season that few commanders would take the risk of leaving their quarters for any reason. At this point, Villeroi and part of his forces were in Cremona while the balance of his Franco-Spanish army was scattered about Northern Italy. If successful, the move would place Eugène right in the middle of the Po plain, between the allied armies.

Major O'Mahoney was in command of the portion of Dillon's Regiment who were stationed within Cremona's walls.[2] The full Irish contingent in Cremona was composed of members of the Dillon and Bourke regiments, but there was only one battalion of each.[3] A total of about 7,000 men in the French army were wintering in the city, of which the Irish numbered about 600. But they and their leader performed near miracles of military success, for which they became justly famous.

Prince Eugène had a contact in Cremona, a priest named Cozzoli, who provided him with a perfect entry into the town. A dried-up sewer led under the north walls of the town and directly into the priest's own cellar, while one of the city's gates was opened to let in the enemy cavalry. Eugène's soldiers were able to surprise most of the garrison, but not the Irish who were on guard. O'Mahoney had asked his landlord to wake him early in the morning, but was startled to awaken instead to the rumble of heavy cavalry and musket fire in the town.[4] His landlord appeared and O'Mahoney demanded to know what was happening. He was told that the enemy cavalry, having surprised the guards, was in the town, and the situation was desperate. O'Mahoney grabbed his sword, carefully made his way past the Austrians and safely reached his men. There, with drums beating the call to arms and his men in only their shirts and underwear, he had them quickly fall into formation.

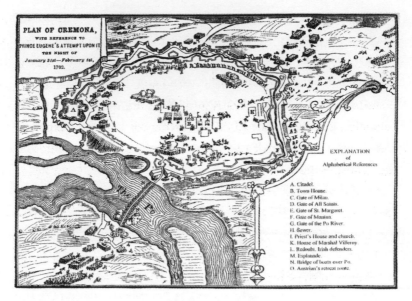

Battle of Cremona from Quincey's Histoire de Militaire

Within a few hours the situation within and outside Cremona drastically changed. The Irish troops who had been stationed in the redoubt at the Po River gate managed to hold Eugène and his troops on that side of the city. Many attempts were made to take the redoubt but the Irish stopped the Austrians from advancing further towards the bridge. The two Irish regiments earned the most laurels for their dogged determination and obstinate defence, for which O'Mahoney has been given the credit. O'Mahoney's biographer, a Frenchman, named him 'le fameux O'Mahoni' after the battle for this city.

Because of his performance, O'Mahoney was given the honour of delivering the report on the battle and his personal observations to King Louis XIV at Versailles. He was received by the King with great attention 'proportioned to the importance of the intelligence from Italy'. When the King rose from his dinner he had O'Mahoney accompany him to his private quarters. O'Mahoney gave the King his briefing and Louis is reported to have said, 'You have said nothing of my brave Irish.' Colonel O'Mahoney replied, 'They fought in conjunction with the other troops of your majesty.' However, despite his reticence, his men's reputation had obviously preceded the messenger. Louis awarded him, in addition to his colonelcy, a knighthood, 1,000 louis d'ors for his travel expenses and an annual pension of 1,000 livres. Being a zealous Jacobite and thus considering himself still bound in allegiance to King James II, O'Mahoney proceeded from Paris directly to Saint Germain-en-Laye where he was knighted by James III. From then on he was frequently identified, after the French style, as *Sieur Mahoni*.

King Louis had every reason to be pleased with the Irish. According to the English historian Forman:

> … the Irish perform'd there the most important piece of service for Louis XIV, that, perhaps, any King of France ever received, from so small a body of men, since the foundation of that monarchy. This action of the Irish, by an impartial way of reasoning, saved the whole French army in Italy; the destruction of which, according to the account itself, as well as the opinion of all military men, *must* have been the infallible consequence of the loss of Cremona.[5]

However, the victory came at a cost. The Irish lost over half their command, the French another 1,100 men, and the Austrians at least 1,600 officers and men. The Irish may have saved Italy for France, but at a price. However, as a result of their exertions at Cremona Louis upgraded the rate of pay to Irish officers and to a lesser extent the enlisted soldiers as well. This increase put them on a par with the regular French army, something only Dillon's Regiment had achieved before this point. Not only was the pay of Bourke's Regiment increased but the other four Irish regiments then in Italy: Galmoy, Albemarle, Clare and Sheldon's Dragoons were recipients of the largesse as well. Dillon's men also received an additional gratuity as proof of the King's pleasure with their services.

This was not the end for O'Mahoney in Italy. The new commander of French forces, Marshal Louis Josef, Duke of Vendôme, grandson of Henri IV, assumed command of the army in Italy and pursued Eugène's forces. Unlike Villeroi he was a skilled professional who gave the imperialist leader the most memorable battles of his career. Although Eugène was usually given credit for the ultimate outcome of their encounters, whether he won or lost, more than once he was forced to cede ground to or was defeated by Vendôme. The Frenchman frequently had the best of it, usually because he commanded larger forces than Eugène. With the French army were five battalions of Irish – from the regiments of Albemarle, Bourke, Dillon, Galmoy and Berwick, plus 'Sheldon's Horse'.[6]

The year 1702 was a very active year in the war in Italy. First Vendôme forced Eugène to lift the siege of Mantua and fight on ground of the former's choosing. Even though Eugène retained the field he had a hard time retaining the ground his army won. Between 27 May and 1 June Colonels O'Mahoney and Bourke distinguished themselves at the reduction of Castiglione delle Stiviere. On 26 July O'Mahoney, an officer named O'Carroll and Dominick Sheldon, commander of Sheldon's Dragoons, distinguished themselves in the ambush of four of Eugène's squadrons led by General Annibal Visconti at Santa Vitoria.[7] The Irish infantry decimated the horses and their riders, and Sheldon's Horse cleaned up those who remained in their saddles. Visconti's troops were no longer useful or available to Eugène.

Following this success, Vendôme moved his army to the small town of Luzzara on the right bank of the Po River, where Eugène had a garrison. Eugène took up defensive positions around

Borgoforte at the confluence of the Po and Mincio Rivers. A battle was fought on 15 August: the French forces had thirty-seven cannon and upwards of 35,000 troops but only 20,000 to 22,000 could engage in battle, as the rest were scattered in various locations. Prince Eugène had fifty-seven guns and somewhere between 24,000 and 26,000 men. The battle began at about 5 p.m. and continued until 1 a.m. the following morning. It was mainly a musket and cannon contest. The ground was rough and broken and allowed for entrenchment by both sides. The casualties were modest, about 2,500 each side, and each army stood its ground.[8] Neither really won nor lost, though *Te Deums* for victory were sung in both Paris and Vienna.

Following Luzzara, O'Mahoney wrote to the French Secretary of War, M. Chamillart in Paris, requesting that he be allowed to leave the French army to organise a regiment of Irish dragoons to serve the French King's grandson, Philip V of Spain. If approved, he would be serving Spain and its King, and this seems to be the first official mention of any Irish regiment for Spain during this period. During the previous century the Irish had formed regiments for Spain in Flanders. But following settlement of that war their reason to continue service for Spain was deemed unnecessary and they were eventually disbanded. It seems O'Mahoney's request was not granted at this point – he did organise a regiment of dragoons and transferred his services to Spain, but not until later.

On 28 July 1703, the important fortified town of Brescello, located west of Luzzara on the Po River, surrendered and O'Mahoney was appointed its governor. He spent a few more months in Italy but later that same year was back in Paris. There he was promoted to brigadier-general and also ennobled by Louis XIV. He was now a count, but he continued to be identified in contemporary writings as Sieur Mahoni. Just two years after

Cremona he was transferred from French to Spanish service to support Louis' grandson, Philip V.

The allied armies of Portugal, England and the Netherlands, also known as the Grand Alliance (or Allies), were now carrying the war into the Spanish peninsula and there were Spanish soldiers, as well as Irish and Italians, fighting on both sides. Leopold I, King of Austria and Emperor of the Holy Roman Empire, carried the burden for the alliance in Italy, providing the bulk of the forces there. Great Britain and the Netherlands wanted to divide up the Spanish colonies, especially in the western hemisphere. Austria, which had been denied the crown of Spain for Archduke Charles of the Habsburgs, wanted the extensive Spanish holdings in Italy to combine with their own.

By 1701, Philip V had been generally accepted as the new Spanish King, having been appointed by King Carlos as his successor, though Charles was proclaimed King of Spain later that year in Vienna. Leopold I never entirely gave up on winning that crown and the empire for his son. Portugal wanted as much Spanish territory as they and their allies could gain by military action. But it was Great Britain that came out best. They took Gibraltar and have held it ever since. All the rest was up for grabs and has changed hands many times since.

In 1703 Marshal Berwick, who was leading the French forces in Spain, had been holding the Allies quite successfully. Although the Allies had crossed the Portuguese-Spanish border they had made little further headway. The bulk of the force was Portuguese. Besides being poorly trained they were also badly led at nearly every level. Antonio Luis de Sousa das Minas, a reasonably good soldier in overall command, made earnest efforts to improve their training and morale. He was embarrassed by their previous performances and did the best he could, but was fighting a losing battle. The same could be said for the other Allies' overall performance in the months to come. General Marlborough and later Eugène were working wonders along the Rhine River but so far the peninsula campaign was a disaster for the Allies.

In 1704 Sieur Mahoni, now serving in the Spanish peninsula for Philip V, was pitted against Portuguese troops. Even though the town of Monsanto in Portugal had been taken, a French captain with fifty troops still held the castle in the town. O'Mahoney and his dragoons were sent with a small detachment to relieve the Frenchman and were soon arrayed against twenty Portuguese squadrons and sixteen battalions of infantry. The Portuguese, fighting in their own country and supremely confident with their superiority in numbers, attacked the flank and rear of O'Mahoney's Dragoons. He repulsed the attack with such vigour that they were stopped in their tracks. O'Mahoney then called upon the Regiment of the Queen (of Spain) which attacked the Portuguese so effectively that they were driven back in great confusion.

However, soon more Portuguese infantry were brought up into line and their superior numbers forced the Spanish to retreat. Meanwhile, O'Mahoney and his dragoons were protecting the rear of the retreating infantry with musket and pistol fire. This stopped the Portuguese from turning the defeat into a rout. His loss of fifty men during the retreat was small compared to their previous successes. When his dragoons arrived at the Portuguese town of Idanha Velha, they found that the Spanish troops had vanished in disorder upon hearing erroneously that O'Mahoney's cavalry had been defeated.

The following year the Régiment de Mahoni Irlandois was provided for the protection of the city of Cadiz when it was learned that there was to be an attempt to take the city for Archduke Charles.[9] In the meantime, with the capture of Barcelona by the Austrians, the French marshal, Prince de Tilly, was dispatched from Madrid to protect the region of Aragon. His second-in-command, O'Mahoney, was at the forefront of efforts to curtail and defeat the Austro-Carlist forces, especially the *miquelets* (Spanish guerrillas) who were causing as much trouble as all the other Allied forces combined. One unknown source from Madrid dated 18 December 1705, relates that O'Mahoney was engaged with the guerrillas when they 'advanced on the side of the Mequinença [River] which was put to flight by Colonel Mahoni; and 40 of them, who had rushed into a boat to save themselves, on the opposite side of the river were all drowned'.[10]

By 1706, the Allies had secured most of Catalonia for Charles. In order for the Earl of Peterborough and the English army to reach Valencia, they had to pass Murviedro. There O'Mahoney awaited him with his regiment of dragoons and other troops stationed across the river. Peterborough realised that to engage O'Mahoney he might very well be forced to also engage the Duke of Arcos, then besieging troops disloyal to Philip based in Valencia. There were but five miles between the two Spanish forces and Peterborough was naturally cautious. Realising the difficulties he faced if he tried to attack and defeat O'Mahoney, Peterborough arranged a truce under a white flag and suggested talks. Suspecting nothing ill from another professional soldier, who was also a distant relative through marriage, O'Mahoney accepted the proffered interview, at which Peterborough tried to suborn his host, offering high rank in Austrian or English service. O'Mahoney politely refused. Peterborough then sent two of his dragoons to the Duke of Arcos as pretended deserters. They were allowed into the Duke's presence and told him that they had witnessed a meeting between Peterborough and O'Mahoney in which the former handed the latter a bag of gold. They recounted hearing the former promising the latter a promotion in the English army to major-general with a force of 10,000 Irish Catholics to command. O'Mahoney was only to entice Arcos to come to his aid so that Peterborough could catch him without adequate defences on an open plain. And, of course, the Irishman would just stand aside and let it happen. Arcos doubted this story but still had O'Mahoney arrested and sent to Madrid. Once there, he sought an audience with Philip V who, when O'Mahoney had explained the situation, immediately saw through the false subornation and promoted him to Maréchal de Camp (major-general).[11]

Upon his promotion O'Mahoney was sent with a small force to the province of Valencia to attempt to preserve or retake areas still faithful to Philip. In April 1706 he called on the town of Enguera to surrender and return their loyalty to their lawful King. Failing in this peaceable attempt his army then stormed and sacked the town. This action prompted more towns to return to their allegiance to Philip than actual loyalty did.

During the summer O'Mahoney was in command at Alicante when it was attacked by Allied sea and land forces. The attack on the coastal town was commanded by Vice Admiral Sir John Leake and Brigadier Richard Gorges. By 8 August the Allies had breached the walls and entered the town, whereupon O'Mahoney, though wounded, and some of his troops, retired behind the castle walls to continue their defence. Not having a surgeon present, O'Mahoney asked Gorges for the brief loan of one, which he generously granted. When O'Mahoney's wounds had been tended to, Leake then demanded his surrender. O'Mahoney refused and continued the defence for twenty-seven more days, until all his provisions were gone. On 4 September he surrendered on honourable terms. He and his remaining men, about 134 in all, plus four cannon and two mortars, were to be transferred via English ships to Cadiz.

What is interesting is that the treaty terms were negotiated with O'Mahoney's 'old friend' Peterborough, who had just arrived on the scene. The latter had encountered some delay in attempting to take the town of Monteza, which lay on the path to Alicante. It seems that the governor, Colonel Oliver O'Gara, had held up Peterborough and his force for several days because he wouldn't surrender. According to the memoirs of Captain George Carleton the town never actually changed hands.

Upon being ennobled as Count of Castile in 1706, O'Mahoney was also appointed as governor of Cartagena, another important port south of Cadiz. Within a few months he was recalled to Madrid for consultation and instruction. On 10 February 1707, he left to join his new command in Valencia. Meanwhile Captain Daniel O'Carroll, with 100 Irish dragoons at the Castle of Seron, had been assailed by over 1,000 of the Allies' regular troops and 'he received them with so much bravery that, after a combat of six hours, he obliged them to retire'.[12] While O'Carroll was making a name for himself on the frontier of Aragon, his countryman, O'Mahoney, was extending his forays against Alicante, making life unpleasant for the 'disloyal'. The important coastal towns may have been held for Charles but the balance of the country was nearly all held for Philip V.

The next most important event in O'Mahoney's military career was the Battle of Almansa, in the province of Albacete, Spain, on Easter Monday 25 April 1707, with an Englishman, the Marshal Duke of Berwick, commanding a Franco-Spanish army and a Frenchman with an Irish title, the Earl of Galway, commanding an Anglo-Dutch-Portuguese army. The battle was part of the War of the Spanish Succession, which had at this stage been grinding on for five years with victory going first to one side, then the other. In the Battle of Almansa at least two Irish units were present with Berwick, his own Berwick Regiment and O'Mahoney's Dragoons, and both were in the forefront of the fighting. There were also Irish serving on the opposite side, the majority of whom were Roman Catholics and probably serving under duress.

The Earl of Galway, a French Protestant named Henri de Massue, formerly Marquis de Ruvigny, was the leading opponent of the Duke of Berwick. Galway had fought bravely for William of Orange in Ireland, hence his Irish title. While not entirely successful in Spain he was a reasonably gifted soldier. At this time he had forty-two battalions of infantry and fifty-three squadrons of cavalry. These forces were composed heavily of Portuguese troops but with strong elements of English and Dutch troops to bind them together into a commendable fighting force.

Galway and his second-in-command, the Marquis de Sousa das Minas, who commanded the Portuguese and was over eighty years of age, agreed that they must occupy Madrid. They were also aware that Berwick was expecting a large group of reinforcements from France led by the Duke d'Orléans. To make the fight more balanced Galway needed to get between the two forces before they combined and to defeat the force in Madrid before dealing with Orléans' men.

The Franco-Spanish forces under Berwick consisted of fifty-one battalions and seventy-six squadrons, but the ranks were sparsely filled.[13] The numbers between the two armies were probably roughly equivalent, that is, until the arrival of Orléans to join Berwick. In an effort to force Galway into battle on Berwick's chosen ground he set up a stratagem that played into Galway's game plan, which was to intercept Berwick before his reinforcements arrived. To encourage Galway to fight, Berwick ordered two of his Irish officers to make their way to the enemy's army pretending to be deserters, with a story about the approach of Orléans' men.[14] According to them the Frenchman was marching rapidly towards Berwick with an additional 12,000 men, horses, guns and infantry and would be on the field within two days. Galway was at this point laying siege to Villena, but upon learning this 'intelligence' immediately marched towards Berwick's army for a confrontation. His army travelled at least six miles in the heat of a Spanish day, and when they arrived at the site of battle on Easter Monday morning at about 8 a.m. the Allied army was exhausted. Unbeknownst to Galway, Orléans himself hadn't arrived but his troops had – Orléans did not show up until the following day.

Very pleased with his easy deception, Berwick had already decided where his field of battle would be. He had drawn his forces up before the town of Almansa, on a flat, treeless plain with a rather modest hill on which stood the dilapidated castle. When Galway's army came down into the plain they found awaiting them a considerably larger army than anticipated. Sir Winston Churchill, in his description of the campaign, wrote, 'the wine was drawn and must be drunk'.[15] Berwick had cleverly drawn the enemy into his trap.

The very perceptive Galway rapidly noted the discrepancies between the two forces; about 26,000 to 16,000. For some reason he co-mingled his horse- and foot-soldiers, which was the opposite of what his opponent had done. Berwick's forces were drawn up in the usual formation – infantry in the main centre line, with cavalry on both flanks. There were two battalions of Berwick's Regiment in the second line of the centre.[16] Four squadrons of O'Mahoney's Dragoons were posted on the right wing. As the battle commenced Galway did his best as a military commander but the effort was doomed to failure. His personal courage was exemplary and in one mêlée he suffered several sabre cuts to his face, one of which cost him an eye. Yet blinded as he was, he re-entered the contest with great courage.

Meanwhile the Franco-Spanish artillery on the right opened up on the Allied infantry facing them. However, the Allies advanced and after some confused cavalry fighting, they managed to drive back the Spanish infantry in the front line. Berwick then ordered his brother-in-law, Francis Bulkeley, to advance. Bulkeley led the Brigade of Maine, named for the oldest French regiment in the group and including Berwick's Regiment, within thirty paces of the five English battalions. Having taken fire, his brigade of four regiments approached the enemy and opened fire with their muskets at point-blank range. They then went to work with bayonets. The English were thrown into such disorder that they fled the scene. As they retreated in a near rout they were forced to pass through a ravine, where they were slaughtered.

In the centre things were entirely different. The British Grenadiers and Coldstream Guards advanced against Berwick's centre and drove several Spanish regiments back almost to the walls of the town. O'Mahoney's Dragoons then launched an attack against the Guards and smashed them totally.[17] The dragoons captured two lieutenant-colonels, three majors, three subalterns, fourteen sergeants and 110 guardsmen, thereby placing the balance of the English Guards in a desperate position. The dragoons themselves had suffered severe losses with two captains, seventeen subalterns and 110 troopers killed.

The Allies were now in a bad way. Their left wing had been routed. The Portuguese on the right had retreated and the centre was almost surrounded and very badly diminished. Under the circumstances, Galway decided to try to withdraw. He and das Minas managed to pull back some of the horse and a mix of 1,500 British and Dutch infantry, but no guns. Another thirteen battalions managed to avoid capture by withdrawing to a hill two or three miles from the scene of the disaster. The next morning, realising they were entirely cut off, those men elected to lay down their arms and capitulate to the inevitable.

Captain Miles MacSweeny, who commanded a squadron of O'Mahoney's Dragoons, was granted the Cross of the Military Order of St Jago by Philip V for his personal bravery. Moreover, 135 Irishmen serving in the British army changed sides and joined O'Mahoney's Dragoons. Additionally, another 215 Irish went into Dillon's Regiment and another 189 joined Bourke's Regiment after this battle.

The Carlists were still active in the north-east region of Spain. By 4 October they had managed to collect 1,000 regulars, 2,000 *miquelets* and ninety cavalry at Molinete and they then moved on Pego which they easily took. However, the suburb of Pego was a more difficult proposition. Three hundred English troops plus 800 *miquelets* were detached to take possession, but they failed as it was so well defended by a Spanish colonel. They were forced to retire to the town itself, having suffered considerable losses. In the meantime, intelligence of this move reached Lieutenant-Colonel Cornelius O'Driscoll, now commanding O'Mahoney's Dragoons at Olivia. Taking a hundred of his troopers, double that number of French infantry and a hundred loyal Valencian militia he made a diversion and attacked the main body of Carlists at Ondara. So thoroughly did he confuse and abuse them, 'they were pursued even to the gates on Denia'.[18]

O'Driscoll and his force then attacked the enemy in the suburbs at Pego, smashing them in the first shock of his charge. They later counted over 300 of the enemy slain in this vigorous action. The Irishman's loss was put at fourteen dragoons and eight other troops, killed and wounded.

The following month General O'Mahoney moved his force against the small town of Muchemiel, demanding money. However, the English governor Brigadier Charles Sibourg had strengthened the place from his post at Alicante and O'Mahoney, with his diminished forces, was unable to capture the town. Instead he burned down seven villages as he retired in the valley of Gallinar. This reduced cover for any Carlists during the forthcoming winter.

On 2 January 1708, O'Mahoney, with 6,000 regular troops

including the Franco-Irish Corps of Berwick, Bourke and Dillon, appeared before the town of Alcoy. Two days later his guns had breached the walls and on 5 and 7 January his men assaulted the town unsuccessfully and experienced great losses. On the 9 January they once again went forward and this time were successful. The English defenders were made prisoners of war but it was planned to put the 'disloyal' pro-Carlist inhabitants to the sword. Instead they were taxed 48,000 piastres. Meanwhile O'Mahoney continued his reduction of towns and villages along the coast. He maintained strict discipline amongst his troops. The residents were said to be amazed that they hadn't suffered worse privations such as massacre and pillage.

In March that year O'Mahoney was appointed to command the troops in Sicily. With 3,000 Spanish troops and his 500 Irish dragoons he reached Messina in April. The Allies had already made moves against the island and were planning to add it to their conquests. They already possessed the kingdom of Naples and whoever had Naples usually added Sicily to the prize. In addition, they had the English navy aiding the cause of Charles. Sir John Leake, was still able to throw this considerable naval weight about in the Mediterranean, having already helped to reduce the island of Sardinia and force it into the imperialists' cause. The Austrian claimant 'King' Charles had substantial help in the area and O'Mahoney would be hard pressed to hold Sicily.

Somehow his polished and generous manners and wit helped O'Mahoney to make friends with the Sicilians, whereas his predecessor, the Marquis de los Balbases, had earned Philip numerous enemies. The strength of O'Mahoney's abilities and reputation inspired the Sicilians with confidence. His preparations for the defence of Sicily were so effective that the Allies were unable to make any successful landings during the period of O'Mahoney's rule, whereas during the same period Philip's fleets sailing from Sicily caused the Neapolitans much grief. They even sailed into the Port of Naples and exacted tribute from the rulers of that city.

By 1709 Sicily was so well organised militarily that the Allies were wary of invading the island. Consideration of such an enterprise in the past had estimated necessary numbers at around six ships with 3,500 men; now they spoke of 10,000 men. On 30 July, Leake decided to make a move. Two squadrons appeared off the coast between Trapani and Castellamare and the other off Melazzo. But the Sicilians, sustained by veteran Spanish troops, vigorously repulsed their enemy, so much so that the enemy was forced to re-embark and withdraw, though not before losing about 600 men.

In June 1710, Lieutenant-General Daniel O'Mahoney returned to Spain with great honour. With 2,600 men, he soon successfully seized Cervera, in the province of Lerida, at which time its magazines, loaded with food and clothing for 4,500 men and other goods, became the property of Philip V. He also destroyed the castle of Calaf and a large quantity of provisions stored there. O'Mahoney moved within a dozen miles of the Carlists' great port of Barcelona.

On 20 August the two contending armies came into contact once again near Zaragoza. Charles' army was substantial, at about 24,000 men, whereas the 'loyalist' forces were down to 15,000. General Starhemberg commanded the Carlists, whereas Philip's army was commanded by the Marquis de Bay. The cannonade began at daybreak and by 3 p.m. the defeat of Philip's army was convincing.

O'Mahoney was in command of the right wing of the loyalist army. With the King's Guards and the Spanish Dragoons he charged the Portuguese so furiously they broke, and routed the Allied force led by General Hamilton. Many of them perished in the River Ebro. He then attacked the guns and though he couldn't haul them all away, he had 400 mules hamstrung so that the enemy couldn't either. Surrounded by Lieutenant-General James Stanhope's cavalry and a substantial force of infantry, O'Mahoney managed to break through and brought back five captured enemy standards.[19] He then escorted Philip, who had come to watch the battle, and his entourage on their retreat.

Later, for some reason, O'Mahoney was blamed for the loss of the day. The concern was that he had pressed the enemy too hard. His reply was that if his inferior numbers were able to accomplish what they did, how much better it would have been if the rest of the army had equalled their efforts. At any rate the Irish Brigade of Castelar, which meant at least the newly formed Regiment of Hibernia, was in attendance, as were the battalions of MacAuliffe (later Ultonia), Comerford (later Waterford) and MacDonnell, all of which were equally distinguished.[20]

For the next few months, the forces of Philip V regained the offensive from the successful Allies. The latter were forced by Philip's avenging army to fall back on Catalonia. Stanhope, with seven battalions and eight squadrons of English troops and one battalion of Portuguese, fell back on Brihuega. Starhemberg, with the main body, was encamped about six miles away.

The Duke of Vendôme, now commanding Philip's army, made a surprise attack on Stanhope and after breaching Brihuega's walls on 9 December, Vendôme affected a successful assault. Stanhope surrendered and his surviving men became prisoners of war. Now it was Starhemberg's turn. The latter had under his command experienced forces totalling approximately 13,000 foot and horse. Vendôme's army was numerically stronger at 17,000 but over half of them were new levies. Each army had about twenty-two guns. On 10 December the two armies met near Villaviciosa some time after 1 p.m. and for the next five hours the battle was fierce. Starhemberg was defeated with a loss of several thousand, including all his guns, colours and standards. Possibly worst of all, he lost his military chest with upwards of 30,000 Spanish doubloons. The losing army was pursued vigorously and lost so many men that when he finally reached Barcelona, he was reduced to around 4,000 men.

O'Mahoney was in the forefront of the victory at the head of the King's Dragoons which now included Crofton's Dragoons, another Irish formation which was now the property of David Sarsfield, Fifth Lord Viscount Kilmallock.[21] O'Mahoney had pushed Starhemberg up onto a height and had him surrounded. Sending a parlay message by a drummer, he asked for Starhemberg's surrender. But the latter, seeing that night was coming on and a fog or mist descending, refused. Keeping the Spanish drummer with him, Starhemberg's force broke through O'Mahoney's men, and O'Mahoney's horses and men, exhausted from the day's exertions, were unable to effect an attack or a follow-up to Starhemberg's retreat that night. In addition O'Mahoney had no cannon. What O'Mahoney did obtain was a train of 400 mules laden with 'the plunder of Castile'. He was also the recipient of a Commandership of the Order of St Jago which produced a rent of 15,000 livres annually. Additionally it was noted that the 'Sieurs de Magdonel, Makaoli, Combefort, Colonels of the Brigade of Irish Infantry of Castelar, each acted at the head of his battalion with a great deal of courage and conduct as they had already done at Zaragoza'.[22]

As he hurried towards Catalonia, Starhemberg was continually harassed by O'Mahoney and his rapidly moving dragoons. The latter captured the castle of Illueca with 666 Carlists and an unfortunate Spanish lieutenant-general who had deserted Philip's cause for Charles. Of the lower ranks 150 were formerly officers who had lost their companies at Villaviciosa or on the retreat with Starhemberg.

In the meantime an unnamed Irish lieutenant-colonel (possibly O'Driscoll) entered Zaragoza with King Philip's troops on 31 December 1710 and wrote that he 'had ended this wonderful year well'.[23] The Irish Dragoons, led by this same Irish officer, were ordered to occupy the castle of the inquisition in which there was an unmovable magazine loaded with arms and munitions. Before vacating the premises, Starhemberg's orders had been to set a match to the whole thing. A reported thousand pounds of powder was set to blow up everything including the intruders. According to the account quoted in O'Callaghan, 'the match, which was in a very forward state, would have effected its purpose, but for the precaution of an Irish lieutenant-colonel, who had been dispatched there to command those dragoons, and who, having detected this stratagem, rendered it useless'.[24]

Following Villaviciosa, the Archduke Charles' candidacy for the throne of Spain was all but concluded. More Irish prisoners deserted the British army and quickly found a home in Spain. Although winter had arrived and most of the Spanish army had gone into winter quarters, the campaigning wasn't over. Aided by Count O'Mahoney, Vendôme had bottled up the Carlists in Catalonia by February 1712 and reduced their territory by at least two-thirds.

In 1714 Daniel O'Mahoney died at Ocana, Spain. He had attained the rank of lieutenant-general in Spain's service. O'Mahoney had two sons from his first marriage, neither of whom left male descendants. The oldest, James O'Mahoney, rose to the rank of lieutenant-general and inspector-general of cavalry in the service of Naples, was governor of Fort St Elmo and Commander of the Order of St Januarius before his death in 1757. James' granddaughter married Prince Guistiniani of Naples, while his younger brother Dermod (or Diarmuid) became the lieutenant-colonel of the Regiment of Edinburgo and colonel of the dragoons of Pavia. Following that he became a brigadier and finally a lieutenant-general.[25] He assumed his brother's title as a count of Spain upon James' death, later becoming commander of several orders and ambassador from Spain to Austria. He died in Vienna in 1776.[26] He was the host of a famous St Patrick's Day party in Vienna in 1766. The attendees, most of whom were not Irish, each wore the Irish Cross for the occasion, in honour of the fête.

When he died, O'Mahoney's contemporary and acquaintance, the Chevalier de Bellèrive said:

> He has always been not only brave, but indefatigable, and very painstaking; his life is, as it were, a continued chain of dangerous combats, of bold attacks, of honourable retreats. If he has mounted to the first dignities of the army, he has raised himself by degrees; he has passed through all the military grades so as to make himself master of their respective duties; he has learned to obey before commanding, without having been precipitately elevated to these glorious employments, which he has exercised, during this war, with so much applause.[27]

CHAPTER 5

GENERAL ALEXANDER O'REILLY
'FREDERICK THE GREAT OF SPAIN'[1]

Spain was always short of good men for her armies and navies during the many wars following the expulsion of the Moors and Jews in 1492. By 1715 more than three regiments of the Spanish line were Irish in name and in composition. Many famous and less famous individuals also made a positive impact upon Spanish arms. Alexander O'Reilly is one of the best known of those of the eighteenth century.

O'Reilly was born at Baltrasna in County Meath, in October 1723. For many centuries the O'Reilly family was concentrated in Cavan, Longford and Meath. The family provided numerous churchmen to the Roman Catholic church. But they contributed an even greater number of soldiers in Ireland and to foreign nations. During the war of 1689–1692, sometimes called the 'War of Three Kings', Edmund O'Reilly's Regiment included thirty-three officers of that name and Mahon's Regiment had another sixteen, most of whom eventually became segments of the 'Wild Geese'.

While Alexander was still very young his father, Thomas, to

escape the oppressive penal laws, took the family to Spain for a new and better life. There Alexander entered a Catholic school at Zaragoza, the Colegio de Padres de las Escuelas Pias, where he received a brief but evidently significant education. Like so many other sons of Irish emigrants in Spain, he entered the army at the very young age of eleven. As was to be expected, he joined the Regiment Hibernia, a formation of mainly Irish soldiers. It and its sister regiment, Ultonia, had been formed in 1709. By 1735 Hibernia (La Columna Hibernica) and its sister regiments of the Royal Spanish Army, Ultonia (El Immortal) and Irlanda (El Famoso), had already repaid in their own blood and that of the King's enemies, the courtesies extended to the Irish by the crown of Spain.[2] There were several other Irish regiments but those three continued to exist for more than a hundred years, well into the Napoleonic age.

While the regiment was in Catalonia in 1740, O'Reilly was promoted to the rank of *sub-teniente* (sub-lieutenant, equivalent to an ensign). When Great Britain made a declaration of war upon Spain in 1739 the regiment moved to Cartagena, an embarkation port in south-east Spain.[3] Having waited fruitlessly for a British attack the regiment embarked for southern Italy, arriving there in 1741. Upon arrival, the Duke of Montemar, commanding the Spanish army, moved northward with Spain's allies, the Neapolitan army, in hopes of bringing the Austrian allies of the British into battle. Hibernia, commanded by the Marquis of Castelar, was part of the main army in its journey northward.[4] Their intent was to capture the Austrian Duchy of Milano, but they were generally out-manoeuvred by the Austrian Marshal Traun and the Neapolitans were forced to return home to provide protection against a possible British amphibious landing.

Over the next few years Spaniards and imperial troops fought each other several times. Because O'Reilly had served prominently in each encounter Montemar promoted him to infantry lieutenant. In February 1743 O'Reilly was badly wounded on the bloody field of Camposanto and was left all night with the dead and dying.[5] The following morning an Austrian soldier was about to kill and rob him when O'Reilly managed to convince him that he was the son of a Spanish nobleman, the Duke of Arcos. The soldier, obviously expecting a grand reward, spared his life and O'Reilly was brought before the Austrian commander Field Marshal Maximilian von Browne, another Irishman.[6] O'Reilly made Browne aware of who he was and the latter, very much amused by the young man's ingenuity, had his wounds taken care of and returned him to his own troops with some ceremony.

Unfortunately his wounds hadn't completely healed; he had a limp for the rest of his long life. Regardless, shortly after his release he was again in action and fought in the Battle of Piacenza where the French and their Spanish allies were separated and forced to retreat, and again at the Battle of the Tanora River. The Duchess of Arcos learned of his claim about their relationship and took the young man under her wing. The Duke was a grandee of Spain and their interest in his welfare meant that, for the next few years at least, his future was assured.

Upon the signing of the Treaty of Breslau in 1742 which brought peace between Austria and Prussia, O'Reilly was again promoted, for meritorious service in Italy, to sergeant-major, making him third in command of the regiment. But back in Spain he soon despaired of peace-time duties and requested a foreign assignment. Prussian armies led by Frederick the Great had earned themselves an enviable reputation in the First Silesian War. The Austrians were once again fighting the Prussians, the peace having broken down in 1744, and O'Reilly asked to be sent there to learn war from an acknowledged master.[7] The tactics of Prussia as well as its army's superb training went far towards advancing the cause of their King, which O'Reilly was likewise anxious to do for his King. The request was approved and he spent the next several years in the Austrian army fighting the Prussians. At this time many Irishmen were serving Empress Maria Theresa in the imperial officer corps so O'Reilly undoubtedly found many kinsmen to aid him in his quest. During his three years in the Austrian service, O'Reilly earned a medal and respect from his peers in that country.[8] However, he was outspoken about the weaknesses of the army and so left the imperial service for the French armies of Marshal de Broglie.

Upon his return to Spain in 1745, O'Reilly presented his findings on Prussian tactics in a special report which was received by the high command with considerable enthusiasm. Indeed, they were so impressed that he was promoted to the rank of colonel and to command of the Spanish Guard Regiment with directions to implement his findings in his own regiment. His success in developing the new system earned him another promotion, this time to brigadier-general in 1760.

Anglo-Spanish relations were always tenuous at best. England had recently taken Canada from France and forthwith closed the Newfoundland fishery to Spain, indicating that Pitt, the English Prime Minister, was looking for trouble with Spain. Because England couldn't control Spain's sea-borne trade, she declared war upon Spain on 2 January 1762. Brigadier Alexandro O'Reilly, as his Spanish friends called him, led the army into Portugal, a British ally of many years. There he defeated the British-Portuguese Brigade but elsewhere, under different leadership, the Spanish armies were not as successful. They were forced to retreat out of Portugal and back into Spain where they remained for the balance of the war. Britain's success in her various colonial wars had an impact upon France and Spain, the two other major imperial nations. Neither could forget that their outposts required special military and naval attention, otherwise Britain with its huge navy would take everything. Both countries immediately set to work to repair any damaged fortifications and manpower weakness and rebuild their navies.

During the Seven Years' War with Spain, Britain had taken Havana in Cuba but evacuated that city when the peace treaty was signed in Paris on 10 February 1763. The Count of Ricla was placed in command of the Spanish expedition sent to recover Cuba and he requested that O'Reilly accompany him as his second-in-command. Their party arrived in 1763 and after much effort by O'Reilly, the defences destroyed by the British and previous neglect were repaired. O'Reilly restored the colonial army and raised a disciplined militia. His militia organisation was so superior to any other then in existence that his alterations were extended to the rest of the empire. While still in Cuba he drafted a report on political and economic conditions that contributed to the 1765 royal decision to open the Caribbean island trade to the major ports of Spain. In his report he highly recommended

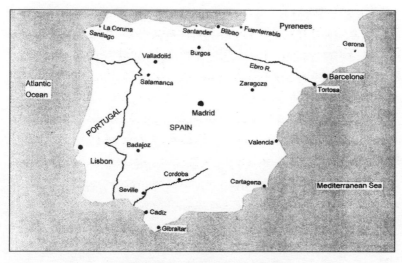

Map of the Spanish peninsula

that the crown implement a plan to send Irish immigrants to the island to strengthen its military presence and to increase its financial status and productive power.[9]

In the summer of 1765 O'Reilly was sent to the island of Puerto Rico to do there what he had done for Cuba. He repaired defences and reorganised the island's regular military forces. It was soon obvious to Spanish military authorities that O'Reilly was not only an efficient soldier but a superb organiser and administrator, and was soon given additional duties along the same lines.

O'Reilly was called back to Spain in 1766 to assume the post of inspector-general of the Spanish infantry and to implement Prussian army tactics which he had studied so intently many years before. Still under its aggressive King Frederick, Prussia was considered to have the leading army of Europe. She had successfully held off numerous enemies during the Seven Years' War. As part of this role, O'Reilly drafted army ordinances which were accepted in 1768.

By the Treaty of Fontainebleu, Louis XV ceded to his cousin Carlos III the Province of Louisiana on 3 November 1762. Antonio de Ulloa, a famous scientist, was appointed governor, but it was 5 March 1766 before he and ninety Spanish soldiers arrived at New Orleans to take up his post. De Ulloa was expecting an additional 300 troops to sustain the Spanish position but they failed to arrive.

Relations between the governor and the primarily French residents went from bad to worse. By 1767, when he formally took possession from the French, de Ulloa had barely seventy-five Spanish troops still able to support his regime. In 1768 a force in Havana, the Louisiana Infantry Battalion, was preparing to leave for the mainland. It consisted of 410 officers and men and was waiting for additional troops from Cadiz to make their move to New Orleans.

But before they arrived, there was a revolution by the local population in and around New Orleans, who were mainly French and had no desire to live under Spanish rule. There were no casualties but the court in Spain was in turmoil because of it. De Ulloa was forced to retire to the island of Cuba which was another insult to the Spanish crown and had to be crushed. Therefore a reconquest of Louisiana was formulated and Alexander O'Reilly was the instrument Spain chose to settle the problem of the French rebels. By 1767 O'Reilly had been promoted to lieutenant-general and admitted to the prestigious Order of Alcantara by the age of forty-four.[10]

In May 1769 O'Reilly left Spain with well-trained troops and an assortment of lawyers, engineers and craftsmen, all bound for Havana, where they arrived on 24 June. Alexander's main task was

Alexander O'Reilly

to put down the rebellion and train the Louisiana militia to meet the high standards for which he was noted. There were 679 officers and men of the 1st Battalion, Lisbon Regiment; 567 of the Havana Infantry Regiment and picquets from Aragon and Guadalajara, Spain, both of which were to be merged with the Louisiana Battalion. In addition he had nearly a hundred gunners of which thirty per cent were with the Louisiana Battalion; a company of grenadiers from a white militia battalion plus eighty men each from the mulatto and Negro militia of Havana. His force was rounded out to include a forty-man picquet from the Volunteer Militia Cavalry Regiment, eight 'distinguished volunteers' and six cadets, all from Havana. His force added up to 2,056 officers and men, supplemented by three engineers. They travelled with an impressive array of artillery, mortars, bombs, rockets, ammunition, tools, rations, provisions and everything needed to reconquer a recalcitrant population.

O'Reilly left Havana on 6 July aboard his flagship the *Volante* leading a squadron of twenty-one ships and arrived in New Orleans on 24 July. On 18 August O'Reilly disembarked and provided an awesome spectacle for the locals when he and his troops marched into the main square, the Place d'Armes. There he greeted the interim governor, a Frenchman named Charles Philippe Aubry. O'Reilly read the official proclamation, signed by the French and Spanish kings, which transferred Louisiana to the Spanish crown. After exchanging salutes Aubry turned the keys of the city over to O'Reilly. Festivities really began when Aubry shouted 'Long live the King'. He didn't say which King, but we can presume that the Spaniards believed it was Carlos III they were saluting. O'Reilly formally took possession of Louisiana that same day.

Within a week of his arrival O'Reilly had investigated the causes and the leaders of the revolt. Six were sentenced to be incarcerated for varying terms and five were sentenced to be executed. The trial has been variously described as 'inquisitorial' or 'eminently fair' according to who was making the charges. There were a great number of co-conspirators who were never charged and were eventually pardoned by O'Reilly. There is no question in many historians' minds that O'Reilly cleverly used a velvet-covered mailed fist to settle the colony's future under Spanish domination. After all, according to the times, they were traitors to their King. Certainly Patrick Henry and John Adams, two of the most outspoken rebels, knew they could only expect death if Britain managed to retain the American colonies.

O'Reilly was well pleased with his men. 'Not an officer or even a soldier has said a single improper word to these people, nor done anything meriting the slightest disapproval.'[11] He immediately set about organising his territory, sending troops to Arkansas and Illinois but retaining most of them in New Orleans. His troops were well trained and obedient in contrast to de Ulloa's force. Inhabitants of Louisiana, expecting the soldiers of Spain to be ogres, were somewhat taken aback to find that they were well behaved and disciplined. A major factor in O'Reilly's regime was to incorporate French residents who had been soldiers in the unpaid militia units. This made for an easier transition since it showed the inhabitants that all was forgiven and that everyone was responsible for the defence of the colony. The British forces were now located along the border of the territory and even though, at this time, peace reigned between the antagonists, no one could foresee when that might be broken. The situation in South America between the two nations was tenuous and of course one could strike before the other even knew that they were at war. But O'Reilly somehow managed to placate the British General Gage, thereby keeping the two forces from an undesired clash.

In addition to his military organising, O'Reilly made many changes. One of his first tactful measures was to have the Spanish code translated into French so that the inhabitants and the new governors could easily exchange dialogue. This allowed the two groups to identify and solve possible problems immediately, before they grew to unmanageable proportions. When discussing any situation relating to the French-speaking post commandants it was their language he used. Another measure was to confirm the positions of former French officials as much as possible, especially those on the frontiers. One improvement, at least for the Indians if not the Negros, was to grant freedom from slavery without compensation to the former owners. Another, very liberal for the age, was to grant settlers plots of 240 acres or more which was adequate to make most people reasonably independent landowners.

Thus Governor O'Reilly sought to skilfully blend intimidation and peaceful persuasion to inculcate a permanent respect for the Spanish crown. Of course he also intended to bring his majesty's new subjects into line without resorting to force, if possible. He did not forget the Spanish King's native American subjects. In October 1769 he invited nine chiefs of various local tribes to a meeting at his home and decorated each with a medal, asking them to kiss the royal effigy. With his sword he touched each on both shoulders and chest with the sign of the cross, then gave a personal embrace and his hand. This was of evident pleasure to the natives who were duly impressed to be paid such manifest respect, and O'Reilly effectively eliminated any potential hostility from that quarter.

O'Reilly's changes and modifications in the government of the colony were extensive. His directives, usually not far removed from French concepts, affected taxes, prices of goods including price controls on important commodities such as rice, and other ideas prevalent in America. Just a few weeks after taking control he instituted regulations governing taverns and other establishments that had been sources of trouble for the government.[12] O'Reilly was undoubtedly Spain's finest soldier and diplomat of the eighteenth century.

O'Reilly created eighteen religious posts for the twelve Louisiana parishes and for New Orleans, believing that a strong church presence might curb the excesses of drunkenness, licentiousness and rowdyism that the colony was famous for. He then dispatched Captain Edward Nugent and Lieutenant John Kelly, two Irish soldiers, to the provinces, to learn from the inhabitants, Indian as well as white settlers, what problems Spain faced and what to do about them. The party went up the Red River in 1769. By January 1770 they had returned and brought back the first detailed information on the government posts at Atakapas, Opelousas, Natchitoches and Rapides.[13]

There were many more Irish involved with the affairs of both Spain and Louisiana but most at a somewhat later period. During this period Charles Howard was a sub-lieutenant in the Louisiana Regiment with earlier service in the Regiment of Hibernia. Five soldiers in the Louisiana Regiment all named Macarty were identified as inhabitants of New Orleans and were probably Irish born.[14] Adjutant Major Arthur O'Neill was born in Ireland and had served previously with both Spanish regiments, Irlanda and Hibernia. Cadet Henry White, also born in Ireland, had wide services throughout Europe and eventually served over twenty years in the Regiment of Hibernia. Edward and Stephen Ross were born in Ireland and a New Englander named Noel O'Brian became an officer in the territory in 1797. There were many more Irish names in later years.

Alexander O'Reilly, having successfully re-established the Spanish crown in the Louisiana territory, was recalled to Spain in 1770 and there resumed his duties as inspector-general of infantry. He was ordered to co-ordinate the military preparations in connection with the Falkland (Malvinas) Island crisis of 1770–1771. From this position he extended military reform to the colonies at Santo Domingo and New Granada. Count O'Reilly was a favourite of King Carlos III and Prime Minister Marquis Jerónimo Grimaldi and in 1772 acquired the title of count. He was made the military governor of Madrid and found time to create the military academy at Avila for infantry, cavalry and engineers. He had studied the Austrian, Prussian and French military organisations and selected what he thought was the best of each for his school. Alexander was the main factor in altering the archaic Spanish method of musket fire. His changes included a three-deep line of infantry which gave a high rate of firepower and depended upon the strictest discipline instilled by ruthless Prussianised Spanish and foreign officers. He also introduced the tactic of heavy cavalry death-or-glory charges, where the cavalry attacked with no regard for losses or casualties. O'Reilly was instrumental in establishing heavy armament factories, turning out new and modern artillery and muskets, with the former being upgraded in quality by foreign experts. O'Reilly thoroughly modernised the Spanish army, making it one of Europe's finest in the final years of the eighteenth century.

In 1775 O'Reilly was Spain's premier soldier and was selected to lead the attack upon the Corsairs of Algiers.[15] The problems between Spain and Algiers were of more than 250 years' duration and not easy to solve. The Spaniards had tried several times to conquer North Africa but were unsuccessful each time.[16] Carlos III decided that Spain must try once again. There had been a long history of ground warfare between Spaniards and Moors over control of the city of Algiers, none of which settled the issue decisively. Spain still had imperial interests of which strong positions on the North African coast were at the forefront. She controlled the city of Melilla in which a Lieutenant-Colonel

William Creagh commanded the garrison; also Ceuta and most importantly Oran.[17] As a defender of the faith Carlos determined that Spain must, once and for all, put the Muslims in their place and in the summer of 1775, Spain went to war with Algiers.

There are at least five differing accounts of what transpired in this Spanish attack against Algiers. One is from O'Reilly himself and another from the naval commander, which basically substantiates O'Reilly's version and was an obvious attempt to tone down the disaster. Two other versions were critical of the overall leadership, one of which O'Reilly himself ordered to be forwarded to the war minister. Interestingly this is the most damaging of all the reports. Another was by an Englishman who wrote his shortly after the fact and is less critical of O'Reilly and his naval commander. Using all five, I will attempt to piece together what might really have happened. Three of the critics seem to place most of the blame upon O'Reilly's lack of planning as to where the armada would land. It is true that he hesitated simply because he had no idea what he might expect from the tides and winds. The admiral was in complete agreement with O'Reilly in not prescribing a landing place beforehand, since the port was well known to be dangerous at almost any time of the year.

The expedition set off from Cartagena, Spain, on 23 June 1775 with fifty-one warships; six of the line, twelve frigates, thirteen smaller ships, including four bomb ketches, and 344 smaller transport vessels. There were nearly 20,000 infantry, slightly over 700 cavalry, 120 dragoons and 900 artillerymen. The latter had thirty 24-pounders, eighty 4-pounders and twelve mortars. There was more than sufficient shot to satisfy any immediate necessity. Among the infantry units were a regiment of the Spanish Guards, Walloon Guards and companies of grenadiers from the Regiment of Hibernia.

The Algerian government knew that the Spaniards were

coming; Spanish plans had somehow come into their agent's hands back at Cartagena. Forewarned they summoned nearby supporters to help, especially from Constantine and Oran, even though the latter city was still occupied by the Spaniards.[18]

The Spanish forces, having arrived at the Bay of Algiers on 30 June and 1 July, were ordered to disembark at midnight on 2 July. Some officers complained that only the senior officers seemed aware of the plans for the attack. The troops could easily see, even in the dusk, formations of numerous Algerian cavalry and infantry all around the beaches. At the first appearance of the Spanish fleet the Algerian guns opened fire and maintained it nearly continuously for the entire day.

As the troops were about to disembark, an easterly wind blew up, creating a choppy sea and making it nearly impossible to effect a safe landing. The weather didn't improve for two days and O'Reilly decided to wait until 6 July and then to land west of Algiers at Cape Caxines. He was dissuaded from this by strong opposition from the fleet's second-in-command. Instead O'Reilly decided to select a beach just west of the River Harrach at about the same place Charles V had landed and been defeated.[19]

The planning and operation were not successful. Not enough landing boats had been assembled by midnight on 7 July and when the troops started to go ashore the Algerians were well aware of what they were doing. In seven columns the landing craft proceeded ashore with warships flanking them for protection as far as their draft would allow. The military organisation on shore would undoubtedly have been sufficient to prevent what was coming if only the Algerians had responded as expected. O'Reilly had the troops formed in columns six deep. The first, second, fifth and sixth were to suspend fire when action was joined, while the third and fourth would hurl grenades. O'Reilly further warned his subordinate officers, much to their apparent chagrin, that failure to follow his precise instructions would be cause for court-martial. He warned them that the Algerians would first attack violently, then feign a sudden retreat. Under no circumstances must his officers be drawn into any traps set by their enemy.

Plans required the Spanish troops to immediately seize the inland dunes, establish batteries of guns there and then advance to Kouba Hill, their main objective for the day. Upon reaching that point they were then to establish a fortified camp which would dominate the city and the surrounding territory.

The Algerians, variously numbered between 30,000 and 150,000, attacked the two inside columns of the Spanish forces which were in advance of the main body, but were soon driven off. When the Algerians seemed to be retreating, contrary to O'Reilly's orders the Spanish followed closely behind. The enemy drew them towards a series of well-concealed trenches in which more Algerians were hidden. Here the advance of the Spaniards was stopped and they were driven back to the beach. All this time a steady well-aimed fire of both muskets and artillery was used against the landing force. It appears that at some point O'Reilly made a fatal mistake. He delayed the second wave until several hours later. Ammunition was sparse and not enough made its way to the more advanced Spanish artillery. Consequently those guns were overrun, taking out the main Spanish fire support.

When the second wave did arrive at the beach the Algerians launched a massive and violent attack upon the closely clustered Spanish troops in disarray. The attack was launched behind a screen of camels, with eight Algerian guns supporting them. According to an eminent historian the companies from the Hibernia Regiment acted as a steadying influence at this point. If they hadn't, the entire army on land would have been in danger of being totally wiped out. Taking the same role the Irish picquets had at Culloden in Scotland thirty years before, they remained in the rear-guard protecting the Spanish forces until they reorganised.[20]

O'Reilly knew the situation was now desperate. Accompanied by several adjutants and aides, all of whom were wounded or killed, O'Reilly made a reconnaissance of the ground. He decided not to risk the lives of any more of his men. In darkness he managed to re-embark his force without drawing the attention of his enemies and without further loss.

At least 530 officers and men were lost and over 2,000 wounded. A Spanish encyclopedia states 1,500 men were killed in total, with an additional 3,000 wounded.[21] O'Reilly blamed the leadership of the two central columns which he asserted had advanced far beyond the other two and their supporting artillery, leading to ultimate disaster. The general commanding on land, who wrote the extremely critical report mentioned above, claimed it was O'Reilly's fault for not stopping the centre columns.[22] It was O'Reilly's first defeat and it did not go down well in Spain. But O'Reilly took full responsibility for his failure and for a short time, after his return, was exiled to the Chafarines Islands, just off Melilla in Africa.

For a while, the man who had been the most popular general in all of Spain was a pariah. Anyone associated or friendly with O'Reilly was shunned in public places. The King knew that his friend and loyal subject was being held responsible for something that was caused more by fate than by his incompetence. Therefore Carlos III refused to allow O'Reilly to accept all responsibility for the disaster and had him recalled from the islands to Spain. Initially he was deprived of his important positions but was created captain-general of Andalucia. Later O'Reilly held several additional important posts, the most consequential being the post of captain-general of the port of Cadiz.

Alexander O'Reilly's friend and protector, Carlos III, died on

14 December 1788 and O'Reilly was exiled to Galicia in north-west Spain where he spent a few years in confinement. O'Reilly still had many enemies in Madrid after the Algerian disaster. Upon release he returned to his home in Valencia and it appeared that he would be allowed to spend his final years in peace. However, now came a new time and a new war and one of the first things the new King Carlos IV, son of his old friend, did was to recall O'Reilly with full restoration of rank and honours. When the French Revolution broke out the personnel at the great naval base at Toulon, France, declared for the monarchy. Spain supported the monarchy as did most other European states and went to war with France. Britain and Spain lost no time in sending support for the French monarchist sailors at Toulon. O'Reilly was made naval base commandant. He boarded the first ship from Cartagena to Toulon in December 1793, but the trip was aborted when it was learned that the French troops under the young General Bonaparte had already taken the naval base. O'Reilly thereupon returned to Madrid for further orders. King Carlos IV named O'Reilly commander-in-chief of Spanish forces which were then preparing to advance north to the Pyrenees to fight the French revolutionary armies. A few days later, as the seventy-year-old Irishman rode to the front, he suffered a stroke at Bonete and died on 23 March 1794. He was buried in the churchyard in the town and a large plaque was placed on his tomb attesting to his character and ability.

In his biography of Carlos III, Sir Charles Petrie relates a contemporary account of what happened to a younger O'Reilly. It seems that O'Reilly, then captain of the Household Guards, saved the King's life. During a revolt in Madrid, insurrectionists entered the Palace of Escurial and O'Reilly rushed into their midst, sword in hand, and was primarily responsible for suppressing the riot. The King promoted and honoured O'Reilly in many ways. When a new road was being built to connect this palace with the palace at St Ildefonso, the workmen came upon a huge sturdy oak tree standing right in their path. The King instructed the workmen, who had built the road as straight and true as could be, to make a circuit around the tree and not to destroy it. He named the tree 'O'Reilly', 'for if I was gone tomorrow, this venerable tree and poor O'Reilly's existence would fall sacrifices to my subjects'. Clearly, Carlos the King, unlike many of his peers and contemporaries, believed in and felt an obligation to someone who had served him nobly and well.

Of all the accolades praising O'Reilly during his lifetime the one which identified him as 'the Frederick the Great of Spain' was one which even Frederick himself agreed with.[23]

CHAPTER 6

THE IRISH IN FRENCH SERVICE

Irish men and women left Ireland and travelled to France from the earliest times. Later, as France hired foreigners for their numerous wars, the occasional Irishman would find his way to wherever the job was located. In the late sixteenth and early seventeenth centuries it was usually in Flanders. Later, entrepreneurs would gather a flock of men from the British Isles or Ireland, bring them to Europe and sell them as company or regiment to France or Spain. The group would then fight until killed, wounded or crippled for life, occasionally being paid some of the money they were owed.

Until the 1620s the army of France was technically a feudal force, with units belonging to various members of the French nobility. Cardinal Richelieu assumed power and, in his tenure as Prime Minister, changed that structure to form a King's army. When he died in 1642, his successor Louvois completed his plans.[1] England was supportive of those Irish who wished to leave Ireland for foreign shores, placing no restrictions on them, and some of the first levies began arriving in France after 1635. An O'Reilly was authorised to recruit ten companies of a hundred men each and although negotiations were completed in November 1634, those numbers were never achieved. More negotiations with other Irishmen led to several regiments over the next few years which were hastily thrown into France's many battles, including the Thirty Years' War which was blazing all over the western and central parts of the continent.

In the early 1640s many Irish already on the continent began leaving Spanish and French service to return to Ireland for what would become the Irish Confederate War, in which a Catholic confederation rose up against their English overlords. Following the defeat, those who survived and were able to, escaped from the Cromwellian scourge. Within a few years Cromwell and his kind were out of power but the damage visited upon Ireland was never undone.

Because the French government strongly supported the Stuart family in exile and their restoration in 1660, Irishmen in return fought for the French. During the latter part of the century more began going to France, not only as soldiers, but also to engage in mercantile and other professions. Those who went to lead soldiers were members of several families. The Hamiltons were among the first, raising several Irish regiments for Louis XIV in his various battles with Spain.

Next came Justin MacCarthy, Lord Mountcashel, who was born at Blarney in Cork, the son of Donogh, Viscount Muskerry, and his mother Eleanor Butler, the sister of the Lord Lieutenant Ormond. Though tried for treason by Cromwell's judges, Donogh was acquitted. The family was, like so many others, deprived of their estates and went to France. Their the eldest son, Cormac, led a regiment of men from his father's estates. When the treaty between England and France was signed in 1656, Charles Stuart left France for England, and so did Cormac's regiment. Later, Cormac named the regiment after Charles' brother, James, the Duke of York. Following the restoration, Viscount Muskerry and family returned to Ireland but it is unclear whether he, unlike so many other Jacobites, had his estate returned.

Justin MacCarthy joined the Hamilton Regiment in 1671 and fought in the Dutch War, earning a respectable reputation. When in 1676 the Duke of Monmouth was granted colonel-proprietorship of a French regiment, his commander was a Lieutenant-Colonel Scott.[2] However Scott was an ill man and the regiment was soon very badly in need of a commanding officer who could enforce discipline. Justin MacCarthy, whom Monmouth called 'Macartie' when he recommended him to Louis XIV, was appointed to command in November 1676. Justin soon turned things around, even making sure the men were paid regularly, not very common in any army of that period.

During the following years the regiment fought in the Netherlands where MacCarthy and his men gained valuable experience and skills. MacCarthy became acquainted with Patrick Sarsfield who was then serving in the Hamilton Regiment.[3] Following the Dutch war MacCarthy served in Denmark during their war with Sweden and then returned to England.

James II, formerly the Duke of York, had succeeded his brother Charles II. He and his wife, Mary of Modena, both Roman Catholics, had been making changes which the English Protestants had been barely tolerating. When she gave birth to a son, James, the child was supposed to be baptised in the faith required by English law. Nonetheless the parents had him baptised a Roman Catholic. Whigs, the extreme right wing, enticed James II's protestant son-in-law, William, and daughter, Mary, to come over to England and take over the crown and throne. They did so in 1688. James and his family left for France, where they were well treated by Louis XIV.

However, that wasn't the end of it. In Ireland a large group of clan leaders under the overall command of Richard Talbot, Lord

Deputy of Ireland, First Earl of Tyrconnell, formed an army. Talbot had cleared the military forces as well as the local government in Ireland of Protestants and invited James to come and take command of his army. The forces of James, limited in muskets and artillery, performed as well as they could. However they were defeated in most battles and after the Battle of the Boyne on 1 July 1690, James travelled to Dublin complaining, 'You Irish ran.' To which someone responded, 'But not as rapidly as your majesty', or words to that effect.

Following the disaster most of the Irish, still in military units, accepted the invitation in the Treaty of Limerick to leave Ireland. They moved to France in October 1691 and were soon involved in the wars of Louis XIV. The English parliament refused to accept William of Orange's agreement and many Irish soldiers who hadn't left in 1691 followed them to France. Some of the leaders were of Celtic stock, many more were the 'Old English' which included Norman stock. Examples of the former were the O'Briens, and of the latter, the Dillons. Norman names such as Tracy, Burke and Lacy were numerous. But they were all Irish.

Their wars in France were fought during the 1690s until the Treaty or Peace of Ryswick in 1697. One important issue for the stateless Irish was France's agreement to end their support of the Stuart family. This technically terminated King James' Irish Army and its regiments, which could have left the soldiers without employment. Nevertheless, France, like Spain, was always in need of military manpower and a number of Irish regiments were formed in the French army as an Irish Brigade. Those not assimilated drifted elsewhere. Many also went to Spain.

For the next hundred or so years those Irish who remained or arrived in France served that nation extremely well. There were many thousands who could not tolerate the conditions prevalent in Ireland which resulted in an almost continuous flow of new blood into France for the next century. One of those who arrived there was Peter Drake, perhaps better known than many of his countrymen because of his memoir.[4]

Several members of the Barnewall family arrived in 1691. Later, Nicholas Barnewall, born in Ireland in 1725, went to France and made a huge fortune, but he lost it all in the chaos of the revolution at the end of the century.

Thomas Betagh, son of Francis Betagh of Moynalty, County Meath, who lost his estates upon the restoration of Charles II, moved to France and resided and died at St Germain-en-Laye. His son, Thomas, entered Nugent's Cavalry Regiment, married Marcelle Tyrrell in 1707, and had two sons. Thomas Tyrrell Betagh was born at St Germain-en-Laye in 1714, and later entered FitzJames' Cavalry Regiment attaining the rank of colonel-commandant of the regiment, having been wounded at Fontenoy. He especially distinguished himself at the Battle of Rosbach in 1767 against Frederick the Great's Prussians. Thomas' brother Jean Patrice was killed there.

The many O'Connors in France held rank in several Irish regiments with some coming over in 1691 and others during the next century. Thomas Roe, born in County Roscommon in 1710, entered Dillon's Regiment, serving through most of the battles of the Austrian Succession. Brave to a fault, at Fontenoy he earned an appointment as a Knight of St Louis. Next were the battles of the Seven Years' War during which he was especially noticed at Marburg in 1761. He was promoted to Brigadier des Armées du Roi and in 1780 to Maréchal du Camp. He returned to Roscommon and died there.

Nicholas Glascoe was born at St Germain-en-Laye in 1715, the son of Christian, a captain of the Irish troops who had left after Limerick. As a cadet, then ensign, in Dillon's Regiment he was wounded in the knee at Fontenoy. He went to Scotland with Prince Charles in 1745, where he was noted for capturing Keith and its entire garrison on the morning of 20 March 1746. After the Battle of Culloden on 16 April 1746, where the Jacobite army was destroyed, he, like so many others, was in irons in London for almost a year. He was allowed to return to France after his trial and he resumed his career in Ogilvey's Scottish regiment.

John Fitzgerald, from Waterford, entered Dillon's Regiment in 1730. With them he fought in the German wars; was at the siege of Kehl in 1733 and at Philippsburg the following year. Captain Fitzgerald fought at Dettingen in 1743 and in 1744 became company commander in Lally's Regiment, fighting at Fontenoy in 1745. His regiment was singularly distinguished, as was he, receiving a colonel's brevet. In 1747 he was at Lauffelt and managed to survive even though the Irish Brigade regiments took major casualties. Marshal Saxe won the battle but his opponents managed to withdraw towards Maastricht. Following the German wars of 1760–1761, upon the death of Charles O'Brien, Seventh Viscount Clare, Fitzgerald was appointed colonel of Clare's Regiment. At the end of the Seven Years' War, Fitzgerald retired and died on 9 February 1773.

Three Irish soldiers, Major Richard Gaydon, Captains Luke O'Toole and John Misset, plus Misset's wife and her maid, joined with Sir Charles Wogan in a special mission in April-May 1719. They were to go to Innsbruck in the Tyrol and free a royal captive, already selected by Wogan as the future wife of James III, hereditary King of Britain.[5] The captive was Princess Maria Clementina Sobieski, granddaughter of John Sobieski, formerly King of Poland. It was a dangerous – and successful – task to bring the princess to her intended, who was based in Rome. She married James and became the pretender Queen of Great Britain.

The Hennessys sent many men to serve France, but several

of note are included here. A native of Kilkenny, John Hennessy, entered Bulkeley's Regiment and by the time the Battle of Fontenoy on 10 May 1745 was fought, he was a captain. After Lauffelt he was promoted to lieutenant-colonel. He took early retirement and returned to Ireland, eventually being buried at Derrynahinch, County Kilkenny.

Another Hennessy, first name unknown, came to Ireland in 1730 to raise recruits for the Irish Brigade of France. He had managed to obtain a letter of support from the English Prime Minister, Sir Robert Walpole, to Primate Boulter in Dublin recommending his mission. As soon as Walpole's permission was made public, a storm was raised over this support of France's armies, and it was rescinded.

Richard Hennessy was born in 1720 at Killavullen, County Cork. At twenty years of age he went to France and became an officer of Dillon's Regiment. With them he fought at Dettingen, later at Fontenoy and other battles of the War of the Austrian Succession, during which he was wounded. That caused him to retire from the military and in 1763 he married his cousin Ellen; two years later they settled in Cognac and established the distillery which still bears the family name. He and Ellen had a son, James, who was born at Brussels on 11 October 1765, a few days before his parents set out for Cognac. Richard died in 1800.

James Hennessy also sought service in Dillon's Regiment, but eventually resigned and joined his father at the distillery. He married Martha, daughter of M. Martell, also in the cognac business. Meanwhile he had been actively involved in politics and served in the Chamber of Deputies until his death on 22 April 1843. His son and namesake was born in 1795 and married Sophia, daughter of Baron de Marcuil, French ambassador to many courts.

The O'Shee family also delivered sons to France to fight their many wars. The family was closely connected to the same Clarke family as Henri, Duke de Feltre, Napoleon's Minister of War.

Robert Richard O'Shee was born in Cloneen in County Tipperary on 24 December 1736, the son of Richard and Elizabeth O'Shee. At age sixteen he became a cadet in Bulkeley's Regiment in 1752 and participated in the Seven Years' War, following which he was promoted to captain. In 1759, along with most of the Irish Brigade, his regiment was based in Brittany for the planned invasion of Ireland, which never came off. Destruction of Admiral Hubert de Conflan's fleet at Quiberon Bay on 24 November 1759 effectively ended France's naval power for the balance of that war. As aide-de-camp to Marshal Broglie and Chevalier of St Louis, Captain O'Shee was in Dillon's Regiment in 1775. As commander of the National Guard he was at the attack on the Bastille on 14 July 1789, and in 1792 was a major commanding a battalion in the same regiment, now known as the 87th Regiment. Four years later he was on half pay as commandant of the École Militaire. Lazare Nicholas Marguerite Carnot, a member of the Directory, thought this man was dubious because he supposedly did not have a high reputation in Paris, and this undoubtedly had something to do with his reduced circumstances. Robert died aged seventy on 5 December 1806.

The son of Marcus and Thomasina O'Shee, Richard was born on 13 May 1740 at Castletown, County Kilkenny. Also emigrating to France at age sixteen, Richard became a cadet in the cavalry regiment of FitzJames and in 1763 transferred to Berwick's Regiment. In 1768 he became a captain in Roscommon's Regiment. With the Legion of Artois at the Île de France in 1788, Captain of Grenadiers O'Shee didn't return to Paris until 1791. He supported the revolution and was appointed a colonel of the 87th Regiment (Dillon's) in 1792, then a general of brigade in 1796. Carnot suggested sending O'Shee to Ireland as an emissary while preparations for Hoche's invasion of that island were underway, but neither event happened. Richard became commandant at Finistère in 1799, retired on half pay in 1800 and died on 31 January 1801.

Another Kilkenny man, Eugene Bernard O'Shee, son of Henry and Susan Nichols O'Shee, was born on 29 March 1775. Eugene went to France in 1782 at the tender age of seven years, to be raised by his relative Henri Clarke, Duke de Feltre. At age sixteen he was made a cadet in Berwick's Regiment in 1791 and served through most of the campaigns of the revolutionary and Napoleonic periods. In 1809 he had been promoted to colonel of the 13th Regiment of Chasseurs and for distinguished service Napoleon created him a baron. During the Spanish war he had taken prisoner and treated with kindness the Marquis of Anglesea. Twenty years later the Marquis, then Lord Lieutenant of Ireland, referred to that treatment as reason for enlisting Irish men in higher ranks in British service. When the Bourbons were restored he was made general of brigade. Baron Eugene O'Shee died at his home in St Germain-en-Laye in 1839. His brother, William, formerly a captain in Dillon's Regiment, left the service and entered the British army when the French Revolution began. He was shot and killed during a duel with Captain Stack, a fellow Irish officer, in Jamaica in 1797.

Henry O'Shee was born at Landrecies, France on 1 January 1739, the son of William, a captain in Clare's Regiment, and Marie Peponier. He would later become Henri Clarke's step-uncle through the marriage of his sister Louisa to Clarke's father, Thomas, Colonel of Dillon's Regiment. Henry O'Shee entered Clare's Regiment as a cadet in 1755 and fought through the Seven Years' War with special distinction at the Battle of Marburg in 1761. He was colonel of the Duke of Orleans' Regiment in 1785 and for a period was the Duke's military secretary. Because of ill health, he retired from the army in 1791 but returned to active duty in 1795 and was promoted to general of the brigade. He was part of Hoche's ill-fated expedition and at that time became acquainted with Wolfe Tone with whom he continued a close relationship until Tone's demise. In civilian service in 1801, he was prefect of the Bas-Rhin province with headquarters at Strasbourg. He was decorated with the Cross of the Legion of Honour and in 1809 Napoleon created him a count. He became a senator in 1810. He, like his nephew Henri Clarke, sided with the Bourbons and Louis XVIII appointed him a peer of France in June 1814. His daughter Françoise (also known as Fanny) married Jacques Wulfranc, Baron Dalton, and produced a son who became Baron Dalton-Shee. Count Henry O'Shee died on 3 March 1820 aged eighty-one.

Edward Dalton-Shee's parents died not long after his birth on 1 June 1810, and he was adopted by his grandfather, Henry O'Shee. Upon the latter's death, young Edward inherited his grandfather's patrimony. He became a politician and later fought on the barricades in Paris to prevent the ascent of Napoleon III. His stand for democracy was hailed by President Leon Gambetta. He died in Paris on 22 May 1874.

A priest named Henry Kane, also known as O'Kane, was born in County Mayo, earned a degree at the Irish college at Nantes and was ordained in 1788. In 1793 at the outbreak of war between England and France, Kane declared that England was his enemy while keeping Ireland in bondage, and joined the 65th French Infantry Regiment. He fought during the Revolution and in 1798 was staff officer with General Humbert in his expedition to Ireland. He saw distinguished action at the Battle of Castlebar but when the French surrendered he was court-martialled by the English. However his life was saved and he returned to France. Serving during the Napoleonic period his valour in various battles earned him promotion to major and the Order of the Legion of Honour. Kane served in Portugal in 1810 and 1811, but after Napoleon's defeat he retired with a pension.

Lord Kilmallock, also known as Dominick Sarsfield, son of the fourth Lord Kilmallock, had in his youth served in the French army incognito as an enlisted soldier in the Dutch wars. Later he was a colonel in the army of James II and accompanied them to France in 1691. There he became the colonel of the Régiment du Roi and commanded at the Battle of Marsaglia in 1693. He was at the siege of Valenza in 1697, and at the battle of Chiari in 1701, where he was killed while leading his men. Sarsfield was married to Frances, a sister of his kinsman, Patrick Sarsfield.

Another kinsman, Edmund Sarsfield, was born in Ireland and emigrated to France in 1752 and joined the regiment of Rothe as a cadet. He attained the rank of lieutenant-colonel in Walsh's Regiment in 1769 having fought in the Seven Years' War, and was made a Chevalier of St Louis. He remained in France during the Revolution, serving in the 92nd Regiment, and attained the rank of brigadier-general before his demise.

Another family with strong ties in both France and Spain were the O'Connells. They included Daniel Charles who entered the French army, joining the Royal Suedois Regiment as a cadet in 1761, and served during the latter part of the Seven Years' War until transferring into Clare's Regiment. Daniel fought at Minorca and later at Gibraltar in 1782. Although he was wounded there he managed to save the life of the Duke of Artois, later King Charles X. He was later colonel of the Regiment Salm-Salm and appointed inspector-general of infantry. That post earned him the Cross of St Louis and the title of count. During the Revolution he first remained in Paris at his army post, then elected to join the refugees at Coblenz. He went to London and in 1791 he persuaded

Pitt to form a British-Irish Brigade of which he became colonel. Though only partially formed, the brigade lasted two years. He took advantage of the Treaty of Amiens which ended the war between England and France in 1802, and returned to France. When the war resumed, he, like so many other royalists, went to jail and remained there until the Bourbons were returned to power. Thereupon he regained his old rank of lieutenant-general which had been stripped from him in the July Revolution of 1830 when he refused to swear an oath to King Louis Philippe. He retired to his home at Madon, dying there in 1833.

The Allen family of County Kildare sent Luke Allen, one of twenty-one children, to France and he entered Dillon's Regiment in 1735 as a lieutenant. Having fought at the Battle of Fontenoy he joined Lally's Regiment as a major and in 1757 accompanied his colonel to India. Allen was an outstanding and very courageous soldier in the war against England on that sub-continent. Allen was entrusted with the storming of Fort Sacramalous and was first to enter. French warships were badly defeated at the naval battle of Pondicherry in September 1759 and with that the French troops in India were no longer able to receive reinforcements or sustenance. During the siege of Pondicherry he had been promoted to commander-in-chief in India and was severely wounded. When the siege terminated and the French surrendered to the English he returned to France. In 1762 he married Marie de Behague, by whom he later had five daughters and a son, Sir Luke Patrick Allen. His battles for France versus England caused his official loss of family property in Ireland.

The Suttons of Clonard were an Irish family with reputations as superior French soldiers. Thomas was born in Wexford sometime before 1710. He emigrated to France and settled at Bordeaux, soon becoming an officer in the Irish Brigade. He gained the title of Comte de Clonard and married Frances Masterson of

Castletown, Wexford, in 1744. They had four sons and two daughters. John and Richard joined Walsh's Regiment in which the former attained the rank of colonel and the latter became a major. Both left France at the Revolution, joining the British-Irish Brigade. John married a Miss Crosbie of County Kilkenny and upon the Bourbon restoration they returned to France. Miss Crosbie was a relative of Henri Clarke who obtained a pension for her husband which lasted until his death in 1833.

Two other brothers both joined the French navy; Robert attained the rank of captain and served as aide-de-camp to Count Jean Baptiste Charles Henri Hector d'Estaing during the American Revolution. He later died during an attack upon St Lucie.

The name Bugeaud de la Piconnerie, Marshal Thomas Robert, Duc d'Isly, doesn't appear to be Irish, but his mother, Frances, was the daughter of Patrick Sutton of Clonard, County Wexford. Bugeaud was one of the great soldiers of nineteenth-century France. He began as a grenadier in Napoleon's Velites of the Imperial Guard in 1804. Two years later he was commissioned as a result of his courageous actions during the sieges of Zaragoza and Pamplona in Spain. In 1814 he rallied to the Bourbons but switched back to Napoleon during the Hundred Days War (when Napoleon regained power), defeating an Austrian force in Savoy. With Napoleon's defeat Bugeaud retired to his estates, where he remained until 1830 when he was recalled to active duty. Until 1835 he held various military and political positions, until assigned to Algeria. There he completed the defeat of a revolt led by Abd-el-Kader and from 1840 was made governor-general of Algeria. He was appointed a marshal in 1843 and then expanded French control over Algeria. He won the Battle of Isly, which effectively conquered the Moroccans, and he was created Duke d'Isly in 1844. He was sacked over his policies in 1847, but was reinstated the following year and appointed commander of the Army of the

Alps by the new president, later Napoleon III. He died of cholera in 1849.

Oliver Harty, Baron de Pierrebourg, eventually a lieutenant-general of France, was born in Knocklong, County Limerick on 2 December 1746. At age sixteen he emigrated to France and joined the Berwick Regiment. He wasn't alone; three of his uncles were serving in different Irish regiments there. Harty attained the rank of captain of the Grenadiers two years before the Revolution and earned the Order of St Louis from Louis XVI. Following the dissolution of the Irish Brigade he remained in France and was appointed a colonel of the 88th Regiment, formerly Berwick. When the 88th was about to leave France to join the Royalists in Germany, Harty managed to talk most of the officers and men out of going and to remain loyal to the Revolution. He was, however, treated with a certain disrespect, as were most other foreign officers and in 1793 was imprisoned for more than two months. Leaving France he was captured by the English and sent to prison in Bermuda. Harty managed to escape and returned to France.

A French attempt to free Ireland from Britain led by Hoche was planned and several Irish regiments were involved. Lee and O'Meara's regiments were being formed into a 'Brigade Etrangère' with Harty in command in 1795, when he had been restored to his former rank. One of the few French ships to arrive at Bantry Bay in Ireland included Harty and his soldiers. The attempt having failed, Harty was back in France with the 15th Division facing the Chouans uprisings in 1799 and 1800.[6] Harty was exceptionally successful during these campaigns. In one battle his 800 troops defeated 8,000 insurgents under the command of Georges Cadoudal.[7] In 1805 he was briefly inspector-general of the Irish Legion while they were near Brest in another planned attempt to free Ireland. Harty played a part in the Napoleonic campaigns and for his courage and gallantry was created Baron of Pierrebourg (in the Alsace) by Napoleon on 30 June 1811, which honour was confirmed after the restoration of Louis XVIII. With an often strenuous military career of fifty years, Lieutenant-General Harty elected to retire on 1 May 1814. He married Anne Marie de Grenveld with whom he had two sons and a daughter. Harty died at Strasbourg on 2 January 1823 aged seventy-six.

Many Irish men were employed in the service of France. However, two Irish women, sisters, must also be included in the outstanding persons listed here, even though neither was a soldier. Both were married to soldiers and both became queens when their husbands were proclaimed king. They were the sisters Cleary (also French-style 'Clary'). Julie married Joseph Bonaparte in 1794, made King of Spain in 1808; and Desirée was the wife of Marshal Jean-Baptiste Jules Bernadotte, Prince de Ponte Corvo. They later became King and Queen of Sweden.

Napoleon was personally greatly interested in Desirée, and for a period of about a year, her fiancé. But her family didn't feel he was right for her. Desirée had many other suitors, and eventually accepted Bernadotte's offer and helped him to establish the only royal house in Europe which has endured until today. Bernadotte was, according to Napoleon, very fortunate. He remarked that he would have had Bernadotte shot several times if it hadn't been for his tender affection for Desirée.

Bernadotte had treated Swedish prisoners of war with great kindness and many of them never forgot that. When the Swedish royal line died out, he was chosen as replacement. He arrived in Sweden in October 1810 and at once adopted the name Charles John and the Lutheran faith. As king he managed to bring the nation into the nineteenth century insofar as military operations and associations with foreign powers were concerned, and became a popular monarch of that nation.

Known for her simple ways, without pretension, Desirée

remained a Roman Catholic even though her husband changed to the state Lutheran faith. She remained in Paris for a number of years following his installation, arriving in Sweden in 1829. Desirée survived Bernadotte and lived to see her son Oscar I and grandson Charles XV both become King of Sweden. Desirée died at the royal palace in 1860. Her sister, Julie, did not spend much time as Queen because Joseph lost his throne when the French were driven out of Spain in 1813.

CHAPTER 7

GENERAL CHARLES JENNINGS (KILMAINE)

The Jennings family of Connacht played a notable part for centuries in the tumultuous history of their country.[1] Son of Dr Theobald Jennings and Eleanor Saul, Charles was born in Dublin at his mother's residence on 19 October 1751. His father's family, the MacJonins of Tuam, County Galway, were extensive landed proprietors in Galway and Mayo, until their continued adherence to their faith resulted in the loss of most of their property.

Charles Jennings belonged to that branch of the family which was settled at Polaniran (Ironpool) near Tuam. A direct ancestor, Richard Óg MacJonin, was hanged in 1599, because he had joined the revolt of the Connacht chiefs. Richard's son, Theobald, was slain in battle the following year and his estate was forfeited. Two generations later their fortunes were still further lowered when the Cromwellian regime left Theobald, the representative of the line, a homeless man.

Other branches of the Jennings or MacJonin family in the Barony of Kilmaine in County Mayo suffered as well. In the eighteenth century many of them joined in the desolate flight of the 'Wild Geese' across the sea to France. General Sir William Jennings of Ballinrobe commanded a brigade in King James' Irish Army in Ireland and went to France after the capitulation of Limerick. Other Jennings, including Redmond Jonins, a native of Shrule in Mayo, was admitted as an officer of the Irish Brigade to the military hospital at Paris (Hotel des Invalides) in 1721.

Theobald Jennings was born at Polaniran and left Ireland in 1758 when the Penal Law system was suppressing the body and soul of his native land. In France he studied medicine and qualified as a doctor. He married his cousin, the daughter of Laurence Saul, a wealthy distiller and well-known Dublin citizen. He practised his profession at Tonnay-Charente and he became a naturalised French citizen. In the middle of 1751 his wife, finding that she was to become a mother, left for Dublin so that their child might be born on Irish soil. She stayed with her father's relatives at Saul's Court. Thirty years later when he required an official attestation of his birth as an officer of the French army, he furnished the following document instead of the formal birth certificate which was not then available in Ireland to adherents of the old faith:

We, the undersigned, Principal and Provisors of the Irish College, called the College of the Lombards, in Paris, certify to all whom it may concern that Charles Edward Jennings, Baron of Kilmaine, officer in Lauzun's Hussars, son of Theobald Edward Jennings, Baron of Kilmaine, and of Dame Eleonore Saul, his father and mother in legitimate marriage, was born at Dublin in the Parish of Rose Mary Lane on 19th October 1751, and was baptised according to the rites of the Catholic Church.[2]

We also certify that, since the Protestant Reformed religion became dominant in Ireland, the Catholic Clergy have not been able to keep any legal registers of baptisms, marriages or deaths. In faith of which we have signed the present certificate at Paris on the 6th May 1784.

Signed,

Ch. O'NEILL, Principal.

P. Flood, Provisor.

W. Burke.

Young Jennings was reared in Dublin with his relations until 1762 when his father brought the family to Tonnay-Charente. Charles, then in his eleventh year, was educated in that town and became particularly proficient as a linguist, speaking, besides French, the four principal languages of Europe. At the termination of his studies he entered the French army, joining in 1774 the regiment of the Royal Dragoons as a cadet. He studied every branch of military science with much zest and seriousness and at the end of four years became adjutant in the Foreign Volunteers of Lauzun. This corps was sent to Senegal to take part in the French war against England then raging in that country to determine which would lead the slave trade. England had come out on top at the Treaty of Paris in 1763. Though they lost Gorée (Senegal), the French had what they considered to be a successful campaign. During the American Revolution, France and England went at it once again, and this time France came out ahead and Senegal was returned to France in 1779.

In 1780 Charles Jennings, Baron of Kilmaine, was promoted to the rank of lieutenant in the famous Hussars of Lauzun, the first cavalry regiment in the army.[3] In the same year this corps formed part of the French expeditionary forces that participated with the Americans in their War of Independence. Kilmaine distinguished himself in many battles during that campaign, and his experiences there strengthened in him a love of liberty and hatred of tyranny.

Returning to France, Kilmaine was appointed Director of

Military Tactics at the riding school of Lauzun's Regiment, while at the same time he taught the new system of manoeuvres at the important centre of Metz. In 1788, the year preceding the outbreak of the Revolution, his talents earned him a captaincy. Such rapid promotion for one who, in the France of those days, could command no court influence and did not belong to the patrician class, indicated a brilliant future for the young Irish officer.

He and many others remained with the army when the French Revolution broke out. At the outbreak of the Revolution in 1789, Kilmaine became a zealous supporter of the new ideas of liberty that began to spread throughout France. His passionate devotion to the new doctrines impelled him to preach them openly to the Hussars of his regiment at Verdun. He told them that the duty of French soldiers was 'to fight and overcome the enemies of their country but never to draw their swords for the purpose of serving the designs of tyranny'. For this action he was placed under arrest and detained for a short time in prison in the year 1789. This experience, however, did not alter his sentiments nor lessen his enthusiasm. Two years later the question of loyalty to the Revolution or the monarchy became a burning one in the various regiments of the French army. When officers began to leave France in increasing numbers Kilmaine carried on a zealous propaganda campaign in favour of the new regime amongst the higher and lower ranks of his corps. He was extremely popular with both his fellow officers and the men under his command, and the result was that the regiment of Lauzun, which at first seemed disposed to desert, remained loyal to the cause of the Revolution during crises. Following the attempted flight of the King in 1791 he was one of the first officers who came forward to swear the oath of allegiance to the National Assembly and to abjure royalty in all its forms.

Owing to the emigration of officers from the nobility there was an increasing number of vacancies in the higher army ranks, and Kilmaine's growing military reputation secured him promotion as Chef d'Escadron. This was the post he held when war broke out between most of Europe and revolutionary France in April 1792.

The first great conflict between French troops and Austria and her allies occurred at Valmy in September 1792. Kilmaine, with squadrons of the cavalry regiment, played a notable part in that victory for France At their head he penetrated the forest of the Argonne 'to places where a horse had never gone before' and, reaching the important pass of Grand Pré, harassed the Prussians and intercepted their convoys.[4] During the critical manoeuvres of the day the heroic resistance displayed by a body of Hussars under his command saved a whole French division from annihilation by the enemy in the defiles of Croix aux Bois. His conduct was especially distinguished in the Valmy campaign. His superior officer, General Pierre du Riel Beurnonville singled him out for special praise, declaring that 'in skill, resolution and intelligence Kilmaine, that splendid soldier, could not be excelled during those perilous days for France'.

Early in November 1792 Lauzun's Hussars formed the vanguard of the invading army that crossed the frontier into Belgium. Its advance was challenged by the enemy at Jemappes. At its most critical stage the battle seemed lost to France when a French brigade at the centre of the field of operations wavered and failed. But Kilmaine and the Duke of Chartres (Prince Louis Philippe), the future King of France, immediately filled the gap with their regiments, which saved the day. General Charles C. Dumouriez, Commander-in-Chief of French forces, was so elated that he called the Irish officer *le brave Kilmaine* – the name by which he was ever afterwards known – and in January 1793 promoted him to the rank of colonel on the battlefield. Afterwards the commander-in-chief declared that Kilmaine was 'one of the most experienced officers in the army' and had 'saved the centre of the line of infantry on the fateful day'. As a consequence he became general of brigade in March 1793 and in May, general of division.

Having been victorious at Jemappes, Kilmaine had a high reputation as a commander of the advance guard. In that capacity he accompanied Dumouriez in the conquest of Belgium, which was soon in the possession of France. Following that campaign hundreds of men in the French forces, starving and without pay, lacking bridles and saddles, pistols and sabres, deserted daily from the ranks. Kilmaine was tireless in his efforts to maintain order in the demoralised regiments, and out of his own private resources contributed to the support of the soldiers who had already begun to plunder the Belgian countryside.

The French forces experienced continuous reverses during the forced evacuation of Belgium in the spring months of 1793. The disorganised and dispirited state to which they were reduced left France in a perilous position and at the same time the defection of Dumouriez to Austria added to her ill-fortune. His successor was General Picot Dampierre, a bold and enterprising soldier, under whose orders Kilmaine had the responsible task of guarding the frontier from Sedan to Longwy. Here Kilmaine was involved in frequent engagements during the months of April and May. At this time the French fortress towns of Valenciennes and Condé, two of the great gateways into France, were being besieged by the allied army and the Republic was concentrating all her energies on their relief. Early in May Dampierre made a gallant but fruitless effort to relieve Condé. In this he was supported by Kilmaine who, on the first two days of May, led his Hussars in what were described as 'the murderous engagements' among the woods of Vicogne and Saint Amand. Horse after horse was shot under him during the fighting. In the week's skirmishing which followed he 'never had his boots off nor returned his sabre once to the scabbard'. In a dispatch to the National Convention, giving an account of these early operations which failed in their immediate object, Dampierre wrote:

> I tried to drive the enemy from several villages occupied by them on the road from Valenciennes to Quesnoi ... The advance guard under General Kilmaine fought with its usual courage – the killed and wounded of the enemy forces numbered 600. I proceeded from the main body to the vanguard where the valiant Kilmaine had two horses killed under him.[5]

On 9 May another effort, by means of a general attack along the whole allied line, was made to relieve the beleaguered town. At the height of the battle, Dampierre was struck by a cannon ball and fell mortally wounded. Kilmaine continued to fight on with his usual reckless valour but by nightfall the French were routed with heavy loss. The defeat and death of their commander had a most depressing effect on the troops and to Kilmaine fell the task of covering their disorderly retreat back to their camp at Famars. The enemies of France were winning; defeat and demoralisation were falling upon everyone.

Much ill-feeling had developed at this period between the generals of the army and the ruling Committee of Public Safety. At the instigation of the latter, officers were frequently recalled to Paris where imprisonment or the guillotine was generally their fate. It is with some surprise that one reads the tributes from many of the officials of the committee to Kilmaine. In a dispatch one of them wrote:

> Brave, enterprising, energetic Kilmaine, general of the advance guard, would be difficult to replace in the event of any accident to him. He

seems anxious to have supreme command, which it would, perhaps, be imprudent to confer on him on account of his foreign birth – he is an Irishman, and Republicanism does not easily penetrate into Irish heads.

A second representative of the committee recommended him as the only general on whose skill and energy reliance could be placed to crush the insurrection then raging in La Vendée, as Kilmaine had a wise and philanthropic plan for the pacification of that province. And still another representative proposed to the great committee that, by reason of his talents and energy, he should be given supreme command of the Army of Rochelle. On receiving news of Dampierre's death, the Committee of Public Safety discussed the situation that existed along the northern frontier which was seriously threatened by 100,000 of the allied army. Kilmaine was recognised as the only officer available to carry out efficiently the duties of commander-in-chief, and the committee accordingly nominated him for the post. The representatives of the Committee who were in Italy on a fact-finding mission objected, however, to his appointment because he was of foreign birth, and it was instead conferred on General Adam Philippe Custine. But charges of disloyalty were soon brought against the latter, and he was summoned to Paris. There his trial before the Revolutionary Tribunal followed and his life ended on the guillotine.

Kilmaine protested when he was chosen as the new commander-in-chief, claiming that his military abilities were such that he might not be able to satisfactorily discharge the duties of the stupendous task. 'Some other more fitting than I am,' he said, 'should accept the heavy responsibility of leading the troops of the Republic.' With some persuasion, however, he gave his consent, and in a letter to the National Convention he affirmed his own loyalty and that of his troops to the nation, adding that his motto would be 'To strike high, to speak low and little!'

This was a grievous burden. The poorly-equipped and ill-disciplined soldiers of the Republic were faced by an enemy that was treble their numbers. In addition, the surrender had just taken place of Condé and Valenciennes, the fortresses on which France depended so much, and at any moment the great allied army could surge forward on a victorious march into French territory.

Immediately upon assuming command in the early days of August, Kilmaine was entrenched with his troops in a fairly strong position known as Caesar's Camp. If any defeat should befall his army, with now only 120 miles between him and Paris, there would be a clear road for the enemy to the capital. On 7 August they advanced and, appearing in strength before the French camp, threatened it on all sides. In a dispatch to the Minister of War Kilmaine wrote:

> Yesterday morning an enemy column of 20,000 men turned our position and simultaneously made an attack on all our posts. This was maintained with much intrepidity, and I was compelled to retreat ... Pursued by 6,000 cavalry, I had only 2,000 with which to oppose them. Three times we charged the enemy and killed sixty of them. Our audacity bewildered them; our cavalry behaved most heroically. Theirs is treble ours, and there is nothing we are in more need of ...

Next day he complained in a further letter of this lack of cavalry in his command area where, more than anywhere else in his opinion, the Republic was in jeopardy:

> Egoism is our ruin, for there exists among us an egoism of commanders, an egoism of individual regiments, of towns and of departments. It is here in the north, however, that the enemy is making his biggest

efforts, and it is here we must mobilise all our strength; and while this is so, the Army of the North, which is in the direst need of cavalry, has in fact fewer than any other.

The advance of the enemy continued all day and by nightfall on 7 August the allied army of 80,000 threatened the French camp. The situation was critical for Kilmaine. Hurriedly summoning a council of officers, he proposed a retreat as the only thing that would save France and the cause of the Revolution. The proposal was approved and before dawn on 8 May the army of the Republic had fallen back to a strong site behind the River Scarpe. When allied forces debouched in front of Caesar's Camp they found to their surprise that it was completely abandoned. Kilmaine's move proved a masterly one, saving the lives of his entire force, and has been described as 'the most glorious exploit in his career'.

When the news of the retreat reached Paris, however, there was consternation on all sides. The politicians in Paris, including Maximilien Robespierre who had Irish ancestry, had no knowledge of the tactics which Kilmaine employed against the advancing enemy formations. Realising the need for his pitifully small force to gain time, Kilmaine adopted tactics used by the American cavalry against the British during their Revolution. These consisted of using his 3,000 cavalry against varied fronts, then withdrawing when confronted by greatly superior numbers, then turning upon other formations, stopping them as well. Each time the enemy had to deploy and difficulties arose when they were regrouping to advance once again.

According to Louis Adolphe Thiers, 'execrations rose against Kilmaine, the service he rendered [in preserving the army] by his splendid retreat being entirely overlooked'. His fate was that of so many other brave generals of the time: he was immediately dismissed from the army. In addition the extreme Jacobin faction assailed him bitterly. He was Irish and a foreigner; he had family relations with the English; he was a 'Baron' in the days of the monarchy and therefore a noble; and he had prevented the distribution of patriotic papers among the troops. These were some of the charges hurled at him.

Robespierre said his retreat was a crime and dubbed him an Englishman. In a proposal at the National Convention Louis Antoine Saint-Just, a devoted follower of Robespierre, advocated the arrest throughout France of all foreigners whose countries were at war with the Republic. Echoing his master he asked 'how can any Englishman be trusted after Kilmaine, who was loaded with honours by us?' Nevertheless General Jean Nicholas Houchard, the new commander-in-chief, begged the Minister of War to appoint the dismissed general as leader of the advance guard since he was the only officer who had the confidence of the troops and whose ability fitted him for the task. But the request was refused.

Kilmaine received with calm dignity the news of his ignoble treatment. 'I am ready,' he declared, 'to serve the cause of the Republic in whatever rank I am placed and, wherever sent, I shall do my duty.' To the reproach that he was Irish he replied that, while he had the ill-luck to be born in Ireland, he was reared and educated in France. He added that during the retreat the English troops in the allied forces had particularly felt the weight of the swords of his cavalry.

The charge of being Irish was being used against him at this moment in time. Yet later on, because he was Irish, he was highly lauded and in 1798 received command of the army destined to invade England. Such was the temper of the times.

He left the army on receiving the news of his suspension. In a letter to the Minister of War he said that he was retiring into private life without a troubled conscience and without any fear, that he knew not vanity nor ambition, that he had never intrigued for promotion. Despite the calumnies heaped on him and the injustice he had experienced, he continued to be attached to the Republic. And finally he declared to the Minister, 'you have need of men like me to lead the advance guard of your army'.

Having been dismissed from the army in August 1793, Kilmaine retired with his wife to the Parisian suburb of Passy, where he lived quietly for some months. However, the infamous Reign of Terror had just begun and in October a decree of the National Convention ordered the immediate imprisonment of all foreign residents in France whose countries were at war with the Republic. Ireland, dominated by England, which was at war with the Republic, had been committed in opposition to the wishes of the immense majority of the Irish people, to England's war against the French nation. The result was that all Irish citizens in France came within the scope of the convention's decree. Kilmaine and his wife were placed under arrest and imprisoned as foreigners by an order of the Committee of Public Safety.[6] This fresh act of injustice weighed heavily on him. He had given thirty of the best years of his life in unselfish devotion to the nation, had undergone nine campaigns and fought for her cause in forty-six battles. His reward was a prison cell with the knife of the guillotine threatening him! Up to July 1794 he expected that he would be at any time led before the Revolutionary Tribunal like his predecessor Custine and his successor Houchard – both commanders-in-chief who had been tried and executed. While he lay in prison, a somewhat sinister letter from the Minister of War to Fouquier Tinville, the notorious prosecutor of the tribunal, charged him with, among other things, abandoning the camp of Caesar without a blow. The ending of the Reign of Terror, however, and the fall of the Robespierrian faction at Thermidor, saved him from a tragic fate. Many gallant French officers of the time including Theobald Dillon, Maréchal des Camp (on 30 April 1792), James O'Moran,

General of Division (on 6 March 1794), and Thomas Ward, General of Brigade (on 23 July 1794), had been guillotined.

On 8 August 1794 he was released, but was rearrested two days later and detained until December, when an order signed by Lazare Nicholas Marguerite Carnot and other members of the Committee of Public Safety at last gave him his liberty. Eager for military work, he immediately offered his services to the Republic. However, during his incarceration, he had developed a deadly form of dysentery, which plagued him for the balance of his life-span and hastened his demise. He wrote to the committee:

7th December, 1794.

From Jennings Kilmaine, suspended General of Division, to the Representatives of the Committee of Public Safety.

CITIZEN REPRESENTATIVES,

You have restored me to the liberty of which an unjust accusation has deprived me for thirteen months. I have ceased during that time to be of any use to the commonweal. I have a sincere desire to show to those who hold an unfavourable opinion of me how unjust they have been concerning me. Place me in a position, Citizen Representatives, where I may fulfil that desire of mine by making use of my talents and my devotion to the cause of Liberty which I successfully and faithfully served. Attached herewith is an account of my services and my work for the Revolution. You will see therein that no one has shown earlier and more faithful indications of his patriotism than I have.

A similar request to the Minister of War was accompanied by statements from representatives to the army and from generals under whom he served. All testified to his patriotic zeal, to his high military talents and entire trustworthiness, while some as well expressed sentiments of deep respect and warm affection.

The record of his career as shown in these merited at least a fair consideration, and his appeal continued:

> I am an only son. My father and mother died some years ago at Tonnay-Charente, their place of residence. I have no means of any kind. For over twenty years I lived uninterruptedly with my regiment. Coming from an Irish family, I have had no relatives in France except my father and mother, and consequently could not have any relations among the *emigrés*.

The offer of his services received favourable consideration and he was restored to the army. Within a few months he was to play a leading part in the Insurrection of Prairial when he defended the National Convention against the insurgents of the Faubourgs (suburbs). That uprising had its origin nearly a year before when Robespierre fell at the culmination of the Revolution in July 1794. A sharp reaction in public opinion followed the ending of the Terror. The overcrowded jails were soon emptied, the powers of the Revolutionary Tribunal were curtailed and the Jacobin Club was suppressed. A new regime of order and justice developed and was fostered by the overwhelming majority of the National Convention. The only opposition to that body, which now wielded supreme power, came from the remnant of the Jacobin party that had been overthrown at Thermidor. These advocated a return to the Terror, and their leaders, threatened with impeachment by the Convention, plotted secretly for its overthrow. Availing themselves of the deplorable condition of the poorer classes, Jacobin demagogues inflamed their minds against the government. Plans were being made at the same time for an insurrection, and it was arranged that the National Convention should be surrounded.

On the morning of 20 May 1795 armed Jacobins assembled in large numbers, and a tumultuous mob, carrying pikes, swords and muskets, burst into the assembly chamber and assassinated Ferraud, one of the deputies. On the following day the convention, hearing that the main body of the insurgents was mobilised in the Faubourg Saint Antoine, with several pieces of cannon, determined to crush the conspiracy. It issued a decree declaring that, if the rebels did not at once surrender their arms and artillery, the Faubourg would be bombarded. To Kilmaine was entrusted the command of the right wing of the forces numbering 4,000 troops, who were employed to execute the orders of the deputies. The Irish officer left a vivid account of his experiences while carrying out the task:

The Deputies of the National Convention, after conferring on me the command of the armed forces of Paris, gave me an order to mobilise a Division of 1,200 men with two pieces of artillery at the Place du Palais National. My instructions were to proceed with this Division to the Faubourg Saint Antoine, to surround Santerre's house and to search it for Cambon and Thuriot who were in hiding there. As a support, 1,500 or 2,000 troops were to follow.

At 5.30 in the morning I set out from the Place du Carouzel; I followed the quays and almost the entire length of the Rue Saint Antoine. I arranged my troops in battle-order opposite Santerre's house but found no trace of Cambon or Thuriot. At this stage, I received an order (contrary to the first one) that I was not to enter the Faubourg but was merely to guard its approaches while awaiting the arrival of all the troops to surround. I returned to the boulevard and waited there till the entire forces would be ready for the arrest of the assassins and their accomplices and for the disarmament. A rumour was brought that barricades were being erected to bar our passage, and local residents begged that force should not be used except as a last resource – otherwise many good patriots would suffer. The method of persuasion and the use of reason towards misguided men were too much part of our principles not to employ them. We began our march and arrived at the first barricade. We were received with yells and the most shocking insults from a crowd of armed men and from a still larger crowd of women or rather furies. I summoned them in the name of the Law and the national representatives to deliver up the assassin of Deputy Ferraud and to open the barricade at once; and I announced that, if they refused, I would batter it down with artillery, thus placing on the rebels the responsibility of the terrible results of their obstinacy.

After using threats and reason alternately, a passage was at last made through the barricade ... we resumed our march and, on reaching the second barricade, were again greeted with insults. Here the same methods were successfully employed as at the first ... We then met reinforcements coming from the opposite direction who were to co-operate in disarming the rebels ... While the troops were resting, they were surrounded by furies of women; but I knew my troops – we had fought together in Champagne, and I was familiar with their republican sentiments and their hatred of brigandage and anarchy. I spoke to several of the dragoons – 'Au! General,' they said, 'when an attempt was made under royalist despotism to oppress the people by using us as the instruments, it was our duty to stand by the people against tyranny; but today it is different, for a gang of brigands and assassins want us to rebel against the sovereignty of the people of France ... we are here to defend the national representatives against Jacobins and anarchists, and we shall do our duty.'

Kilmaine's narrative goes on to tell how five columns of the troops surrounded the Faubourg Saint Antoine. At its entrance he halted his forces and read a proclamation telling the rebels that, if the orders of the National Convention were not at once obeyed, he would reduce the quarter to ashes. His firmness and tact were successful. Arms were delivered up, the leaders of the conspiracy arrested, and the attempt to revive the regime of the Terror entirely crushed. Its suppression, which meant the triumph of the convention and the establishment of justice and humanity, was received with much relief by the citizens.

A few weeks after the insurrection, Kilmaine was officially informed of his appointment as commander of a cavalry division in the army destined for the conquest of Italy, and requested to take up his new duties early in July. Imprisonment had, however, injuriously affected his health, and his reply stating that it would be impossible for him to do so was accompanied by a certificate from his Irish doctor:

> I, the undersigned, Doctor of Medicine, residing at 75 Rue Honouré, certify that General Kilmaine is suffering from a severe attack of Dysentery and that, despite the best treatment which I have given him for several days, he is still quite unfit to travel.
> Edmund St Leger.
> Paris, 24th June, 1795.

In the autumn Kilmaine was still in Paris, and troubles were again brewing in the capital. A fresh insurrection, which aimed to undermine the power of the National Convention, broke out in Vendemiaire in October 1795. Kilmaine once more took an active part in the military operations that followed and he materially assisted Bonaparte in ruthlessly suppressing the new challenge to the national authority.

Early in 1796 the French government, then represented by the Executive Directory, made active preparations to carry on the war against the European coalition with new vigour on all fronts. It was resolved to pursue hostilities against Austria in particular, and that country was to be struck at in Italy, which was then under her sway. Some time previously a plan for an Italian campaign had been submitted by a then unknown artillery captain, who believed that its adoption would crush the enemies of France and bring renown to her name. A French army was to move swiftly from the Riviera coast across the Apennines and cut the connection between the troops of Austria and those of her Sardinian allies. The former would then be driven north-east out of Italy, and the French forces, crossing the Tyrolese Alps, would join up with the Army of the Rhine and march straight to Vienna.

The proposal seemed too fantastic for serious consideration. One man, however, thought otherwise. Carnot, the military genius of the Revolution and now a member of the Directory, favoured it, and at his suggestion the command of the Army of Italy was conferred on Napoleon Bonaparte who had submitted the daring plan.

Glowing with enthusiasm, the young commander set out at the end of March 1796 on what was to be one of the most brilliant campaigns in history. At the beginning, indeed, the prospects of success for the immense undertaking appeared remote. The allied enemy numbered 60,000 men, against whom the French commander-in-chief found himself pitted with a dispirited army of only 34,000. Recent reverses, no pay and little food; and just who was this new general? The troops had never heard of him and was he any different than those who had been leaders and losers up until this time? No sooner, however, had Bonaparte taken command than a wave of enthusiasm began to sweep over the troops, and the inspiring words of his address roused them to a high pitch of fervour on the eve of the campaign:

> Soldiers! you are half-starved and half-naked. ... I am about to lead you into the most fertile valleys of the world; there you will find flourishing cities and teeming provinces; there you will reap honour, glory and riches. Soldiers of the Army of Italy, will you lack courage?

*Charles Jennings
Kilmaine*

The officers, too, were stirred deeply by his exalted sentiments and by the strange magnetism of his personality; men of shining repute as generals whose valour and energy had been tested on many battlefields. Kilmaine, whose renown as a cavalry officer was again high, was one of them. Ability as a leader of the advance guard was his special attribute and in this capacity he played a memorable part throughout the great campaign that was about to begin.

Bonaparte began by moving quickly from the Riviera coast into Italy between the Alps and Apennines. The allied forces which opposed his entrance retreated at his approach. After a few days he fell upon and cut their centre at Montenotte and by completely separating the Austrian from the Sardinian forces gained his first notable victory. Within a fortnight an armistice with the Sardinians made him master of the rich Italian province of Piedmont. The retreat of the Austrians continued and on 10

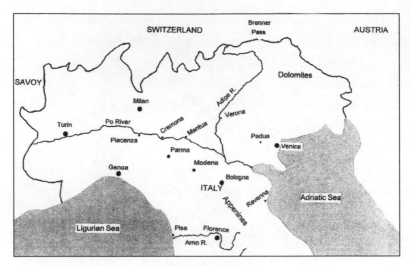

Map of Northern Italy

May he overtook them at Lodi. There another triumph followed and Kilmaine contributed to it by a brilliant cavalry charge at the height of the conflict. In a few days the province of Lombardy was in French hands. Immediately afterwards Kilmaine, at the head of his cavalry division, dashed across its fertile valleys and reached the capital, Milan, which the main army entered in triumph on 15 May. In that city Bonaparte delayed for a week, organising national guards and establishing revolutionary councils for administrative purposes. From his headquarters there he wrote to Kilmaine entrusting him with control of the advance guard:

MILAN,
20th May, 1796.

To General Kilmaine,
    It is decreed that you take command of the advance guard of the Army, composed of 1,600 horse, 5 battalions of grenadiers and 3

battalions of carabineers ... Although in charge of the advance guard, you will still remain at the head of the Army's cavalry.

Bonaparte.

In the meantime Kilmaine was on the heels of the still retreating Austrians and was daily breaking new ground for the advance of the main body of the French forces. On 25 May he entered the important city of Brescia, and four days later came upon the enemy at Borghetto where a conflict took place in which, fighting with much valour, he had a horse shot under him. On the evening of the battle, he pushed on to the strategic centre of Castel Nuovo, from which town he sent a dispatch to Bonaparte on 30 May:

> The enemy has evacuated Castel Nuovo and is in full retreat.
>
> I am taking the cavalry of the advance guard and four pieces of artillery to pursue him. Being much too busy, I am unable to send you a circumstantial account of the affair at Borghetto.

Although only two months had elapsed since the French entered Italy, the Austrians were already driven into the defiles of the Tyrol. Bonaparte, accordingly, turned his attention to the remaining portions of the peninsula. With part of the army he hurried southwards and Tuscany, Naples and the Papal States hailed him on his arrival. The Italian conquest was completed and the splendid dream on which he had set out was in part realised.

In the north, however, the great fortress town of Mantua still remained in the hands of Austria. Within its walls was a garrison of 13,000 soldiers. The possession of this 'Gibraltar of Italy' was of paramount importance to the French commander-in-chief, for with such a dangerous stronghold to his rear he dare not pursue the enemy though the Tyrol and crown his triumphs by joining up with the Army of the Rhine. Realising its strategic value, Austria hoped, through its relief, to recover her Italian possession. During the succeeding six months she was to send four great armies at different times to help the beleaguered town. But on each occasion they were driven back by the energy and strategy of Bonaparte.

The first army of relief, numbering 50,000 men under the command of Count Dagobert Würmser, Marshal of Austria, crossed the frontier in July at three widely separated points. Bonaparte was to make fuller use than hitherto of Kilmaine's cavalry. These days of July soon became perilous ones for the French army and Kilmaine had particularly arduous and responsible work placed on his shoulders. Day or night he was scarcely ever out of the saddle – he became known as 'the Ulysses of the army'. On 7 July he was at Vicenza and wrote to Bonaparte: 'The enemy, who are very near, having been informed of my coming, had drawn up a plan to capture me – or at least to ambush me as I left the town – but I did my business, nevertheless.' Within twenty-four hours he was forty miles away at Verona, and four days later he was a hundred miles to the west at the general headquarters in Valeze. From that town Bonaparte reported to the Directory on 10 July that 'General Kilmaine with 2,000 cavalry stands in readiness here to start for any point at which the enemy might be disposed to attempt a passage.' Finally, at the end of the month he was in the neighbourhood of Castiglione where, within a few days, the splendid tactics of his cavalry helped to roll back into the Tyrol the formidable army under General Würmser.

Würmser sent his troops forward but as they neared the French lines of Massena and Augereau, French guns and the approach of Despino's demi-brigade caused him to send out a recall. At that moment, Kilmaine had launched his attack upon the Austrian armies' left flank, contributing to the rout.

The strenuous weeks preceding this great triumph left

Kilmaine's health temporarily broken. Immediately after it he wrote to Bonaparte:

> The total loss of my strength prevents me, my dear General, from joining you and sharing your glory. Fever and pain have so reduced me that I cannot hold myself upright, much less sit on a horse. I am going to Brescia in quest of relief. With rest and bark I hope to rejoin you.

The respite from his labours was, however, a brief one, for in a few weeks the enemy, despite its recent reverse, was making hurried preparations for a further effort to relieve Mantua.

Early in September a new Austrian army, reorganised and well-equipped, again advanced under Würmser towards the Italian frontier. Bonaparte resolved to proceed against it at once and set out towards the Tyrol, leaving Kilmaine with 3,000 troops at the important strategic centre of Verona. The Austrian commander, mistaking the object of Bonaparte's march, ordered his advance guard to move on Verona with a view to its capture. Outside that town several obstinate encounters took place in which Kilmaine, as Bonaparte reported in his dispatch to the French government, 'was able with his usual sagacity to check and overawe the enemy,' whom he repulsed with artillery every time they tried to penetrate. In the meantime the French commander-in-chief was engaged in attacking the rear of the Austrian forces. He defeated them with heavy losses at Bassano, and by eventually driving them inside the walls of Mantua, crushed the second expedition for its relief.

In the middle of September Bonaparte conferred on Kilmaine supreme command of the 10,000 troops occupied in blockading the great fortress. During the following month Austria, undaunted by failure, sent her most famous soldier, General Josef Alvintzy, to make a further effort for its relief. This too was fated to end in disaster. Finally, four months later, the last of the great imperial armies was repulsed, and Mantua surrendered to the French forces. The fall of the important stronghold was hailed with acclaim throughout France, marking the complete conquest of Italy and removing the only obstacle which prevented the soldiers of the Republic from advancing into the Tyrol. Bonaparte paid due tribute to Kilmaine for his part in achieving the triumph – 'it was Kilmaine,' he said, 'who carried out the second blockade of Mantua and rendered splendid service there'. The French government also acknowledged his labours in a special message of thanks:

> The Executive Directory, on the occasion of the surrender of Mantua, desires to mark its recognition of the success with which you have assisted in the blockade of that city. After giving such repeated proofs of valour and genius in the field, you have now an opportunity, full of interest, for further service equally important. And the Directory always has complete trust in your wisdom and the purity of your Republican principles.

Following the fall of Mantua, Bonaparte prepared to move northwards through the Tyrol into Austria with his main army of 50,000 men. Before starting he entrusted the onerous post of commander of all Northern Italy to Kilmaine, whom he instructed at the same time to keep a watchful eye on the Republic of Venice. Sweeping almost unopposed though the Tyrolese passes and into Austria, Bonaparte was soon dictating peace terms to the enemy plenipotentiaries at the village of Leoben.

Immediately after Bonaparte's departure from Italy, grave troubles arose in that country. Though the Republic of Venice remained neutral in the struggle between France and Austria, its people had suffered severely from the incursions and heavy financial exactions of the French in its territory. Despite this, a considerable part of the population in the towns was favourable to the sentiments of the French Revolution and was secretly organising to throw off the yoke of their oligarchical rulers. On the other hand the peasants and mountaineers were passionately attached to the old order and showed sympathy, if not active support, for the Venetian government. Although Bonaparte advised Kilmaine to maintain neutrality between the two parties, there seems little doubt that the French secretly connived with the democrats. Mutual feelings gradually became more embittered and tension increased day by day until finally several towns were invaded by country people. They were aided by their aristocratic supporters and killed not only the local revolutionary sympathisers but French soldiers and citizens as well.

Kilmaine's position was a delicate one but he at once issued orders to his officers to march into the rural districts and disarm the peasants. At the same time he sent a courier to Bonaparte bearing an account of the serious state of affairs that had arisen. The latter replied as follows:

> I have given much consideration to the dispatch which your aide-de-camp has brought ... You will proceed at once to disarm the division at Padua; arrest the Governor and officers of the city and send them [as] prisoners to Milan. The same is to be done at Trevise, Bassano and Verona ... The mobile columns which, with your usual prudence, you have brought together are to be sent to punish and disarm the mountaineers who have murdered our people. You will take measures to arrest all the nobles of Venice and those most attached to the Senate, so that their lives will answer for whatever may be done to those devoted to our cause. You are not to be deterred by any consideration whatsoever and if this Venetian situation is well handled, as everything you undertake is, these people will soon repent of their perfidy.

In the meantime the ferment was increasing and by the middle of April reached its height at Verona. There the supporters of the Venetian government, assisted by armed bands who had swarmed into that town from the surrounding districts, joined together. They fell unexpectedly on the unarmed French troops and on the Jacobin sympathisers among the citizens and killed them with much brutality. Not even sick soldiers in the hospitals escaped the vengeance of the mobs. When the news reached Kilmaine he at once set out at the head of 3,000 men and after a rapid march surrounded the town. The wild mobs within its walls and the municipality which sympathised with them were struck with abject terror at his approach. Kilmaine threatened to reduce the town to ashes unless there was an immediate and unconditional surrender. When the latter took place and he had executed the leaders who were found bearing arms, a fine of 50,000 lire was inflicted on the place. Cavalry were then sent by him to the country districts and their inhabitants disarmed. Order having been restored, he forwarded a dispatch to Bonaparte and awaited his decision regarding the future treatment of the rebellious town.

Soon afterwards Bonaparte hurried back to Italy. Filled with rage at the treatment of his soldiers, he exacted a heavy retribution from the terrified government of Venice. The oligarchy ceased to exist and was replaced instead with a democratic government along the lines of the French government.

With the Italian conquest complete and the peace treaty with Austria concluded, Bonaparte returned to Paris in December 1797 leaving Kilmaine as chief-of-staff in supreme command of the army in Italy. Kilmaine was, however, summoned in the same month to Paris by the Directory. Plans were being formed for another great expedition which, it was hoped, would destroy the only remaining rival to French supremacy in Europe, England.

The Italian campaign increased Kilmaine's reputation as an officer of brilliant achievements. During its course, Napoleon frequently singled him out for special praise in the dispatches to the Directory. He was particularly fitted, Bonaparte said, 'to take charge of reconnoitring corps'; he was 'calm, of keen discernment and well qualified to undertake difficult or delicate enterprises for which esprit and sound judgment were required'. Napoleon's aide-de-camp, General Count Charles Tristan Montholon, who later shared the exile of his chief at St Helena, expressed similar sentiments:

> General Kilmaine was a superb cavalry officer with coolness and vision He rendered splendid services to the army of which he was, notwithstanding his delicate constitution, one of the outstanding officers. He possessed a masterly insight into the Austrian forces. Familiar with their tactics, he did not permit those rumours, which are spread in the rear of an army, to have any effect on him. Nor did he allow himself to be depressed by those columns of troops which an enemy flings out from its vanguard in order to create deception regarding the actual strength of its forces.

Another famous soldier of the time, Auguste Frederic Louis Marmont, Duke de Raguse, who became a marshal of France, described his Irish comrade-in-arms as 'a man of brains, cool, calculating, brave, full of initiative'. Few of Kilmaine's contemporaries, however, had better opportunities to estimate his worth than his aide-de-camp during the Italian campaign. Captain Landrieux was a typical soldier of the Revolution who played a notable part in its campaigns. In his memoirs he wrote:

> General Kilmaine was Irish and, though very reserved, was an exceptionally fearless soldier who was universally respected for his

high character and estimable qualities. He was the only officer in whom Napoleon ever placed complete confidence. He was capable of the greatest things. His military genius was more profound than even that of the great commander-in-chief, but he did not possess the latter's vivacity, and he would consider it criminal to hold that brilliant man's views. Kilmaine had humanity, honesty and little or no egotism. He was not ambitious. At first acquaintance one was somewhat prejudiced against him on account of his extreme reserve, and Bonaparte, who had not time to understand his character, took some little time to show his appreciation of this illustrious man.

Similar tributes came from various other officers who shared with him the trials and triumphs of the campaigns of the time. These speak of the many merits which marked him out as a brilliant officer – all praised him particularly for that sterling courage which gave him the name by which they always knew him, *le brave Kilmaine*. But there existed among them and, as Landrieux testifies, among the soldiers in the ranks as well – a warm affection for this reserved and seemingly emotionless Irishman.

Ireland responded more sympathetically than any other European country to the ideas spread by the French Revolution. Three-quarters of Ireland, possessing neither rights nor privileges, were in virtual bondage, while a small ascendancy held a monopoly of place and power. Within a few years of the outbreak of the Revolution, however, the new revolutionary spirit generated in that country swept Ireland like a whirlwind. Under its influence an organisation called the United Irishmen, embracing all classes and crystallising popular sentiment, sprang up. Its aims were at first confined to securing by constitutional means a reform of the parliament and the abolition of the grievances weighing so heavily on the population. But the bitter hostility of the all-powerful ascendancy soon showed the hopelessness of achieving these objectives by peaceful methods. Accordingly the United Irishmen developed by degrees into a powerful revolutionary body numbering in its ranks 300,000 disciplined and partially armed men. And by 1797 its objective had become the establishment of an autonomous state separate from England and in alliance with France.

Never did the prospects for the independence of Ireland seem brighter than in the latter months of that year. The French Republic was then dominant in Europe and accredited Irish agents had been cordially received by its ministers, from whom they received definite promises of armed assistance. In December of the previous year one of these emissaries, Theobald Wolfe Tone, had succeeded in persuading the French government to send an expedition to Ireland. And though it failed in its immediate object, it proved that, despite the superiority of the English navy, it was feasible for a French fleet to land men and munitions in Ireland.

We have seen how triumphantly Bonaparte's Italian campaign ended in 1797, leaving the French Republic at peace with Austria and at war with England alone. The Directory, thus relieved of its preoccupation with hostile activities on the continent, concentrated on organising a great army, the Armée d'Angleterre, for the invasion and subjugation of this hated rival of France. Bonaparte was appointed its commander-in-chief on the very day, in October 1797, that he signed the peace treaty with Austria. As he was not expected to return home till December, General Louis C.A. Desaix was entrusted in the meantime with the supervision of the arrangements for the proposed invasion of Ireland. The two Irish agents in France, Tone and Edward J. Lewins, had frequent conversations with this officer and with Talleyrand, the Minister for Foreign Affairs, from whom they received reassuring promises of support for their cause. On the return of Bonaparte in December, they had several interviews with him too, but on these occasions, as

Tone states in his journal, the commander-in-chief was curiously reticent regarding Ireland:

> His manner is cold and he speaks very little; it is not, however, as dry as that of Hoche, but seems to proceed rather from languor than anything else. He is perfectly civil, however, to us; but from anything we have yet seen or heard, it is impossible to augur anything good or bad.

During the early days of 1798 the preparations for the projected invasion of Ireland and Britain went on. The dockyards along the northern coasts of France had become busy centres of activity, and more than 1,000 transports of various kinds were soon ready for the conveyance of troops across the Channel. The army of invasion, composed of forty infantry brigades and fifty-four cavalry regiments, had for its staff officers the most distinguished French soldiers of the day. Among them was Kilmaine, who was to command the centre with 20,000 men under his orders, and was particularly intended for that part of the armada destined for Ireland.

In February, Bonaparte set out on a tour of inspection along the northern coasts of France and remained for several weeks. The results that followed from his mission were far-reaching, for the secret report which he sent to the Directory led to the abandonment of the project. He declared that in view of the inferior condition of the French navy such an undertaking would be 'the boldest and most difficult operation ever attempted'. The fact was, however, that during the time he had permitted preparations to go on, his thoughts were far away. Dazzled with day-dreams of glory in Egypt and the East, he placed before the Directory a project for striking at English power in these regions. And having obtained its sanction for his schemes, he sailed away to the Mediterranean in May 1798.

During the early months of that year Ireland was seething with suppressed excitement. The United Irishmen organisation there only awaited the coming of the promised French aid to revolt.[7] But the harsh regime inaugurated by the English authorities, including the arrest of its leaders, caused active hostilities to commence prematurely in May. On hearing of the outbreak, the Irish emissaries in France redoubled their efforts to send help to their countrymen. Their hopes were dashed when Bonaparte sailed for Egypt taking with him a considerable number of the intended army of invasion. Though apparently sympathetic, the Directory was lacking in money and energy for a new enterprise and by the end of June news reached France that the Irish insurgents had surrendered.

On Bonaparte's departure from France, Kilmaine was appointed commander-in-chief of the Armée d'Angleterre. He had zealously co-operated with the Irish agents in their efforts to induce the French government to send aid to his struggling compatriots, and the news of the early termination of the insurrection came as a severe blow. Wolfe Tone's son wrote:

> General Kilmaine was left in command of the disorganised relics of the Army of England, from which all the best troops were withdrawn. That officer, an Irishman by birth, and one of the bravest Generals of the Army of Italy whose cavalry he commanded in the preceding campaign, was, from the shattered state of his health, unfit to conduct any active enterprise.

Yet Kilmaine still hoped that hostilities might be renewed and it was largely through his influence that two small expeditions were fitted out. One of these under General Georges Humbert, numbering 1,000 men, was to sail at once, the other, under the Irishman General Oliver Harty, Baron de Pierrebourg, with

3,000, was to leave soon afterwards. Kilmaine was hoping to follow them later with a large force of 10,000 men. Humbert arrived in August at Killala, and was well received by the local population. Nonetheless, after a six-week heroic campaign, his small force, greatly outnumbered, was forced to surrender to the British army.

The second expedition under Harty was accompanied by Wolfe Tone and set out from Brest on 14 September. Like Wolfe Tone, Kilmaine was convinced of the comparative futility of sending these small forces, and he now endeavoured to persuade the French government to follow up the smaller expeditions with a larger one at once. Offering his services as commander, he asked for sufficient troops 'to ensure the independence of Ireland'. In a letter to the president of the Directory he wrote:

It is not yet too late to succeed in Ireland, but it is necessary to employ as leader of the enterprise a man who, on account of the dearth of resources, will be most effective with the least means. I am convinced that I am risking nothing in confidentially assuring you that I am the most likely general of the Republic to be successful there. By consulting the Irishmen who are in Paris, the Directory can satisfy itself that my name would suffice to rally round me in Ireland a very large number of the friends of Liberty and Independence, particularly in the provinces of Connacht and Leinster.

He stated in addition that he required 7,000 men as well as 25,000 muskets to ensure the success of the undertaking. The Directory seemed to become enthusiastic regarding his proposal and preparations were hurried on with feverish activity. Even the news of Humbert's surrender did not stop them. But when the report arrived on 19 October that Harty's force had been captured at Lough Swilly, there was extreme disappointment and the new project was given up by the Directory.

The decision shattered Kilmaine's dream of helping to achieve the independence of his native country. On hearing of Wolfe Tone's arrest, Kilmaine at once wrote to the French government requesting that his release be immediately demanded; and that, in the event of refusal, hostages of equal rank from the British military prisoners then in France should be held for the safety of this officer of the French Republic. The appeal of his superior officer to save Wolfe Tone's life was, however, ignored by the French government. Tone and Kilmaine had had frequent conversations regarding Ireland and shared each other's hopes and disappointments during the vicissitudes of that year, and Kilmaine was despondent at the news of Tone's death. Kilmaine had no children and made an offer to adopt Tone's two sons, but their mother refused to entertain the generous proposal. He then successfully used his influence to have them educated by the French nation and, in various ways, helped to soften the tragedy that had fallen on the family of his friend. Years later his many kindnesses towards them were acknowledged by Tone's son, who described him as 'our staunch friend' during the trying period.

Kilmaine's health, which had never been robust because of his time in prison, was seriously affected by his strenuous labours in the Italian campaign of 1796 and 1797. In addition, the onerous duties of commander-in-chief during 1798, the disappointments caused by the failure of the Irish expeditions and domestic griefs, still further enfeebled his delicate constitution. In December 1798 he wrote to the Minister of War from his headquarters at Rouen:

I was hoping that the attack of Rheumatic Gout from which I was suffering would be a mere temporary one, but here I am lying on my back for more than twenty days, helpless in every limb. I am in the same condition in which you saw me three years ago in the Riviera at Genoa. My doctor tells me positively that he believes it will be five or six weeks before I shall be able to walk even with the aid of crutches.

He recovered somewhat from this illness and was, early in the year 1799, appointed commander of the Army of Switzerland which was destined for the conquest of that country. But he soon fell gravely ill again and was compelled to resign from all active duties. Taken by slow stages to his home in Paris, he was attended there by a friend, Dr Edmund St Leger, a notable Irish physician then practising in Paris. Specialists were later called in for consultation, but the old illness, complicated by dysentery, failed to react to any treatment. A visit to Vichy was proposed but he was too weak to undertake the journey. Suffering much pain he grew steadily worse and on 11 December 1799 Kilmaine died in the arms of his aide-de-camp, d'Arbois de Jubainville, who was devoted to him.

Officers assisted at the last rites of a comrade whose bravery and upright character were known throughout the army of France. General François Etienne Kellermann, son of the French commander of the same name, was chosen to deliver an oration and so give expression to the loss which had befallen the Republic. He requested to be relieved of the duty placed upon him, saying 'How shall I, who am but a soldier, speak worthily of this brave man?' He was told, 'You will tell of what he did, and of what he taught others to do.'

General Charles Jennings Kilmaine was the one of the greatest of the Irish soldiers who battled for France during the eighteenth century and added lustre to the name of Ireland throughout Europe. A superb tactician, a dashing cavalry officer, he was also a friend and confidant of Napoleon. His reputation was already high on the continent when he died comparatively young at age forty-eight. There seems little doubt that, had he lived a few years longer, his military genius might have brought him into the front rank of Napoleon's marshals.

CHAPTER 8

HENRI J.G. CLARKE

COUNT DE HUNEBOURG, DUKE DE FELTRE, MARSHAL OF FRANCE

Henri Jacques Guillaume Clarke, soldier, administrator and diplomat, was born of Irish parents at Landrecies in France on 17 October 1765. His father, Thomas Clarke, was a colonel of Dillon's Regiment; his mother, Louise, was a daughter of William Shee (O'Shee) of Landrecies. William Shee, an officer of Clare's Regiment, was the son of Martin Shee of Camas, County Limerick. Martin and his three sons arrived in France in 1725 and upon arrival all entered the Irish Brigade. Their grandfather, William, had come to France earlier from County Kilkenny following the siege of Limerick. He and his wife had settled at Camas, where later a relationship through marriage was established between the Shees and the Brownes, another illustrious Irish military family also located at Camas. Margaret, daughter of Martin Shee, married John Harty of Knockaney, near Knocklong, County Limerick; their son was General Oliver Harty, a famous soldier of the French Revolution.

Clarke's family had been sufficiently patrician to allow him entry to the Royal military schools. Henri Clarke entered the advanced École Militaire at Paris in 1781, and in the following year became a lieutenant in Berwick's Regiment. His father had died while he was still a boy, and he came under the care of his uncle, Colonel Henry Shee, who was secretary to the Duke of Orléans (Philippe Egalité). Much of the young officer's subsequent advancement was due to the support of that prince, in whose royal regiment of Hussars he became captain in 1784. In 1789 he temporarily left the army to take up a diplomatic post in the French Embassy at London and, while there visited Ireland, where he became acquainted with his parents' relatives. It appears that, in later life, he continued an interest in the land of his parents' birth. When Napoleon's Irish Legion was officially formed on 7 December 1803 as part of the Grande Armée, Clarke was, like Oliver Harty, an interested bystander and he was frequently involved in its evolution.

Returning to France from England in 1791, he resumed military life. Clarke distinguished himself during the Rhine campaign, in the first war of the Revolution, as a cavalry colonel. Though we have little record of Clarke's own adventures in the campaign, he appears to have been successful in his endeavours for the Republic. The following best describes what his French compatriots thought of him:

General Clarke is one of the most amiable, and one of the best informed officers of the French army; he is as his name indicates of Irish origin … he entered from his infancy in the service, in the regiments of Bulkeley and Dillon infantry;[1] in 1782 he was a second lieutenant in the Regiment of Berwick; he was a captain when the Revolution broke out; he soon became a lieutenant-colonel, and it was in this grade that he commenced the campaigns of 1792 and 1793.[2]

Afterwards Clarke was appointed Minister Plenipotentiary from France to Florence, at which time he was a general of division and a commander in the Legion of Honour. By 1793 he was a general of brigade and, briefly, chief-of-staff to the Army of the Rhine, but was then caught up in the widespread dismissals of officers of noble birth. Like many other French and foreign officers in the Revolutionary army, Clarke's loyalties became suspect in 1793 – 'most unjustly' as he wrote – and was suspended from military duties. Louis-Philippe, the son of his patron, Egalité, who had been executed during the 'Terror', left France with numerous other *emigrés*. Many joined with the enemies of France, hoping to recover their homeland and return the monarchy to its 'rightful' place. Early in 1795, however, the suspension against Clarke was removed and even though Clarke was always more of a monarchist than a revolutionary, he remained in France.

It was then that Carnot appointed him Chief of the Bureau Topographique, the repository of military maps and plans of the war ministry. He served as a topographical engineer and showed finesse and talent for staff work. His intellect and knowledge procured for him a call to the office of director of the historical cabinet and of military topography, which the government had established. In his new position he proved his talents in the sciences and in soundness of judgement. It was while in this office during 1796 that he had frequent conversations regarding Ireland with Wolfe Tone.[3]

In December 1795 Clarke had been appointed general of division and in November 1796 was entrusted with a delicate political mission. He was sent to Italy ostensibly to open treaty negotiations with the Austrians, which the Directory was anxious to conclude. Clarke was directed to travel via Italy to Vienna, but when Clarke reached Turin he had some difficulty in obtaining a passport which would enable him to proceed. He had no choice but to go to Milan, where the chief result of his sojourn was that he was able to find Napoleon, who controlled all egress and access to Vienna at that time. He still thought of the latter as 'the little protégé of Barras' and thus had no very high opinion of this ambitious man.[4]

When Napoleon assumed command over the French army in Italy in late March 1796 it was in bad shape and rapidly disintegrating. The government in Paris was unable to pay, feed or care for the French armies and was totally ignorant of their strength and dispositions. It was a paper army of 116,000 men but in reality was more like 61,000. There were six battle divisions and three on coastguard duty. By some manipulation, Napoleon managed to collect together slightly more than 48,000 horse and muskets plus a number of guns. Through conquest he also managed to provide the Directory with cash taken from northern Italy. This, of course, didn't anger the 'five kings' then ruling France. Except, for them, it certainly didn't pay to have that sort of independent entrepreneur free-wheeling around northern Italy with a French army. Bonaparte incurred their displeasure when he negotiated what they believed to be an unsatisfactory treaty with Piedmont. Besides, he was rude to and ignored a fellow Corsican, Antoine Salicetti, the civilian deputy sent as a commissar by the Directory. There was no telling what Napoleon might do next.

In addition to his advertised job as negotiator, General Clarke was sent as the Directory's spy in Napoleon's headquarters. His job was not only to 'observe' what Bonaparte was doing but to restrain the ambitions of the man who was frightening the members of the Directory. Henri Clarke, now aged thirty-one, was later described as 'elegant' and 'an honest desk general of Irish descent with moon face, curls and double chin'. From all the evidence, Clarke was able to move easily within refined society, certainly much better than the rougher revolutionary types then so prevalent in France. This was an important asset, since France's enemies loathed the Revolution and its adherents. This ability was demonstrated when he proved to be a satisfactory governor of conquered Vienna, and later Berlin.

He arrived at Napoleon's headquarters in November 1796 and at once began taking notes. With his shrewd eye, his first decision was to closely scrutinise those men who served Bonaparte. Louis Alexandre Berthier, he observed, had high moral standards and took no interest in politics; Jean-André Massena was brave, but slack about discipline and 'very fond of money'. As for Napoleon, Clarke gave this word-picture: 'haggard, thin, the skin clinging to his bones, eyes bright with fever – he had caught a chill after his ordeal at Arcola'. For nine days Clarke secretly watched the chief and then sent back the following report:

> He is feared, loved and respected in Italy. I believe he is attached to the republic and without any ambition save to retain the reputation he has won. It is a mistake to think that he is a party man. He belongs neither to the royalists, who slander him, nor to the anarchists, whom he dislikes. He has only one guide – the Constitution … But General Bonaparte is not without defects. He does not spare his men sufficiently … Sometimes he is hard, impatient, abrupt or imperious. Often he demands difficult things in too hasty a manner. He has not been respectful enough towards the Government commissioners. When I reproved him for this, he replied that he could not possibly treat otherwise men who were universally scorned for their immorality and incapacity.[5]

Clarke recognised that Napoleon's attitude was justified, for he added:

Saliceti [*sic*] has the reputation of being the most shameless rogue in the army and Garrau is inefficient: neither is suitable for the Army of Italy … Please don't conclude that I speak of him out of enthusiasm. I write this in a calm state of mind, and am guided by no other interest than to inform you of the facts: posterity will rank Bonaparte among the greatest of men.

Clearly Clarke was one of the first to judge Napoleon in such a way as would his supporters and enemies alike. Nevertheless, Clarke proved to be a man who had his own private thoughts that occasionally ran counter to his hero.[6] Although not much of a republican himself, Clarke nonetheless saw Bonaparte as 'the man of the Republic'. It is quite obvious now that Napoleon had made another conquest; Clarke, the 'closet' monarchist, was genuinely fascinated by this man whom he further described, with great insight, as one who would never 'be a party man'. Nor, he added incorrectly, would he ever 'be a threat to his nation' meaning, of course, to the regime. How wrong he was on that point.

Austria's alliance with England precluded the negotiation of an independent peace treaty. Nevertheless, a Baron Vincent was sent from Vienna to Italy to confer with General Clarke in an effort to establish a treaty. Napoleon interceded before the agreement was ratified as his troops had been reinforced considerably since the Battle of Arcola and he was determined to continue the war against Austria. He believed firmly that he must completely destroy the Habsburgs' ability to recover and once again threaten revolutionary France. The future emperor completed his conquest of Clarke by demonstrating that it would be necessary to inflict a few more defeats on Austria before thinking of negotiating with her. To get better peace terms he would have to pin both shoulders of the Habsburg Emperor, Francis II, to the ground and thus far he was only down on one knee. But the time would soon come when he would have to beg for mercy. In a letter to the French government Clarke explained: 'The [Austrian] Emperor's ideas differed from those of the Directory. The Gordian knot had to be cut. The new Alexander [Napoleon] did it with the intention of serving the Republic effectively.'[7]

When the Directory read Clarke's report, they mistakenly decided that their suspicions about Napoleon were unfounded. They then promised Bonaparte their full support, and in their letters and orders showed renewed confidence in whatever decisions he might take. This came just in time, for Napoleon was facing his gravest threat: a powerful resurgent Austrian army in northern Italy.

To counter this threat Napoleon decide upon a thrust north and eastward directly into the heart of Austrian territory. By March 1797 the French army, having forced the Austrians to retreat, was deep into the Tyrol. Clarke remained in the field with Napoleon and was a part of the negotiations that led to the temporary Peace of Leoben on 17 April 1797, by which time Bonaparte was very happy to conclude. The French army was now within ninety miles of Vienna and well beyond Napoleon's own line of communications, which were threatened every mile of the way. Napoleon worried that his forces, thinly spaced out as they were, might be an easy target for an Austrian envelopment. At about this time Clarke was sent on another secret diplomatic mission to Vienna where, on 17 October 1797, he concluded the Treaty of Campo Formio which ratified the peace agreed in the Peace of Leoben. France appropriated all of Belgium and changed the face of western Europe. While in Vienna Clarke made an agreeable impression among the city's elite that greatly helped him when he became governor of that conquered city.

Jealous of the growing power of Napoleon and regardless of Clarke's own protestations to the contrary, members of the

Henri Clarke

Directory apparently believed that Clarke was so taken with Napoleon that he was becoming a minor threat, so he was recalled and deprived of his rank as general of division and of his post at the war office. However, after Napolean's *coup d'état* in the month of Brumaire (9 November 1799) he was reinstated to his rank and posts. He returned as director of the historical cabinet and of military topography, a safe sinecure in the backwaters of the Republic.

In 1804 Clarke entered his most important position yet when he replaced Bourrienne to become private and confidential secretary for military affairs to the Emperor Napoleon.[8] As a member of Napoleon's personal staff Clarke soon became indispensable. Other staff members included Caulaincourt, Duroc and, temporarily, Corbineau.[9] The Emperor's cabinet had three main divisions, but the secretariat, which handled correspondence, was the busiest and most sensitive. Napoleon was an active letter-writer, issuing thirty or more dictated letters almost every day, whether in the field or in camp. In later correspondence we find that Clarke was often able to ascertain what Napoleon desired even before the great man had considered or finalised those thoughts for himself.

In December 1805 at the Battle of Austerlitz, Napoleon and his army completely destroyed any chances that Austria might have had to continue the war. He also forced their Russian allies to retreat hastily back to Russia. At the Treaty of Pressburg on 26 December, Austria not only withdrew once again from war with France, but also surrendered territory in Germany and Italy, thereby greatly increasing Napoleon's power in central Europe. Then, on 9 July 1806, the Russian envoy Mr d'Oubril arrived in Paris. He presented papers from Czar Alexander I which empowered him to negotiate peace. 'The Emperor Napoleon was pleased to nominate, as his plenipotentiary, General Clarke, Councellor [sic] of State, Secretary of the Cabinet, and Grand Officer of the Legion of Honour', and gave him authority to treat, conclude and sign a peace, with powers corresponding to those of Mr d'Oubril. In addition to this role with the Emperor, Clarke also represented Bonaparte in negotiations in 1805, when he was still the King of Italy.

At this time Napoleon refused to negotiate with England and Russia at the same time and with the same terms. The British bickered about this for several months but finally agreed to negotiate separately and sent the Earl of Yarmouth to Paris, who was soon replaced by the Earl of Lauderdale. Clarke was appointed to negotiate peace with the British on 22 July 1806. Within a few days his official appointment papers were presented to Yarmouth who in turn passed them along to Secretary of State Charles James Fox in London. Certain letters exchanged between Clarke and Fox make clear Clarke's refusal to give in to British demands. In one letter Clarke explained why France refused to negotiate with Britain for the release of the Hanoverian German states conquered by Bonaparte. Napoleon had promised some of the British King's territory in Germany to the Prussian King as part of their alliance treaty. Clarke was less than direct about Napoleon's plans for 'territorial aggrandisement'. He indicated that 'His Britannic Majesty' had plans for such in other parts of the world in which France would not interfere. In effect Clarke inferred, 'stay off the continent and we won't argue about what you grab elsewhere'.

A letter from Lauderdale dated 9 August 1806 complained about Clarke's position and 'manner' towards the British 'plenipotentiares [sic] to His Britannic Majesty'. Clarke complained that with Yarmouth now in Paris, he was facing two British plenipotentiaries, and insisted that negotiations be discontinued until another French representative was assigned. Shortly after, M. Champagny joined the trio. Regardless of Clarke's controversy with the English, it doesn't appear that France gave up much.

A peace treaty was signed between Russia and France on 20 July 1807. Several times during the years of their relationship Napoleon used Clarke's abilities as a diplomat, but during much of this period Clarke was also still a soldier. In the rank of general, he fought under his master in the successful German campaigns at Ulm and Jena in 1806, where the Austrian and Prussian armies respectively were comprehensively defeated by the French.

On 1 November 1806 Napoleon appointed Clarke Governor-General of Berlin and Prussia, quite possibly as a reward for his satisfactory performance as a treaty negotiator. In the sixty-ninth bulletin of the Grande Armée, 'His majesty [Napoleon] bestows great praise on General Clarke, Governor of Berlin, who displays equal activity and zeal in the important post confided to him.'[10] In 1807, having held governorships in Austria and Prussia, Clarke replaced Berthier as Minister of War.[11] It was a post he occupied until April 1814 when Napoleon abdicated his throne for the first time.

Berthier, possibly Bonaparte's most distinguished bureaucrat, left the war ministry in 1807 to concentrate on his duties as Napoleon's major-general (chief-of-staff). He had handled his dual responsibilities efficiently, but the workload had become too much. His replacement was Henri Jacques Guillaume Clarke. As Napoleon already knew, he was a hard worker, methodical and painstaking; also, he was financially honest and a foe of swindlers and looters. Like Berthier he was not a 'ground pounder'. Even though Clarke had fought bravely and well along the Rhine and later in Germany he was essentially an administrator. He spent a lifetime as an army officer without becoming an all-important field soldier. Lavalette described him as 'possessing all the suppleness of a man who wished to succeed in life' and also 'that species of conduct you expect from an Irishman'.[12]

Soon he was widely known throughout the army as the 'Desktop General and the Field Marshal of Ink'. Nonetheless, in administering his duties he showed much ability and initiative, and this zeal and success earned for him in 1808 the title of Comte d'Hunebourg. In October 1809, he again received high praise for the vigorous measures he had adopted to oppose a British army in Holland.

However, this was the beginning of serious times for Napoleon, his administration, his army and his family. Whereas Berthier had the good fortune of being Minister of War as Napoleon's star was rising, Clarke would come into that role as it was setting. The main trouble emanated from Spain where Napoleon's brother, Joseph, sat on the throne but was unable, even with French bayonets, to control the populace. Neither the Foreign Minister, Jean B.N. Champagny, nor the Minister of War, Clarke, could prevent the daily disconcerting news from reaching Paris. Even though the wording was as carefully phrased as possible, each bulletin was clearly articulating what seemed to be a relentless debacle.

It was evidently not apparent to Napoleon that his Spanish 'ulcer' should have been seriously attended to. Otherwise he might not have left the fighting almost entirely to his subordinates. In the autumn of 1808 he was having serious thoughts about how to cope with Czar Alexander. He decided to use his usual method of putting up a strong offensive front. On 4 September he issued a letter of instruction to Clarke to draft 140,000 men, the largest single number ever called up at one time. This order was distributed throughout the nation and immediately cries and moans of objection emanated from every corner of the domain. There was considerable dissent. The French people had become quite fed up with Napoleon's continual wars.

Meanwhile, Napoleon was influencing his followers by creating an entirely new nobility in France. The new ranks of nobility were heavily dispensed among his most loyal soldiers and Clarke was one of those favoured.[13] Napoleon also took great care of his own family, most notably his brother, Joseph, whom he had proclaimed King of Spain. Other members of his family gained thrones in the Netherlands and Italy. But none would ever be as troublesome as that throne in Spain.

The trouble began in the early months of 1808. Carlos IV and his son Ferdinand had been forced to renounce the throne of Spain and were replaced by Joseph Bonaparte. Spain had been in constant turmoil and now matters became worse. Eventually by April 1814 an estimated 250,000 French soldiers were in that peninsula. Clarke had a hand in most of what transpired within the army during that period. His name appears regularly and almost monotonously in orders, letters and in memoirs of the individuals involved. When orders were given for officers and their men to go to Spain, Clarke usually issued them.

The Emperor ordered Clarke to keep French troops moving into Spain. Replacements for the casualties were essential but sometimes it seemed that only a portion of what was needed actually arrived. When he was in Spain, Napoleon wrote to Clarke in late 1808 that, of 500 soldiers sent to him, only 400 managed to show up, and that was probably the norm. On 24 January 1809 Napoleon wrote again to Clarke, telling him that every man leaving the hospitals 'must return to his unit, if it is on a frontier'. He ordered Clarke to form depots for isolated men to join together. By this time, unlike the early days of the Republic, Bonaparte and his cohorts were beginning to lose direct contact with their soldiers. Not only did they not know the individuals, but the new men didn't know them and the replacements were disappearing as rapidly as they were able to escape. This continued for several years and no matter how desperately Clarke searched for and shipped replacements, many disappeared en route.

Early in 1809 the Emperor was continuing his frenetic schedule. Daily he met with the finance minister Martin M.C. Gaudin and Clarke. There were many duties to attend to; it wasn't just an army they were running, it was an empire. The imperial troops in the conquered lands needed almost as much attention as those in Spain and later, Russia. As time went on, when the Russian campaign and the quicksand of Spain were concurrent, administrators were swamped. Clarke, certainly one of the busiest of Napoleon's bureaucrats, began to be overwhelmed with his responsibilities and with dwindling supplies of raw and human material.

The real struggle in Spain was, and would continue to be,

against the guerrilla forces. In May 1809 the French estimated partisan strength in Upper Aragon at 8,000. Frequently the French replacements Clarke judiciously sent to the peninsula were subject to the guerrillas' attention and frequently intercepted. Eventually it was taken for granted that not all replacements would arrive safely.

Because of his position, Clarke was often the recipient of Joseph Bonaparte's attention. There was a series of conflicts between the two brothers, in which either or both would attempt to drag in a loyal servant to their side against the other. Clarke was often in the middle. He walked a tightrope and somehow managed for most of the period to avoid appearing to side with either against the other. Obviously Napoleon's staff had to always support the Emperor, which angered Joseph and caused more disagreements.

Before Napoleon's victory against Austria at Wagram (July 1809), a hostile undercurrent against the Emperor once again raised its head in France. The police minister Fouché was a constant irritant to Napoleon and eventually attempted to usurp his throne.[14] He warned Napoleon not to lose the battle or 'there will be an immediate insurrection against Napoleon'.

For many months news about a proposed British landing had caused Clarke to prepare a force to defend the coasts of the Netherlands. As the months went by Clarke agreed to hold a couple of battalions along the Scheldt River for just such a possible eventuality.

News reached Paris that a long-anticipated British armada had indeed arrived off the Dutch coast and was preparing to land troops at the island of Walcheren. On 11 August they began landing and went into camps, having captured Flushing. Fouché, without going through the Minister of War or other normal channels, ordered the mobilisation of various National Guard units and directed that they be assigned to Marshal Bernadotte.[15] The latter had just been sent home in disgrace from Austria by Napoleon. Having fought in the Battle of Wagram, Bernadotte was dismissed from the army for actions not conducive to good field operations.

Upon learning of the British landing on the island of Walcheren, within three weeks Clarke succeeded in collecting an army of 60,000 men to oppose the British, who withdrew with considerable losses.

Fouché was serious trouble for Napoleon, but Bernadotte was even more so. For him to have so much military power while the Emperor was in the field and far from home could have been an unmitigated disaster.

Clarke could see that should the large forces of mobilised National Guardsmen turn against the Emperor, they would be a serious threat. 'It's another levée of [17]93 all over again,' he warned. He also warned Napoleon that Bernadotte, who had earlier joined in a plot in Brittany to overthrow Napoleon, was once again grasping for power in Antwerp. 'He is preparing to play a great role ... of grave consequences.' Napoleon, very busy in Austria, advised Clarke that he was well aware of Bernadotte's machinations, but essentially did nothing tangible to counter them.

However, Clarke managed to assume control of the mobilised guardsmen, assigning loyal officers to senior posts, and the problem simmered down. Clarke managed to get the French troops organised and to where they were most needed, on the coast of the Netherlands and opposite the British. Bonaparte was grateful to Clarke whose stock with the Emperor rose appropriately.

Napoleon's France was in constant turmoil. He had to rely upon less able men to administer the nation plus the many countries he had conquered. More trouble began in late November 1809 when

Fouché once again contravened Napoleon's wishes. The Chief of Police of Paris had sent an Irishman, Charles Fagan,[16] with a letter to the British foreign secretary, the Marquis of Wellesley in London.[17] The letter urged that peace be negotiated between France and England. This was all unbeknownst to Napoleon who had decreed that no efforts at peace-making with England would be entered into. He learned further that his brother Louis had made contact separately with the British foreign office. All of these issues Napoleon learned from Clarke and other ministers. He decided that he would settle accounts with his brother later, but he chose to make a severe issue of it with Fouché who had been his *bête noir* for some time.

At a meeting of his council Napoleon asked Fouché, 'You are in charge of making war and peace now? Do you know what the penalty is for such a betrayal? I should march you right up to the guillotine.' However, Fouché had been gathering embarrassing files on each member of the Bonaparte family, including Napoleon himself, since the early 1790s, so Napoleon 'gently' dropped him, when he should have had him executed for treason. He would continue to be a problem for Bonaparte for several years.

Communication between the Emperor and Clarke and vice versa, especially when he was actively campaigning, was by letter. Practically all letters to his brother Joseph in Spain, most of which concerned military matters, were directed through Clarke. In 1809, a very bad year for the King and the French army in Spain, one letter directed Clarke to berate Comte Jean-Baptiste Jourdan, marshal of France (and indirectly Joseph as well), for lack of energy and decision.[18] Jourdan, who wished to retire, advised Clarke that he would do his duty on this occasion, but no more.

Napoleon wrote to Clarke from Vienna on 18 July 1809, while the drums for the dead of Wagram still sounded:

Recommend to the King of Spain that if the English should invade Spain he should not give battle until all his forces are united. He has the 1st and 4th Corps (Victor and Sébastiani) with the garrison of Madrid, which makes more than 50,000 men. The 2nd, 5th and 6th Corps (Soult, Montier and Ney) form about 60,000 men.[19]

Napoleon was convinced the number of troops in Spain was sufficient for victory, because he wrote again to Clarke from Vienna, 'It will be a fine chance to give the English a lesson and finish the war'. If the British could be crushed once and for all, he thought that Spanish resistance would collapse. To Napoleon, the object of the campaign was to crush Wellesley. However, then he heard of the French defeat at Talavera. On receiving Joseph's first reports he wrote hotly to Clarke:

I do not understand the affair in Spain ... Where was the French army on the 29th and 30th [of July]? Where was the English army at that time? The King [Joseph] tells me that he has manoeuvred for a month with 40 thousand men against a hundred thousand men: write him that [if he has] it is his own fault.[20]

When reports of Generals Jean-Baptiste Jourdan, Claude P. Victor and Marshal Nicholas Jean de Dieu Soult arrived, he was furious. 'My army of Spain has been defied by 30,000 Anglais, Jourdan lied to me.'

He sent an order to Clarke:

Make [Jourdan] understand that untruthfulness ... *is un véritable crime* ... that after having been told that the English were beaten ... I find out that *my army was beaten*, that is to say that it took neither Talavera nor the plateau [on which the English stood].[21]

Not all of the communication between the two men, at this time, related to Spain. Clarke made other recommendations, many of which Napoleon gladly accepted. One was the reassignment of MacDonald, a valuable soldier who, because of a *faux pas*, had been dismissed from the Emperor's service five years earlier.[22] He was serving the King of Naples but in 1809, at Clarke's suggestion, Napoleon ordered MacDonald to northern Italy as the Viceroy Prince Eugène de Beauharnaise's subordinate. This transfer greatly annoyed MacDonald, who pictured himself as the younger man's military mentor and later claimed all the credit for Eugène's victories.

Napoleon's other concerns related to instruction, training, supply and other problems concerning the Minister of War. In a letter dated 1 October 1809 Napoleon complained that:

> Our soldiers are not very well instructed. You must occupy yourself with two works, one for the school at Metz and the other for Saint-Cyr. The text for Metz will contain ordonnances [*sic*] on fortified cities, the decisions that have disgraced all commanders who have thoughtlessly surrendered a fortified city entrusted to their defence, and, finally, all ordonnances of Louis XIV and of our own day that prohibit surrendering a fortified city until a breach has been made and the passage of the ditch is practicable.[23]

Napoleon didn't just complain, he also described specifically what he wanted taught at the schools. Fortunately he was well served by his Minister of War who readily understood what the Emperor wanted and successfully carried out his instructions.

In a letter dated 10 October 1809 Bonaparte wrote:

> I desire that you write the King of Spain [Joseph] to make him understand that there is nothing more contrary to military principles

than to make known the strength of his army, whether in Orders of the Day and proclamations or in the gazettes. Tell him that when he is induced to reveal the strength of his forces he should exaggerate and present them as formidable by doubling or trebling the number, and that when he mentions the enemy he should diminish his force by half or one-third. In war everything is mental, and the King strayed from this principle when he stated that he had only 40,000 men and proclaimed that the insurgents have 120,000. This discourages the French troops by representing enemy numbers as immense, and gives the enemy a poor opinion of the French by proclaiming his weakness throughout Spain.[24]

In another letter dated 19 December 1809 he wrote:

I order that the map of Germany, which has been made at the *Dépôt de la Guerre*, be sent back. It is so bad that I cannot use it. I would rather have the first map captured in a library. This mixture of good and bad portions is fatal – worse than if all the parts were bad – for it serves only to jeopardise important operations. I know of nothing more dangerous. When it comes to maps, we must have only good ones, or else the dubious or poor sections must be coloured to indicate that one should not trust them. Moreover, I am not pleased with the map that you presented me for the four departments of the Rhine. I want it to be on the scale of that of Cassini ... and you propose a map on a scale one-eighth smaller ... The Depot of War is poorly managed.[25]

Napoleon continued sending out 'millions' of orders and instructions. In 1810 he sent Clarke a notice complaining, 'the vast ignorance of the officers commanding the coastal batteries render useless the cannon entrusted to them. The projectiles do not reach the target because, with the vessels beyond point-blank range, they have not removed the bushings.'[26]

He was also concerned about expenditure on fancy uniforms that some of his colonels were purchasing. The expense was becoming intolerable. Money was never available for such 'luxuries'. Bonaparte insisted that the soldiers be fed and provided with satisfactory clothing, nothing more elaborate. Soon Clarke was bombarded with protests from commanders, which took time from more important work.

He learned that the French army had no complete uniform regulations and he proceeded to correct that problem as quickly as he could. He found that many directives were out of date and frequently incomplete. The regimental commanders had done whatever they wanted and Clarke was convinced that now was the time to alter that freedom. He sent Napoleon the results of his research and recommendations, and the Emperor set up a committee to look into the matter. Regulations were issued in 1812 and over a period of time, the old uniforms being used up first, new clothing began making its way to the men in the lines.

From February 1809 to February 1810, Marshal Louis Gabriel Suchet and General Andoche Junot attempted to enforce King Joseph's political authority in Aragon, establish a royal administration in the province and convert Aragon into a base of operations for the Third Corps. Junot wrote to Napoleon but the Emperor was engrossed in the Austrian war and instead the Minister of War replied to Junot's queries in May. Clarke urged that harmony should reign between Joseph's bureaucrats and French military officials, since they were opposing a common foe. However, should discord arise, if possible, deference should be shown to the Spanish. Clarke warned Junot: 'You must understand that in no circumstances can you infringe upon the authority of HCM [His Catholic Majesty] who unites with his power of sovereignty, that of commander-in-chief of the French army.' Clarke reprimanded Junot, asserting that he had completely exceeded his authority by issuing decrees and imposing martial law throughout the province. He added that Junot's duties in Aragon were to pacify the province, protect the inhabitants and their property, ensure the welfare of his troops, and assure the execution of the orders of the King with regard to the administration of the country. Clarke did concede that he might encounter difficulties with Spanish officials in his efforts to provide for the Third Corps personnel. In such cases, Clarke empowered Junot to take all measures necessary to guarantee the well-being of his troops. But Clarke cautioned that he should resolve such conflicts by enacting provisional measures and then submitting them to Joseph for final approval. Unless Junot followed these procedures, 'the King would find himself without authority, and his government absolutely helpless'.

Upon the change of command from Junot to Suchet, Clarke instructed the latter in a similar vein: 'It is up to HCM to govern his kingdom, and the generals should execute his instructions with all the means at their disposal.' Like Junot, Suchet was authorised to enact coercive measures to ensure the provisioning of his corps if the Spanish officials failed to co-operate; but he was to act in concert with the royal personnel if at all possible and submit to Joseph an account of any punitive actions taken against royal authorities. Clarke believed that such difficulties should not occur because the 'French and Spanish officials ought to be striving for the same goal'. He seemed unaware that a common foe had not produced common objectives between the *afrancesados* (friends in Spain) and the French.

Early in Suchet's transitional period in January 1810, he complained to Clarke about the guerrillas' interfering with his plans for logistical efficiency. He was just beginning his trials and tribulations with the real defenders of Spain's autonomy. They never gave up nor went away, as the French learned much too late.

Clarke's instructions clearly defined the duty and authority of a military commander subordinated to Joseph. He was to avoid civil-military administrative conflicts while fulfilling the obligations imposed upon the commander to provide the sustenance of his personnel. He was to recognise Joseph as his military superior as well as the administrative sovereign of Spain. Of course, the major problem with these guidelines was, as Junot and later Suchet complained, that the Spanish officials would not or could not assure the welfare of the French troops. French military authorities therefore had to undertake this activity without regard for the Spanish bureaucrats' titular control over governmental affairs. Compounding this problem was Aragon's relative isolation from Madrid, which did not allow for quick resolution of the ensuing administrative conflicts. Despite Clarke's guidelines the contest continued between civilian and military authorities for the administrative control of Aragon.

From the various complaints directed against Spanish officials by French generals, Clarke recognised that Joseph's administrators were reluctantly supporting the French war effort. On 12 June 1810, he wrote to Joseph complaining that the Spanish officials in Aragon were failing to fulfil their duties towards the French army. As he noted, 'These Spaniards were supposed to assist French generals, furnish the sustenance of the imperial troops and guard the countryside by organising an effective police force.' Instead, as Clarke lamented, 'A complete inertia reigns in the administration, and it is unfortunately maintained by Madrid's [Joseph's] silence.' Clarke asserted that since the capture of Zaragoza, the royal government in Aragon had received no instructions from Madrid.

The Emperor Napoleon had sought to end the discord between

native administrators and French military officials by ordering his commanders to assume control of the local administration in Spain. Clarke transmitted Napoleon's decision to Suchet:

> The Emperor directs me on this occasion to warn you not to allow the Spanish authorities to betray you. It is up to you, General, to take the proper measures in order to form and replenish the military magazines; to secure provisions, transport, and in general, everything which is necessary for your troops.[27]

In 1811 Napoleon wrote to Clarke stating that all his troubles in Spain were the result of his brother's inadequacies. 'All the follies in Spain are due to the mistaken consideration I have shown the King [Joseph], who not only does not know how to command, but who is incapable of recognising his own limitations.'[28] Although Napoleon had become less active in military affairs after his marriage to Marie-Louise in April 1810, he was, by the summer of 1811, his dynamic self once again. Letters poured out to any member of his official 'family' and that included almost everyone in the employment of France.

The Emperor responded to the Minister of War's letter concerning weapons and armaments for cuirassiers and lancers. His letter of 6 November 1811 described how bad it would be if 3,000 or 4,000 [cavalry] men were trapped in their encampments by a company of light infantry with carbines or muskets if they were only armed with lances and swords. He went on to describe how he wanted his units to be equipped. Clarke responded as always by putting into motion orders through the quartermaster's offices. Cuirassiers and lancers were subsequently equipped with carbines.

Late in 1811, Clarke did a survey of the number of French Imperial Eagle standards and the types of flags in each regiment.

Generally he found that most of the latter were in decrepit condition and because of battle conditions were generally missing in the older units. Napoleon intervened on 24 December 1811. He was very unhappy that regiments were supplying themselves with eagles even though they had not been officially awarded and sat down and wrote his decision in his own hand. There would be but one eagle for each regiment, including cavalry and artillery, and any excess would be turned in. In the meantime, independently, Clarke had been busy designing flags, mostly green ones. Napoleon wasn't amused. He deplored the idea that the flags in blue, red and white should be supplanted and said so. Once the eagles' matter was settled according to Napoleon's dictate, Clarke proposed that each branch receive a different coloured flag; white for infantry, green for light cavalry and so forth. Napoleon accepted the point expressed by his Minister of War that the current flags from 1804 were ill-designed for adding battle honours. A subordinate of Clarke's suggested that the flags be enlarged with three vertical bands of equal width allowing for additional battle honours. That solved this major problem before Napoleon went off in 1812 to visit Alexander in Russia. The newly issued flags also went on the trip but how many returned is difficult to determine. Those that survived would have been suitably enlarged for the many new honours heaped upon each unit.

The Irish Legion had been formed in 1803 by Napoleon, and it subsequently became the Third Foreign Regiment, Irish. It was awarded an eagle in 1804 and this was retained for the length of their service for France. In 1809, the Legion saved its green flag and eagle from capture in the doomed island fortress of Walcheren when Major, later Lieutenant-Colonel, William Lawless and Captain Terence O'Reilly slipped through the British fleet with it in a small boat. Their eagle was also preserved at Katzbach where, because of MacDonald's blundering, they were trapped against the river. As the Prussians pounded them, around thirty Irishmen with fixed bayonets and their musket butts wielded wildly, broke through the 'Dutchmen's' lines and swam to safety with their eagle and their honour. Napoleon never had cause to regret having those Irlandais in his army. As a matter of fact, no French ruler ever did. Clarke had this to say of the Legion:

> To maintain the existence of this Irish regiment, I have carefully brought together the United Irish and the ancient partisans of the Stuarts [sic]. This regiment is a sort of bugbear to England, which is always worried about it.[29]

Although he had shown great interest in the regiment, Clarke was apparently not well liked by its officers. They believed that he showed favouritism towards the few French and German officers accepted in the regiment, even though he struggled to maintain its 'racial purity'. Morale fell in 1811 when the name was changed to the Third Régiment Étranger but by then there were few Irish survivors in the ranks and definitely more Germans and Poles, though the officer corps remained mainly Irish.

Although they supposedly didn't like Clarke, he took care of a lot of them, like a Colonel Daniel O'Meara who he placed as Marshal Jean Lannes' senior aide-de-camp; the French general, Baron Jean Baptiste Antoine Marcelin de Marbot wrote that O'Meara was 'brave, but unable to do much'.[30] Clarke also managed to have two of his Shee cousins appointed to the Legion.

Napoleon was dissatisfied with the conduct of the Fourth Régiment Étranger, Preuss (Prussian) because it was less than worthy in Spain. He wrote to Clarke in July 1813 to check it out and take any and all corrective action. He was also very dissatisfied when Clarke began dismissing Dutch officers in various Dutch units and replacing them with some of his French friends.

Napoleon told him that Dutch troops were to be commanded, whenever possible, by Dutch officers. When Spanish troops loyal to Joseph were driven out of the peninsula, as was their King, they were absorbed into the French army. Marshal Soult was anxious that they be treated with due respect because they had performed at a very high level. They were disarmed and supposedly converted to Pioneers, engineering labourers who carried out what were considered menial tasks such as digging ditches and erecting fortifications. Clarke made an issue of that by speaking up and declaring that 'pioneer' was a foul name for such faithful soldiers. Why that should be, we have no record, nor of the outcome.

Napoleon instituted a fresh flow of orders to his Minister of War which meant he was once again preparing for a major war. This time he was going to Russia. Russia had 'recognised' Napoleon's actions in Prussian Poland, but Czar Alexander became angry when Napoleon created the Grand Duchy of Warsaw in 1807. To the Russian Czar this move meant a new Poland on his borders, with its consequent threat. Relationships between France and Russia then began to fray badly and by 1811 the two were once again seriously at loggerheads. From 1811 until May 1812, Bonaparte assembled nearly 450,000 French and allied soldiers in Poland. It was obvious to Alexander that Russia was about to be invaded.

In October 1812, while Napoleon was invading Russia and beginning to find that he had tackled a bear which was no longer sleeping, General Malet, a long-time foe, had escaped from his 'mild' house-arrest.[31] Malet had prepared plans to usurp Napoleon with some help from those who were not on the Russian campaign and who were unhappy with the Emperor. The plans called for the enticement and usurpation of the National Guard regiments on duty in Paris and the arrest of Napoleon's numerous 'house-keepers' including Clarke and the Arch-Chancellor Cambacérès[32]

– in effect, the men who were running the empire while Napoleon was away conquering new territories.

Malet's plans worked up to a certain point. He gave a set of written orders to former Colonel Doucet, promoted by Malet to brigadier-general. Doucet very slowly reviewed the situation. He was ordered to arrest his commanding officer, General Henri François de Laborde, who was also brought into the fracas. Then Laborde told Malet he was 'unauthorised to leave his maison without my permission'. Consequently the two, Doucet and Laborde, had Malet arrested along with all the other conspirators. All were tried and almost everyone involved was executed. Clarke, who was never taken by the conspirators, and his fellow officers were safe to continue what they did best – administer the Empire.

While deep in Russia, Napoleon was still concerned about his manpower and wrote to Clarke about the soldiers in Italy. His concern was that as young recruits for the most part, the 'morning air in Italy is deadly' and that they should be moved to the higher localities rather than [be] in places like Mantua. Otherwise, according to Napoleon, they 'were so many lost men'. Even when conditions weren't always the best for him, Napoleon's thoughts were on his army. It is not clear why the morning air in Italy would be injurious.

Upon his return from Russia, Napoleon had learned several things. The most important was that he should not try to carry on more than one war at a time. Suchet was still having trouble in Spain and had requested 'Please send me several battalions so I don't have to give up Zaragoza.' It isn't known whether Clarke had several, or even one battalion to send. Most had been used up in the trip to Moscow and Suchet would have to do the best he could with what he had.

The *29th Bulletin of the Grande Armée* admitted the enormity of the catastrophe in Russia, where Napoleon failed to take Moscow and in the retreat back to France, lost the majority of his army. All of Paris saw it in the *Moniteur* of 16 December 1812, but his brother Joseph did not see it until a month later.[33] On 4 January 1813 Napoleon ordered Clarke to instruct his brother 'El Rey José Bonaparte to withdraw from his capital at Madrid … moving temporarily [northward] to Valladolid'. The reason, according to the Emperor, was that Joseph's primary mission must be to protect the southern frontier of France. Clarke so informed the King by letter on 4 January 1813:

> The Emperor thinks Your Majesty will have been informed by the 29th bulletin, of the state of affairs in the north; it is easy to comprehend that they require all our attention and effort, and that it is consequently necessary to subordinate the affairs of Spain. In these circumstances the Emperor [orders] … that Your Majesty move personally, with his headquarters, to Valladolid, and occupy Madrid only as one of the extremities of the line.[34]

Joseph claimed he did not receive Clarke's important instructions to head north until 16 February 1813, adding that he did not know until then that he was no longer to have a capital, but only a headquarters, and that in the north of Spain. Joseph complained that Clarke's orders to him to vacate Madrid limited his 'freedom of movement'. Bonaparte then assailed Clarke because his brother still hadn't vacated Madrid. 'Where is he and what is he doing?' At about this same time Napoleon told Clarke that his family was the cause of 'all the setbacks in Spain … [which] are the result of my misplaced trust in the King [Joseph]'. As conditions deteriorated for France, Napoleon lashed out at everyone within reach of his relatively efficient Minister of War.

In January 1813 Suchet continued to plead with Clarke

for reinforcements for his now ragtag army in Aragon. On 22 January, Clarke told Suchet not to let the guerrillas bother him. His attitude seemed to be that if Suchet ignored them, they would probably go away. Clarke is blamed, appropriately it seems, for not knowing how desperate the situation was in Spain. This was perhaps because he was far away or, more likely, because he had no reinforcements to send. Possibly Clarke believed that pretending the problem didn't exist would make it go away, but it didn't.

In a letter to Napoleon in February 1813, Clarke warned the Emperor that it was useless to send National Guard troops to Spain, or at least to the frontier, and recommended sending regular troops instead. Bonaparte refused because he needed them elsewhere. At this time he was fighting on numerous fronts and had left garrisons throughout eastern Europe, further dissipating his trained troops. Prussia had revolted against French rule in January, and their contingent of the Grande Armée joined the advancing Russians.

During the latter part of the Spanish campaign Clarke made various recommendations to Joseph, most of which the latter angrily rejected. Joseph was still seething against the decree of 8 February 1810, which had divided his kingdom into military governments. Perhaps as revenge, he informed Clarke on 5 June that he knew nothing about the situation in Aragon because he had 'never had a report from the provincial commander nor knew the name of the governor'.[35] Besides, he added, 'I don't have any spare troops.' Clarke was wise enough not to let Napoleon know Joseph was angry.

Clarke, with strained circumspection, tried to inform Joseph of the conditions in the empire, and goad him into action. 'The Emperor orders me to declare that Your Majesty can expect nothing [additional] from him considering the circumstances in which France finds herself ... His Imperial Majesty orders me once again to tell Your Majesty that to command an army well, one must work at it without ceasing.' Clarke then asked why Joseph's armies were stagnant and the British moved about at will. Despite Clarke's urging, Joseph kept his armies dispersed.

As a result of Wellington's triumph at Vittorio on 21 June 1813, General Bertrand Clausel, commander of the Army of the North in Spain, found the allied army of English, Portugese and Hanoverian troops placed squarely between his 12,000 men and Joseph's beaten force. Clausel decided to retire to Zaragoza so that his corps could serve as liaison between Suchet's troops in Valencia and Joseph's force rallying at Bayonne. Clausel told Clarke he would remain in Zaragoza unless ordered to leave, and the French Minister of War fully approved of the general's manoeuvre.

On 3 July, when Marshal Suchet received confirmation of the defeat at the Battle of Vitoria, he wrote to Clarke complaining that this defeat had ruined the accomplishments of five years of devoted service and hard work. The battle was the ultimate defeat of the Emperor's forces in Spain. Not only did Joseph lose 7,000 men but he also lost his treasury of 5 million Spanish dollars, plus huge masses of stores. Joseph fled towards the French border and Marshal Soult assumed command of what was left of the French army in Spain.[36] In November Joseph crossed the frontier back into France and was placed in charge of the National Guard.

As the year 1814 began, Napoleon was getting into deeper trouble. He was winning many of the battles, but each time he flattened one opponent, several others, usually stronger than he, avoided him and marched on Paris. By mid-February, Clarke promised Napoleon 27,000 men from Poland and Germany and although he managed to gather together that number, he also promised another 180,000, from where we can only guess. The

French and conscripted foreigners grumbled and cursed Napoleon as they marched to 'the sound of the guns'.

Finding war material was another very serious problem for Clarke and, ultimately, Napoleon. Sometime in the early months of 1814, the Emperor was literally begging Clarke to find him bridging equipment. However, he couldn't locate any until mid-March, and then only a small train appeared, 'horrible and immobile' and practically useless. Things got worse. The dry wood set aside to be used for musket stocks had long since disappeared and soft pine was being used instead. Locating stocks of cloth was becoming very difficult, since so much wool had already been used for the new uniforms for recruits going to Russia. New recruits were even harder to locate. Many soldiers of the Grande Armée had found ways and means to disappear in many lands through which the army had marched. Frenchmen, especially former soldiers, were scattered all over Europe.

On 11 January 1814 the Emperor wrote to Clarke, 'My plan is to make Paris a fortified city. Should the enemy succeed in his avowed design of reaching it I intend to wait for him here and in no circumstances to leave Paris.' As things went from bad to worse Napoleon sent captured flags to Clarke to publicly present to Empress Marie-Louise before transfer to Invalides. It was another of Napoleon's public relations efforts which by now were overdone and often overlooked by the people of Paris. Dutifully, after the reception, 'Clarke and the official cortège proceeded to Invalides to lay up the glorious standards'. On 17 February Napoleon sent Clarke another ten flags taken at Montereau and Montmirail to keep up the Parisians' spirits and Clarke loyally made the trip once again.

In March 1814 Napoleon raged at nearly everyone. 'So everybody has lost his head! That's what comes of employing men who don't have common sense or energy … That swine of a

Joseph, who thinks he can lead an army as well as I can! ... And that bastard Clarke, who can't do a thing once you take him away from his office routine!'[37] Regardless of what he said, Napoleon was in constant contact via letters with his Minister of War who was doing what was possible to 'create new armies'. Most orders to his various field commands went through Clarke's office.

By late March it was becoming obvious to everyone, including the Emperor, that his world was crashing down. He sent orders to Joseph that the Empress and his son should vacate Paris at once. She was reluctant to leave because of the appearance that would give to the French people and to the enemy. But Clarke sent an officer to urge her immediate departure, since Prussian cavalry had been seen within the city walls. She still refused to leave until Joseph failed to return one day and then gave the most difficult orders of her life, to abandon the capital and make for Tours.

By 25 March the Emperor tried, with Clarke's help, to establish resistance within Paris but it was too late. Napoleon began swinging at anyone and everyone. He blamed everyone, especially Clarke, for his 'incompetent defence of the capital'. This charge has to be reviewed based upon the facts, which were that the allies were upon and in the city, Napoleon and his forces were somewhere outside, and the city and residents were in danger. Whoever was responsible for the outcome, certainly Napoleon himself must absorb much of the condemnation. He had run his race, and even though he had won many times, he was finally overwhelmed by his many enemies who had finally united. On 6 April, following a mutiny by his brothers Joseph and Jerome, some generals and some of his marshals, Napoleon Bonaparte signed his first abdication.

With the downfall of Napoleon, in April 1814 Clarke ceased to function as Minister of War. Though Clarke had served Napoleon, upon Bonaparte's defeat he became associated with the newly restored Bourbons, and when Napoleon later returned during the 'Hundred Days', Clarke was called upon to serve Louis XVIII in March 1815. Soult was the first appointed Minister of War under the restored monarchy. But he was a disaster, appearing as disloyal to the Bourbons as he had been to Napoleon. He was fired for treasonable activities but not charged. Saint-Cyr, the next Minister of War, tried to preserve as much as possible of the existing order, but that merely resulted in his being replaced by Clarke.[38] Both Clarke and Berthier were berated by Napoleon's supporters because they led Louis' carriage to the Tuileries upon his triumphant return, the two having been long considered Napoleon's most loyal subordinates.[39] Later, like so many of Napoleon's followers, Clarke gave his loyalty to Louis XVIII and accompanied him to Ghent.[40]

When Napoleon landed in France, Clarke called out every French military unit available that might be reasonably loyal to King Louis. It has been said that he had such energy and diligence that if he had had the time, 'the entire nation would have been in the field against the enemy of the Bourbons'.[41] Napoleon's enemies were primarily based in Paris, the countryside being more inclined to accept his return. However, it was not enough and Napoleon swept through France, forcing the monarchy to flee.

During Louis' exile, Clarke was temporarily given the post of Minister of Marine. He had been and remained very close to the King. For some reason, Clarke did not live in poverty as did so many of the other officers who attended Louis in Belgium. Stenger claims that he alone 'was in a position, owing to his great wealth, to live in solitary luxury'.[42]

Following Napoleon's defeat at Waterloo, Wellington's army stalked the retreating French forces on their journey back towards Paris, and the entourage of King Louis followed closely behind. Wellington wrote a rather long letter to Clarke, who was travelling in the King's carriage, describing his activities and those of the defeated army of Napoleon:

> We already find the white flag flying above the towns and villages. The defeat of Napoleon's army is more decisive than it appeared to be at first. The soldiers are dispersing, in small bodies, to their own homes. The cavalry and train of artillery are selling their horses in the districts through which they pass. The infantry are throwing away their arms and dispersing to their homes. There are more than 2,000 muskets waiting to be picked up in the forest of Mormal.[43]

Upon return to France, Clarke became Minister of War for the third time in September 1815. Unfortunately for Clarke and several other loyal members of Louis' entourage who went to Ghent with him, they were summarily fired, probably because of the conflict between Talleyrand and Louis and his loyalists.

Despite his dismissal as Minister of War, Clarke accompanied Louis in his triumphant return to Paris. There was to be a large gathering of people to cheer on the King when he entered the city in victory. But upon arrival, near Paris there was another large segment of the populace who opposed the reintroduction of a Bourbon regime and stood in solemn silence along the path leading to the entrance of the city. Louis and his followers feared a violent reaction, perhaps even a riot, but all went well. The King's carriage was preceded into Paris by the royal bodyguards (Swiss, foot, horse and gendarmes) and in the middle of the formation were Marshals Marmont, Victor, Oudinot, MacDonald and Gouvion Saint-Cyr; and Generals Clarke, Maison, Dessolles and Villate.

Soon after this, Clarke's replacement as Minister of War was found to be inadequate and Clarke was once again reinvested in this position. The allies, and many monarchists, regarded the survival of any recognisable element of the Grande Armée a menace to the general tranquillity, but Clarke ignored this and went zealously to work. He made numerous changes in the army, most of which were to alter the 'menace' and create a new professional force loyal to the King. Impressed by his diligence and skills, the Bourbons made him a marshal on 16 June 1816. He also found the time to have a full-length portrait of himself in full dress painted, baton prominently displayed, his face beaming and (as Elting added) 'like that of an unjust Hibernian publican who had just successfully unloaded a consignment of watered ale'.

In September 1817, Clarke resigned his portfolio and retired to his country estate at Neuville (Bas-Rhin), where, worn out and ill, he died aged fifty-three on 28 October 1818. The ducal title became extinct with the death of Clarke's son, but was restored in 1864 by imperial decree (Napoleon III) in favour of his great-great-grandson, Charles de Goyon.

Henri J.G. Clarke has left behind a mixed, and in some ways, a convoluted memory. To those writers in English, most of whom were Irish, he was a shifty individual who took care of number one. Others claimed that officers of the Grande Armée found him as harsh to his subordinates as he was 'wiggly' to his superiors. Having been accepted by the Bourbons it is said that he turned completely against his old colleagues. He treated Madame Ney, wife of Marshal Michel Ney, contemptuously.[44] When one of Napoleon's generals, Comte Lavalette (to whom Clarke supposedly owed a debt of gratitude from their old days with the Army of Italy) asked his help to ensure that Ney died by shooting rather than hanging, Clarke rebuffed him, telling him to recommend Ney's wife and daughter to the King's inexhaustible benevolence.

When he had provided the Bourbons with his skills in managing the army, he set about completely revamping each unit.

His first step was to eliminate, as much as possible, those officers and men who were Bonapartists. He laboured enthusiastically with the cavalry; officers and men were sent home on leave and horses put out to pasture. Thereafter the regiments were rebuilt with officers and men drawn from various former units, making each one a collection of strangers. Regimental numbers were replaced by departmental names: for example, the six retained Hussar regiments were dubbed Jura, Meurthe, Moselle, Nord, Bas-Rhin and Haut-Rhin. Most of them lost their traditional uniform colours. Much the same thing happened to the artillery. It was a thorough piece of work, one that completely mixed-up the unit lineages and battle honours of all but one French regiment. The carabiniers, being the Comte d'Artois' (later Charles X of France) special favourites, were exempt from these changes.[45] Regimental customs, some more than a century old, were scrapped. The new organisations had no past, no traditions and no reputation, neither bad nor good, to contend with.

These legions and regiments were activated with some pomp and ceremony. Their new flags were taken to the local cathedrals to be solemnly blessed, while the troops fired a salvo of musketry outside. Usually a member of the royal family made a formal presentation. When Clarke finished with the 'new army' it was just that, brand new. At the time, this was essential for the safety of the returned royal family and continued stability in France.[46] It was also required because the Allies were hovering on the borders of France; waiting for any sign of a return of French empire-building.[47] The regime required many years of peace and this revamping of the armed forces was more acceptable to potential enemies than had been the imperial armies of Napoleon Bonaparte.

Clarke was an astute diplomat, but was never very scrupulous (it has been said) on points of honour or conventionality; his character has been severely criticised by some French historians. They state that he saw Napoleon's star rising and knelt down and worshipped it. Some of his Irish compatriots, who were acquainted with him, were not very enthusiastic about his virtues. Wolfe Tone alternately praised and criticised him, while Miles Byrne charged him with expelling from France a number of officers of the Irish Legion after the return of the Bourbons, 'because they had remained faithful to the very Napoleonic Eagles of which Clarke was supposed to be such a champion'.

Subordinates found Clarke conceited, rough-spoken and often harsh. He was much more willing to commission a 'wet-behind-the-ears sprig' of the nobility than a deserving enlisted man. As an example, his attempt to squeeze Arniel, a soldier of note, out of the 27th Chasseurs à Cheval, to make room for a useless relative of his own, caused an uproar and he was forced to back down.

He had, according to writers like Elting and Lachouque, a frequently unpleasant disposition. When Napoleon abdicated the first time, for some reason he was, according to some of them, especially hard on the Irish who had joined Napoleon's Irish Legion. For the most part they damned him in letters and later in memoirs. He has been criticised for being the ultimate bureaucrat. At times when men and officers were desperate for the issue of clothing or musket balls he backed the dispensers who demanded that the proper forms be submitted and filled out. He always stood for 'conformity' at the expense of smoothness. Often he suggested methods of uniformity, many of which Napoleon intelligently refused to consider.

Frenchmen were also baffled by his fascination with his own genealogy and his researches to prove himself a descendant of the Norman Plantagenets who once ruled England.[48]

When Napoleon returned after the first abdication, Clarke was criticised for refusing to give up his new relationship with the Bourbons. Of course he wasn't the only follower who didn't return to his side. Unlike many of the other 'turncoats' he even went into exile with Louis XVIII to Ghent, later returning with the King when Bonaparte was defeated at Waterloo. He was, after all, a monarchist – no one could or did call him a revolutionary or even a common man. Although he loyally served Napoleon for many years, his real loyalties were to the Emperor, not to the man. When that Emperor resigned he transferred his monarchist tendencies to the new King. As for the Irish critics, he saw himself as a French soldier whose responsibilities were to his commander. When he could help the Irish *émigrés*, he did so. But they were not his first concern.

Obviously he had many faults, but he served Napoleon more honestly, faithfully and successfully than most other administrators. When Napoleon abdicated in 1814, Clarke switched allegiance as did many others. After all, he had paid his dues to a relatively ungrateful monarch, and was still able to provide loyal service to another monarch. Why not? The restored Bourbons were of the royal line and the republicans were temporarily out of office. Regardless, as time would prove, France was badly served by both.

Are ye mad or in a trance?
Waken, gentlemen of France!
(Shout, boys, Erin's the renown!)
See your lilied flags are flapping,
And your Marshal is caught napping
In Cremona town.

Emily Lawless,
Cremona, 1704

CHAPTER 9

THE IRISH IN THE HOLY ROMAN EMPIRE AND AUSTRIA

'The more Irish in the Austrian service the better ...'
Emperor Francis I, Holy Roman Empire

When the imperial forces entered the Thirty Years' War in the early seventeenth century, there were already a few Irishmen in their ranks. Some of the many Irish individuals who had become unemployed following the Twelve Years' Truce of 1609 between Spain and the Dutch, had drifted eastward from the Spanish Netherlands. Some went to the many German states, some to the Holy Roman Empire. Many stopped in numerous countries along the way. Some remained in Denmark; others went to Sweden and to various parts of Germany, often the Protestant principalities; some went further east to Poland and Russia. I will concentrate here upon those who headed for, or ended up in, Austria or the imperial lands.

The wandering Irish soldier found a good home in the imperial domains and its extensive empire of the period. The Irish soldier was a very desirable commodity in that community. As Emperor

Francis I said: '… our troops will always be disciplined; an Irish coward is an uncommon character, and what the natives of Ireland even dislike from principle, they will generally perform through a desire for glory'.[1]

No imperial regiments were filled with eager Irish rankers as they had been for Spain in Flanders, and later for France, but there were many Irish who were looking for work, and soldiering was their trade.[2] References to Irishmen then serving in the armies of the German states can be found in a book by Carve entitled *Itinerarium*, which was published in Germany in 1640.[3] Assorted names appear, usually in a German variation, and one has to step gingerly when identifying them as Irish. Carve did so but used the diverse terms that always confuse the issue, such as: *Ibernia Scotiave, Scoti seu Iberni* or even *Scoti et Iberni*. The word 'Scot' or variations, always meant Irish, in pre-seventeenth-century Europe.

Carve's book references various names, which have been translated into versions of well-known Irish names. Examples abound: Dermitz Carthii (Dermot MacCarthy), D'esmond (Desmond), Geraldin (FitzGerald), Onell (O'Neill) and Barnaby Patrirch (Patrick). These show that at least some Irish were serving in Germany during the early years of the seventeenth century. Inferences from Carve's book are that there were contingents (units) of Irishmen which became diluted as casualties increased and the Thirty Years' War raged on.

Carve's work is not the only source that provides a small amount of information about the Irish in Germany during those years. There were records of an entire regiment of Irish being shipped from France to the Holy Roman Empire for service in a war in Hungary between the empire and the Turks. Those Irish proved to be more bothersome than useful, and consequently any record of their exploits was not recorded for posterity.

One of the earliest Irish names to appear in Central Europe, of which there were at least six members, was the Butler family. At the battle of Ostrode (Ostroda), Poland, in 1628, a Polish citizen named James Butler was prominent at the defeat of the Swedes.[4] He may have been a colonel, and was serving in the imperial forces when he brought his regiment to relieve Tiefenbach at the siege of Frankfurt on Oder in April 1631. The following year he returned to serve Sigismund of Poland where he remained for the balance of his life. One of Butler's sons (or nephews), also named James and a colonel, was the proprietor of a Polish regiment commonly called the 'Young Butler' regiment.

What we do know is that Irish officers of Colonel Walter Butler's Regiment of Dragoons were involved in the assassination of General Wallenstein, who was considered a threat to the Emperor, in February 1635. They also managed to bring two Scotsmen, Lieutenant-Colonel John Gordon and Major Walter Leslie, into their plot. The Irish have been identified as Butler himself, Major Robert Geraldine, Captain Walter Devereaux and Captain Denis MacDaniel, who guarded the gates. While the Emperor did not directly order nor even suggest that Wallenstein be assassinated, after the deed he raised Butler to the rank of Count and Imperial Chamberlain, besides granting him the late Wallenstein's Hirschberg estate, then worth 225,000 gulden. The others were all appropriately rewarded in large sums, including Leslie and Gordon. There is no suggestion that any were punished or refused the largesse for their part in the deed.[5]

If Butler had a regiment as early as 1635, he was a person of some prominence in the empire. Several other Irishmen served as officers in his regiment, as well as Scotsmen.[6] It is possible that the lower ranks of the regiment were composed entirely or largely of Irishmen. In April 1631 Butler's Regiment fought the Swedes at Frankfurt on Oder, including Hepburn's 1,500-man Scots Brigade which opposed them.

King Gustavus placed Hepburn and his force opposite the Irish who were defending the walls. Hepburn and his men had been badly treated by Butler's men that same year at New Brandenberg, and Hepburn was out for revenge. Colonel Robert Monro of Mackey's Regiment had the following to say about Butler and his Irish:

> The yellow and the blew Briggads, being esteemed of all the Army both resolute and courageous in all their exploits; they were to enter on the *Irish* quarter, where they were twice with great losse furiously beaten off, and were cruelly spoyled with fireworks throwne by the Irish amongst them. But at last they having entred, notwithstanding the inequality of their strength, the Irish though weake stood to it, and fought with sword, and pikes within workes a long time, till the most part of the Souldiers fell to ground, where they stoode fighting, so that in the end, Lievetenant Colonell Walter Butler, who commanded the Irish, being shot in the arme, and pierced with a pike through the thigh, was taken prisoner, so that the next day, it was to be seene on the poast where the best service was done: and truly had all the rest stood to it as well as the Irish did, we had returned with great loss and no victory.[7]

And again '… but if all those within this Towne had stood to their defence, as Lievtenant Colonell Butler did and the Irish, Francford had not bin taken.'[8]

The battle between the two sides was fierce. Butler lost four lieutenant-colonels, Wade, O'Neill, Patrick and MacCarthy; a Captain Grace and Lieutenant Brown, and an ensign named Butler. Walter Butler himself was badly wounded. The losses to the Scots are unknown but Hepburn's memoir states 'the Scots fought the Irish to the last man'. It didn't say whose last man. When Irish resistance was overcome, Gustavus Adolphus invited the badly wounded Butler to supper, having him carried into the King's presence on a stretcher. During the course of the dinner the King asked Butler, 'Are you the Butler senior?' to which Butler replied, 'I am not.' The King replied, 'The gods are kind to you, brave soldier. Because if you had been the elder one, my royal right hand would have smitten you.'[9] Butler was kept prisoner for eight months, until a large ransom was paid for him. Upon his release, Butler then went into Poland, where he raised another regiment of dragoons for imperial service.

Several times Carve's book mentions that the Swedes held the Irish in high esteem, especially when they fought them. 'When the Swedes heard that *Scoti Ibernique* opposed them, they quickly withdrew.' That may have been literary licence carried to an extreme. In those days Gustavus and his army didn't run from anyone. In that Swedish army was a modest gathering of Scotsmen which Carve embellishes as a 'Scottish Brigade'. Included were Drummonds, Leslies and Monroes as well as a regiment named MacKay's (or Mackey's). There were also Irishmen, albeit mostly of the Protestant persuasion.[10]

There are several illustrations in Carve's book which purport to represent Irishmen, though they look as though they might have been wearing Scottish costumes. They were identified as *Irrländer* and Carve relates: 'Such dress is worn by the 800 *Irrländer* or *Irren* arrived at Stettin.' And as quoted in John Henning's book:

> The *Irrländer* are a strong enduring people, contented with plain (or little) food; when they have no bread, they can endure hunger for three or four days, feeding instead on water, cress, roots and grass; when necessary, they can walk more than twenty miles a day; apart from their musquets [*sic*] they have their bows and long knives.

Following the battle for Leipzig on 15 September 1631, when General Tilly took the city for the Holy Roman Empire, Colonel Monro requested permission to recruit from the prisoners any Britons (including Irish) for his sadly depleted ranks. Permission was granted but as Monro tells us: 'When I had made try all to finde out the number; there were but three *Irish* amongst them all, and being disappointed of a strong Recruet, I did oversee those, to follow their Camerades.'[11]

Another description of the Irish soldiers, in verse form, credits them as coming from Hibernia:

That nation is enduring and hardy; swarthy like gypsies, stocky of build, war-loving ... they are so swift, that in one day they can cover sixteen miles. Their dress and caps are altogether barbarous, almost entirely black in colour, because, as is well known, all the sheep in their whole country are black. Their shoes are mostly made of straw. They are contented with plain (or little) food. When they have no bread and are hungry, they dig up roots from the ground and thus satisfy their hunger.[12]

Individually and collectively, Irish soldiers were serving in Germany during the Thirty Years' War, some for the Empire and, it appears, some for Sweden as well. And the latter, according to Carve, were Roman Catholics as well as Protestants, which is confirmed by Fischer.

The great Austrian Wallis (also Walsh) family had its beginnings when Colonel Richard Walsh of Carrighmain, County Dublin, arrived in Germany in 1612. He was wounded in action at the head of his regiment during the Battle of Lutzen, and subsequently died as a result of those wounds at Magdeburg in 1632. But in the next two centuries there would be many more to replace them.[13]

Another of the same breed, but spelled Wallis, was Oliver, also born at Carrighmain, in 1600. His arrival in Germany was about the time that the Thirty Years' War began. By 1642 Ferdinand III created Wallis a baron and imperial chamberlain. He had been promoted to major-general and was the first Count Carrighmain. As major-general, between 1644 and 1667 he raised four different regiments of infantry for his Emperor, all of which he commanded successively. He died in Hungary in 1667. Another Wallis, Lieutenant Field Marshal Ernst von Wallis earned many plaudits before dying in 1689.

The Taaffes, an Irish family which had its origins in County Sligo, arrived in late seventeenth-century Austria. An Irish priest named Taaffe served Prince Octavio (Count) Piccolomini, an Italian general in the imperial service, as his personal chaplain. Interestingly, the origin of both names, Wallis and Taaffe, in Ireland, signified Welshmen who landed with the Norman invasion. Walsh simply stated meant 'Welshman' and Taaffe translated to 'David', a common Welsh name. The diminutive nickname 'Taffy' is as Welsh as 'Pat' is Irish and 'Jock' is Scots.

Possibly the most famous of the Taaffe family during this period was Count Franz (Francis) Taaffe, Third Earl of Carlingford and Fourth Viscount Taaffe, who was born at Ballymote, County Sligo in 1639.[14] Franz was educated at Olmütz in Moravia and he was found a place in the imperial service as page to both the Emperors Ferdinand III and Leopold I. As a youth he and Charles Leopold, the exiled heir of Lorraine, served as soldiers together and developed a friendship that lasted until the latter's death in 1690. Charles gave Franz a company of his own *kürassiers* (Dragoons) in Hungary in 1670. In 1673 Franz commanded his company at the siege of Bonn and in the following year at the battles of Sinzheim and Mülhausen. In 1674 he was selected to press (unsuccessfully) Lorraine's candidacy in the forthcoming election for the Polish throne. The following year he commanded the right wing of the imperial army at Neider-Sasbach.

When Lorraine approached the Emperor asking that his friend be rewarded, Taaffe was made colonel-proprietor of his own regiment of *kürassiers* in 1677 and retained it until his death in 1704.[15] When he was informed that there were no vacant *kürassier* regiments he resigned his own and it was then awarded to his friend Taaffe. In 1682 Taaffe was a general and still under the command of Lorraine in Hungary where they fought a Turkish onslaught, but were soon overwhelmed and forced to retire. At the relief of Vienna in 1683, Franz Taaffe was in command of the left wing of Lorraine's army. There he is credited with greatly assisting in defeating and driving back the huge Turkish army. Because of his services he was promoted to General of Horse in 1687. In 1694 he was made a Knight of the Golden Fleece, one of the most exclusive orders in the world.

When Lorraine died in 1690, Taaffe was named in his will as his best friend and caretaker of his widow and heir, Leopold. Taaffe took the boy's place at negotiations, which culminated in the Treaty of Ryswick in 1697. The family's sinecure, the Duchy of Lorraine, had been lost by a frivolous duke some years before and it was now restored. This resulted in Franz Taaffe becoming the young Leopold's chamberlain, Prime Minister and Minister of Finance. He was also made governor of the fortress of Metz and colonel of his guard.

In 1676 Taaffe had married Elizabeth Maximiliana Traudisch. She was the widow of two successive counts Schlick, and died herself in 1700. She provided Franz with much valued property and also a daughter, Anne, who predeceased him. In August 1704 he died while at Nancy, then part of the Duchy of Lorraine.[16]

Another Taaffe, Nicholas, Sixth Viscount Taaffe, was born in 1677 at Castle O'Crane in Sligo and in later years was appointed chancellor to Emperor Leopold II. As the colonel of the *kürassier* regiment Lanthieri, he distinguished himself fighting the French in 1734 and 1735 during the War of the Polish Succession. Two years later he was in Hungary with his regiment and fought the Turks at Widdin and at the defence of Fort St Elizabeth, where he gained additional recognition for saving the army's artillery and baggage. In 1738 he was at Pallesch where he covered the retreat of the army, as he did again at Semlin. In consequence of his bravery and skills he was promoted to general in 1739 and to lieutenant-general in 1752. He wrote a letter in the third person to Emperor Francis Stephen and his wife, Empress Maria Theresa, which read:

> ... because he was afraid that his descendants pressed by the Penal Laws would not resist the temptation of becoming Protestants. He therefore took refuge to a Catholic country where his ancestors were well-known by the military services they had rendered at different intervals to the House of Austria. He had abandoned his relations and his estate and the rank and liberty he had in his country to prevent his descendants from deserting a religion to which their Imperial Majesties so fervently adhered ...[17]

Upon the death of his kinsman, Nicholas Taaffe succeeded to the title, the Fourth Earl of Carlingford. There were many more of both names, Wallis and Taaffe, that continued their service to Austria for many years to come.

The Burkes of Gallstown, County Kilkenny, were another Irish family some of whose members found their way to imperial service. The best known was Colonel William Count Gall von Bourch, whose four brothers also made their way east. Patrick Gall Burke joined the Spanish army and was killed at Torgau in 1637 while David, Thomas and James all joined the Austrian service, the latter being killed at Leipzig in 1631.

William had first taken service with Poland and in the 1630s had joined the imperial army, possibly at the same time as James Butler. In 1633 he became governor of Neisse. That same year William raised a regiment of dragoons and remained proprietor of it until 1644. Between 1640 and 1642 he also commanded and was proprietor of a regiment of *kürassiers* which was incorporated into another corps in 1644. He was imperial chamberlain to both emperors, Ferdinand II and Ferdinand III, and the latter made him a count of the Holy Roman Empire in 1637. He purchased an estate in the barony of Holstein, near Limberg in Silesia, and died there in 1655.

Following the Treaty of Ryswick, many French soldiers were set adrift. The Irish in French service, with no home base, or with relatives to aid them, found their way to other European armies or became part of the huge unemployed mass. The 'gentlemen' had less trouble than the thousands of rankers who had no station or influential friends to fall back on. It was following this period that the Irish began going into the imperial service in large numbers but almost always as officers, as they had already been in foreign armies. No records of permanent units of Irishmen can be found in any armies other than those of France and Spain.

At least one Irish regiment, or perhaps two, was formed from those regiments who were in England when William of Orange landed there in 1688 and effectively disposed of James II. Those 1,800 Irish were sent to detention in the Isle of Wight but in 1689 were transferred en masse to Hamburg to serve the Emperor. Nearly half of them deserted while the remainder had to be clothed and weapons found for them. Less than 1,000 Irish were sent to fight the Turks in Hungary and on their trip eastward they made quite a reputation for themselves. They plundered all the towns and villages they passed through in Silesia and Moravia, but saved the real destruction for Bratislava in September 1689. Their lack of enthusiasm for the Emperor's cause was probably because they were opposing Louis XIV, host and ally of their exiled King, James II. That regiment of Irish was disposed of and the Emperor was prepared to write them off as a loss.

The next formation of Irishmen shipped to the empire from France was a volunteer mass of approximately 2,200 men. They too were shipped to Hamburg and, under German supervision, seem to have behaved somewhat better than the first group. Unfortunately for the Irishmen and their employers, many became ill, some from homesickness, others from prevalent diseases. There was also violence between them and the non-Irish in the army, and so in the summer of 1693 the regiment was disbanded. In 1710 another scheme was put forward by Christopher Taaffe, a cousin to the Earls of Carlingford, to recruit a regiment of Irish for imperial service but apparently that concept never went any further than discussion.

The War of the Spanish Succession, 1701–1714, provided employment for many Irish in France, Spain and Austria. It was a war to determine who would succeed the deceased Carlos II on the throne of Spain – Louis XIV's second grandson, Philip of Anjou, or the Habsburg Archduke Charles, second son of Leopold I of Austria. By Carlos' will, Philip was the designated heir and on 1 November 1700 he was proclaimed Philip V, King of Spain. The main opponents were Austria on one side and France and Spain on the other, but England and the Dutch also had interests in the outcome. Both had the same ruler, William III, and under no circumstances would he allow Spain and France to be united, as this would form too powerful a force on his borders. Consequently, both nations sided with Austria.

Captain Francis MacDonnell of the Bagni Infantry Regiment made a name for himself during this period. MacDonnell captured Marshal Villeroi, the French commander of Cremona, and refused his victim's entreaties to be allowed to go free, even with an appropriate exchange of gold. But he became infamous when he tried to suborn the Irish defenders of the town. It angered them and they took him prisoner, even though he was under a flag of truce at the time. He was later released. As a lieutenant-colonel he was in the process of forming a battalion from Irish deserters from the French army, when he was killed at Luzzara in 1702.[18]

His father, Henry MacDonnell, managed to survive him by many years. According to his own records he was born in Ireland in 1654 and initially served in the French army, later shifting to Austria. His death was reported in an English periodical as having occurred in October 1772 in Croatia, but that would have meant he survived to be 118 years of age.

Irishmen continued their journey from their homeland to the imperial domains for many more years. They were mostly the younger sons of dispossessed families, but with wit and skill, plus family connections, they soon created a new aristocracy from their position in the military forces of Austria. Actually they did much better in Austria than in France. In France to progress beyond the rank of major-general, one had to be able to prove lineage denoting nobility. In Austria it was more often *what* you were rather than *who*. Consequently the Irish did very well in all of middle Europe. General, or even field marshal, was not an uncommon rank for Irish immigrants. During the same period they were barely accepted in the British service as private soldiers.[19]

The Irish brought in numerous relatives from home. Soon many Irish junior officers were holding together companies and regiments which had formerly been the personal provinces of the gentry of the empire. Their ever increasing presence in higher ranks and position generated some complaints against them. Like so many of the foreigners in the Austrian service they were frequently guilty of nepotism. But most Irish officers were competent, which couldn't always be said of those who were displaced. Fortunately for them, collectively, they never had to worry about serious intrigue against them.

Christopher Duffy has brought forward a thesis created by Ernst Schmidhofer entitled 'Das irische, schottische und englische Element im kaiserlichen Heer', in which Herr Dr Schmidhofer offers the following tribute to the Irish:

> The Irish need not fear comparison with any other national element in the Austrian army. There were occasions when they played an absolutely dominant role in the ranks of the senior officers. It is no exaggeration to say that the fate of the Austrian state often lay in Irish hands.[20]

Schmidhofer adds that in 1761 three of the nine full generals were Irishmen. And 'We may almost speak of a dominating role of the Irish in the leadership of the army.'

In addition, James O'Neill, writing in a later issue of *The Irish Sword*, quotes Dr Schmidhofer as follows:

> The example of the Thirty Years' War, in which the Irish served in the most widely diverse armies, demonstrates a characteristic Irish taste for adventure, allied to the hope of gaining personal reputation and wealth, which fostered the decision among many Irishmen to prove their courage in the turmoil on the Continent.[21]

In one issue of *The Irish Sword*, William S. Murphy revealed that over 300 Irish-named officers appeared in Austrian army records and added that at least a hundred were field marshals, generals or admirals. Most of the balance were colonels, lieutenant-colonels, or majors.[22]

The Browne family added much lustre to the imperial service.

George Browne was in the first generation to arrive following the Treaty of Limerick. His career, which began in the 1690s, was one of courage and ability. In 1708 he reached the rank of major-general, in 1709 he obtained a regiment of his own and in 1716 was ennobled and promoted to lieutenant field marshal, then in 1723 to general. But his trials and tribulations in active field service led to an early grave; he died in 1729. His son-in-law, Francis Patrick O'Neillan, assumed proprietorship of Browne's 57th Infantry Regiment.

General O'Neillan was born near Limcrick about 1670. He joined the Austrian army and made his way upward through the officer ranks until he became colonel of the 22nd Infantry Regiment in 1718. This regiment was also known by the name of its proprietor, Graf Franz Moritz von Lacy (see Chapter 10). O'Neillan distinguished himself in its command and Emperor Charles VI awarded him the title Baron Laimpruch zu Epurz. General O'Neillan died on campaign at Mantua, Italy on 3 October 1734.

He and his wife, Barbara Browne, gave Austria five healthy sons, all of whom served in the army. Edward served in his father's 57th Infantry Regiment and was wounded at Mollwitz in 1741. In recognition of their services to the crown, two sons, Alexander and Eugene, were awarded the rank of Counts Onelli [sic] by the Empress Maria Theresa. Alexander assumed command of the 42nd Infantry Regiment in 1734 and became lieutenant-general in 1735 but died in 1743. Brother Eugene was born at Lodi in north-western Italy in 1724 and served as a captain in the 59th Infantry Regiment. He was captured by the Prussians at the Battle of Hohenfriedberg in 1745 but escaped. He was wounded in Italy on 10 August 1746 and died two weeks later at Pizziglione. The fourth son, Francis, was born in Ireland in 1729. He served in the 22nd Infantry Regiment but in February 1757 was killed in action at Hirschwald in Saxony.

The youngest, Michael, was a lieutenant in 1758 and served in the oldest German regiment of Austria, Hoch und Deutschmeister, the 4th Infantry Regiment.[23] George Browne's nephew, Maximilian Browne, became more famous than any other officer of Irish antecedents in the imperial service, including his father Ulysses. The latter resigned with the rank of colonel of cavalry in 1713, and went to live in Frankfurt-am-Main where he died in 1731. Maximilian's son Joseph, was a major-general who died of wounds at Hochkirch in 1758. Maximilian's eldest son, Philip, was promoted to general in 1758 and, shortly after, retired to his estates where he died in 1803, the last of the family. There were at least another dozen men named Browne in the Austrian service, most of whom seem to have been wounded or killed in action.[24]

The Nugent family also served Austria very well. The first of that name in Austria was James Robert Nugent, born at Castlenugent in Ireland in 1720. He entered the Austrian army at the age of fifteen and took part in the Turkish war. In 1737 he was stricken with the plague but regained his health and as a lieutenant-colonel on the general staff, took part in the Seven Years' War. Having served as Austria's ambassador in Berlin, Robert was promoted to field marshal and proprietor of the 56th Infantry Regiment. He fought in the War of the Bavarian Succession and served as fortress commander at Prague, where he died in 1784.

His son, Count Laval Nugent, the most famous of the family, was born in 1777 near Dublin. He entered the Austrian army as a lieutenant of engineers in 1794 and fought in Italy. By 1807 he was colonel and then in 1809 major-general at the Battle of Aspern. For services rendered to the crown he was awarded the Commander's Cross of the Order of Maria Theresa in 1814. He was promoted to privy councillor and made a Roman prince by Pope Pius VII. With permission from his Emperor, he entered the service of King Ferdinand V as captain-general of Naples, but returned to Austrian service in 1821. He took part in suppressing revolts in both Italy and in Hungary in 1848 and was promoted to field marshal the following year. Nugent died at his estates in 1862.

The Bradys are well represented by Thomas, Baron von Brady, who was born in Cavan, Ireland in 1752. He joined the 15th Infantry Regiment as a cadet in 1769 but remained a lieutenant for fifteen years. In 1788 he went to the general staff with the rank of captain. He earned the military order Knight's Cross of the Order of Maria Theresa for his part in the storming of Novi on 3 October 1788. His ability brought him further up the ranks to general in 1796. At the beginning of Napoleon's career he was serving in Italy. As a reward for his many services to the crown, he was granted the proprietorship of the Kaiser Infantry Regiment Number 1 in October 1803. His next successful appointment was as military and civilian governor of Dalmatia and Albania, and later as privy councillor. He served at the Battle of Aspern in 1809 and later that same year retired because of ill-health. Brady was greatly affected by asthma of which he died in Vienna on 16 October 1827. Late in life he had married Countess Deyn, but the union produced no children and she predeceased him. He named his nephew, James O'Brady of the 32nd Infantry Regiment, as his heir.

A codicil to Brady's will provided funds for the education of any poor youth selected by the Archbishop of Dublin. For some reason that did not happen and the sum, with collected interest, rose to 16,000 gulden by 1843, and the Baron von Brady Foundation was created. The fund provided (as late as 1964) five foundation scholarships at the Technical Military Academy, bestowed by the Austrian War Ministry.

There were at least six more of the name Brady in the officers list. Two were named Bernard, two named James, and one each,

John and Patrick; all were born in Ireland and all in about the same decade.

Meanwhile, the O'Kellys are represented by several notable men of that name, including Count William O'Kelly von Gallagh und Tycooly who was born in Aughrim, County Galway in 1703 and joined the Austrian army in 1722. In the war against the Turks he served at sea and later as lieutenant-colonel and aide to Field Marshal Reinhard Niepperg. In 1744 he was the colonel commander of the Pallavincini Infantry Regiment and was promoted to major-general in 1752. During the Seven Years' War he was wounded while commanding a brigade at Breslau on 22 November 1757. For his actions and courage there he was awarded the Cross of the Order of Maria Theresa. O'Kelly was a lieutenant field marshal at Hochkirch and commanded eight battalions at Kunersdorf. At the Battle of Torgau he again distinguished himself, and was awarded the Commander's Cross of the Order of Maria Theresa. Following the end of the Seven Years' War, O'Kelly was made grand master of ordnance and proprietor of the 45th Infantry Regiment. In 1763 he was promoted to general. Less than four years later he died in Vienna on 5 February 1767. The family contributed another seven or more of the same name, and all performed their services creditably, sometimes to the ultimate sacrifice.

The O'Donnell (O'Donnel) family held some of the most important posts, military and political, of the many Irishmen who served Austria during the eighteenth century. But certainly Karl (or Con or Conan) Claudius, the second son of Hugh O'Donnell, is the most famous of those who attained the highest rank. He was born in Ireland in 1715 and in 1736 with his elder brother John, travelled to Austria at the invitation of their uncle, General Hamilton.[25] He began his military career in his uncle's 7th Kürassier Regiment and followed the usual path upward from captain in the Turkish War where he was wounded, to major, lieutenant-colonel, and colonel on 8 December 1742, following which he assumed command of the 2nd Dragoon Regiment. During the War of the Austrian Succession he was promoted to major-general and again distinguished himself in combat. In the Seven Years' War he participated at the Battle of Lobositz, was promoted to lieutenant field marshal and awarded proprietorship of the Kürassier Regiment of Condova.[26]

The year 1757 was not the best for him – he was wounded at Leuthen and captured. It was announced that he had been killed in action but on being ransomed he was able to lay that rumour to rest. Karl resumed his career and won praise at Hochkirch on 13 October 1758. Two years later, on 3 November 1760, he fought the Prussians at Torgau. Leading three of his five regiments, he launched a counter-attack against a superior body that forced the Prussians to flight, but not before re-capturing numerous guns and General Finckenstein as prisoner.

Unfortunately, the Austrian commander, Field Marshal von Daun, was wounded and had to leave the field. He assigned senior command to O'Donnell who tried to restore Austrian fortunes but was unable to accomplish anything more than a well-constructed retreat.[27] In 1762 he commanded in the Austrian Netherlands, then went back to Vienna where he was elevated to the Privy Council and in 1765 became inspector-general of the cavalry. The famed St Patrick's Day entertainment put on by O'Mahoney (son of 'Le Fameux Mahoni'), Spanish ambassador to Vienna in 1766, included Karl O'Donnell as one of the many guests. Others included Franz Moritz von Lacy, Johann Sigmund Macguire, William O'Kelly, Philip George Browne, Thomas von Plunkett, and an officer named McElligott.

Karl O'Donnell became governor of Transylvania in 1768, resigning nearly three years later. In February 1771, as he was preparing to accompany Emperor Joseph on a trip to Hungary, Karl became seriously ill, dying on 26 March 1771, unmarried.

His older brother John, also had a distinguished career as a soldier for Austria, attaining the rank of field marshal. He married Anne Corr of Kilkenny and had one son, Hugh, and a daughter, Therese. Hugh was killed in action while a major in his Uncle Karl's regiment at the Battle of Neerwinden in 1793.

A list of the names of Irish-born officers in Austria, or those from Irish parents, includes Barnevals, Burkes, Butlers, D'Altons, Fitzgeralds, FitzPatricks, Hamiltons, Kavanaughs, MacCarthys (in various forms), MacDonnells, Macguires, O'Byrnes (or O'Bernes), and O'Conors. There were O'Neills and O'Neilans, O'Mulrains, O'Reillys, Piers (or Pierce) and Plunketts (and Plonquet or Plunquet). The Taaffe family, mentioned above, in over a hundred years gave Austria at least eight well-known officers. The Wallis family numbered at least twenty.

By the nineteenth century the few remaining Irish born were rapidly thinning out in Austria. The Nugents were still well represented and also a few members of Taaffe, Wallis and the O'Donell families, but the other famous names of the seventeenth and eighteenth centuries had changed somewhat. Many names had picked up German connotations or the male line had died out, leaving descendants with non-Irish names. The four names mentioned above continued in the highest ranks during most of the reign of Franz Joseph. In fact, one of the O'Donells saved the Emperor from an assassin's attack on 18 February 1853.

It so happened that Colonel, later Major-General, Maximilian Karl Lamoral, Count O'Donell, was walking in Vienna with Emperor Franz Joseph near the Kärtner Gate Theatre when a man brandishing a knife lunged at the monarch. With great presence of mind O'Donell leaped for the man, grabbed him by the collar and threw him to the ground. The man inflicted a wound upon

O'Donell, but it proved not to be life-threatening. O'Donell's rewards included the privilege of 'impaling the Imperial Arms of Austria' with his own. Only one other subject had been allowed that honour; Prince Swartzenburg for his part in the Battle of Leipzig in 1813.[28]

In later years, the Wallis family provided Austria with several more of her sons. Count Oliver Wallis, Baron of Carrighmain, was born at Güns in Hungary and joined the army in 1837. He took part in the Hungarian campaign of 1848–1849. The rebel army was led by Lajos Kossuth, who later also became famous in the US Civil War. Wallis became a colonel in 1860, a major-general in 1867 and a lieutenant field marshal in 1873. Wallis retired in 1877 and died at Vienna in 1887.

Another, Count Franz Wallis, also listed as Baron of Carrighmain, served from 1855 to 1857 in the 10th Ulan Regiment, later the Gendarmes of the Life Guard and then the 7th Hussars. He was a colonel in 1880, major-general in 1886 and lieutenant field marshal in 1891. Franz died at Ebelsberg, Austria in 1895. He must have been related to Oliver, possibly his son.

Count Eduard Franz Josef Taaffe, an old friend of the Emperor, was appointed Prime Minister of the Austrian administration to counter the Liberals, who were becoming the bane of Franz Joseph's existence. As Rothenberg described it:

> By political manoeuvring and some chincanery [sic], Taaffe put together a heterogeneous coalition. The Czechs, who for a dozen years had boycotted the Reichsrat and received concessions, returned and voted with the government, while the Liberals split and lost power. Passage of the army law was secured. In the long run, however, Taaffe remained in office for fourteen years, and his policies served to escalate the national strife in Austria.[29]

Taaffe was the 'King's Minister' and not beholden to any political party. Therefore, rightly or wrongly, while he was the chief minister, he ensured that all nationalities within the empire were at odds with each other. Keeping everyone mildly disaffected was the policy of the Emperor's staff.

This brings us to the final Austrian hero who had Irish blood in his veins. His name was Baron Gottfried von Banfield and he was the 'last surviving Irish descended officer of the Habsburg navy'.[30] His father, Richard, was born in Vienna in 1836, the son of Thomas Banfield and Josephine French, both formerly of Castlelyons, County Cork. In 1870 his aunt Elizabeth married well – to John Jameson of Dublin.

Gottfried's family resided in the Austrian territory (now Italian) of Trieste and were engaged in the nautical trade. His father Richard was a captain in the Austrian navy. Gottfried attended the Austro-Hungarian naval academy at Fiume, graduating in 1909. He served aboard various ships of the imperial fleet but made the decision in 1912 that flying was more to his liking and of great value to the navy. He learned to fly in four weeks, and in three months obtained his licence, Austrian No. 67. In that summer he was called to the admiralty. There the authorities gave him funds and a passport and ordered him to travel to Paris to test a flying boat and buy as many Gnome engines as he could obtain. In October 1912 he and a colleague flew the Donnet Company flying boats up and down the Seine River. He later told how he was trying to get his craft up as he approached one of the bridges across the river. Finding that he couldn't make it he throttled back and managed to fly safely under the bridge. The Parisian papers proclaimed 'Austrian Dare-Devil flies under Seine Bridge'. The engines they purchased were used to power the new planes the Austrian navy was then putting into the air.

When war was declared in 1914, the Austrian naval air

force had little to do but patrol the Adriatic looking for French or British subs which aimed their weapons towards the several Austrian naval bases along the coast. It wasn't until Italy joined the Allies on 23 May 1915 that the war for Austria became serious in the Adriatic. Italy was an early supporter of flying and began the war with sufficient planes. Banfield's first aerial victory took place on 27 June 1915 when he destroyed an Italian observation balloon. During the next few months he bombed Italian storage facilities and sank an Italian freighter. On 1 September 1915 he flew an attack upon a Curtis-type Italian plane and downed it near Grado. He and his observer next attacked an Italian Macchi flying boat and drove that into the water, but after minor repairs the Macchi was up again and at 3,500 feet, attacked Banfield. He and his observer managed to shoot the Italian full of holes, forcing it into the water again. Another Italian plane took on Banfield but was forced to land in Lake Grado. When another flying boat attacked them, having used up all their ammunition, Banfield and his observer had to use a carbine and two pistols to fend off the attacker.

From 1916 onward, Banfield, flying a modified model Lohner L.16 with a machine-gun mounted forward, had numerous combats aloft. He managed to shoot down at least twenty enemy craft but, because many were over the Adriatic and not land, only nine were confirmed. During the war Banfield received thirteen decorations from his government. He was so highly regarded that in late 1916 he was summoned to Vienna for a special audience with the Emperor at Schönbrunn Palace. Francis Joseph told him that he, the Emperor, would institute an entirely new award, the Gold Military Cross, especially for Banfield.

Back to the war he went. Single-handedly he drove off twelve Italian Capronis bombers on one occasion and on another broke up an Italian bombing raid. In 1916 he had a conclusive fight with a French naval ace, who as a prisoner of war later proclaimed: 'I was brought down by the hand of a master.' On 1 January 1917 he fought to a draw the famous Italian air ace Major Francesco Baracca.

In 1916 he was sent to Germany with instructions to observe and give an opinion of the German Zeppelins. Travelling in an L.15 as an observer, he was shot down in France and became a prisoner of war. Banfield was the sole air ace of the empire to be awarded the Knight's Cross of the Military Order of Maria Theresa, the highest honour of all. It was awarded on 17 August 1917 by King Karl I.[31]

After the war he spent considerable time in England learning naval architecture. He then returned to Austria to marry the daughter of Herr Tripcovich, Trieste's foremost salvage expert. He joined the firm and later became the managing director. Banfield and his wife had several sons, one of whom became a musical conductor. Upon the foundation of the Irish Military Society in 1950, he was invited to Ireland to speak at their annual dinner. It was said that he was highly emotional at being in the land of his ancestors. Nearly seventy years after the First World War ended, this man, the last to receive the prestigious Order of Maria Theresa, died in Trieste on 24 September 1986 aged ninety-six. In Trieste national flags were flown at half mast in his honour.

This brief overview of some of those Irish who served in the imperial and Austrian service has barely touched upon the many who devoted their lives to Austria's fortunes, sometimes paying the ultimate price for their loyalty. Those who survived the rigours of campaigning usually made a more than satisfactory niche for themselves in their adopted homeland. For good reason, Austria was always needful of top-grade soldiers, and was never dissatisfied with any from Ireland.

CHAPTER 10

FIELD MARSHAL COUNT FRANZ MORITZ LACY

Franz Moritz Lacy was born in St Petersburg, Russia on 21 October 1725. He was the youngest of three brothers, all of whom, like their father and grandfather before them, became soldiers. His father, Peter Lacy (see Chapter 12), was an Irishman, respected both by his Russian comrades and his European adversaries and became prominent in the Russian army and society. Consequently, his sons had a somewhat easier path than their father had.

Franz Moritz Lacy went to Austria as a youth. He was educated in the best Austrian military schools, became a citizen and remained there until his demise in 1801. When he arrived Austria was still a great power. Prince Eugène of Savoy, Austria's greatest soldier, still lived and performed epic deeds. Later, having performed his own great deeds for his beloved Austria, Lacy was considered one of her ablest soldiers. Over many years Lacy reformed the badly weakened Austrian army and established an army that was the equal of any in Europe, during and long after his lifetime. As Frederick the Great's pre-eminence was declining, Lacy was beginning to develop into the man who would become

Prussia's *bête noir*. Even during the Napoleonic Wars the Austrian army was nearly always at Napoleon's throat. Only the problems in Spain and the rout from Russia hurt France more than Austria's continued adversarial role.

Franz Lacy was also partly German, descended from settlers who followed the Teutonic Knights from Prussia eastward along the shores of the Baltic Sea.[1] His mother, the former Countess Martha Philippina von Loeser and widow of the Count von Funk of Livonia, married Peter Lacy and bore him five daughters and three sons. Each son moved abroad and, like their father, served foreign rulers as soldiers, all with dignity, courage and fidelity. The daughters all married well; at least two to soldiers of note.

The eldest son, Michael, went to Austria and joined Prince Eugène as a Rittmeister (cavalry captain), but in 1735 he was mortally wounded during the Austro-Russian-Turkish War. The second son, Peter Andreas, joined the service of the King of Saxony. During the Seven Years' War he was a colonel, general-adjutant and chamberlain of the King and electors. In 1758 he took a trip to Ireland, his father's homeland, but returned and opted to live in London for ten years. Unfortunately, during the final years of his life he was afflicted with a mental derangement (or, as Kotasek so grandly phrases it, 'The shadows of a mental "dimming" fell on his remaining Years'), and died in 1773 in Brussels, Belgium.

The third son, Franz Moritz, not only followed in his father's footsteps, but in some ways exceeded him. Even today he is still fondly remembered in Austria at the Heeresgeschichtliche (Army-Kriegs) Museum in Vienna, with a statue, busts and portraits. There is a display case in which his cane and other personal artifacts are preserved. His statue is in the main entrance hall, along with another fifty-nine of Austria's greatest soldiers. Each of twenty columns displays three statues including also those of Maximilian von Browne and Karl O'Donnell. In Vienna itself his statue composes part of a memorial to Empress Maria Theresa in the plaza bearing her name. The monument includes the greatest men of Austria during her reign. His portrait adorns the Austrian Military Academy at Wiener Neustadt and there is a bust in the imperial War Council building at Vienna. The latter bears an inscription that reads in Latin:

MAURITO LACY SUMMO CASTRORUM PRAEFECTO QUI BELLI AEQUE
AS PACIS ARTIBUS ILLIS VINCEREHIS PATRIAM INVICTAM REDDERE
DOCUIT SUIS IN SCIENTIA MILITARI INSTITUTORIS ET AMICI JOSPEHUS
II AUG. GRATI ANIMI SUIMONUMENTUM HOC PONI JUSSIT.[2]

After Franz's birth the family lived for a time in St Petersburg, but when his father was engaged in his military pursuits, the family settled in Riga. Their mother owned considerable property in Livonia, which had been left to her from her previous marriage. It was here that the boys especially, received a good solid education which prepared them for their destiny. Peter Lacy was popular with the ruling class in Russia and very successful in his trade. The widow von Loeser, by virtue of being reasonably well-born and having entered into a 'good' marriage, gave him not only children but financial support as well, and life was bright for the Lacy family of Riga.

Unfortunately for foreigners soldiering in Russia, after the death of Czar Peter the Great, was a very precarious occupation, so all three of Peter Lacy's sons were instead sent to German lands to find employment as soldiers.

At age twelve Franz Moritz was sent to the Ritterakademie in Liegnitz, Silesia, a military cavalry school established by the Emperor Joseph I in 1708. Two years later he was appointed to the Ingenieur-akademie, a military-engineering school in Vienna. Sometime during this period he also became a chamberlain to the Empress Maria Theresa.[3] This trading of sons back and forth was common practice amongst the upper-class Europeans of the time and it was somewhat easier between Russia and Austria, which were then close allies. The fact that his father was better known than many others in his vocation and that the son's given name was translatable to German, must also have helped to ease the transition.

Franz Lacy's career for the next fifty years followed a path only slightly divergent from that of so many other soldiers of the period. Until the end of the Second Silesian War, he was a field commander of considerable talent. During the Seven Years' War and later, he became a part-time general on the field and a military administrator of great proficiency. His mentor, Field Marshal Leopold Joseph Maria von Daun, could see that Lacy was the man to create a staff which could function as well as the Prussian staff. Not only did he inaugurate training for that purpose, including the selection and preparation of teachers, but he also prepared the army to accept their guidance. From there he went on to full-time administration, eventually becoming the successor to von Daun as president of the War Council or Hofkriegsrat. He instituted numerous reforms with the help of the Emperor which not only expanded but increased the efficiency of an army which had been almost completely disorganised.

In 1743–1744, aged seventeen, he served on the Rhine as sergeant under an Irishman, Marshal Maximilian von Browne. In August 1744, aged eighteen, through his father's intercession, he was Browne's adjutant at the Battle of Velletri in Italy.[4] Young Lacy was a kinsman of Browne's through numerous inter-marriages of the two families in Ireland and on the continent. The young man could have had no better field instructor in all of the armies of Europe. In later times he did not forget his master when, then very close personally to the imperial family, Lacy moved successfully to have the Empress make an overdue public acknowledgment of Browne's accomplishments for the empire.

Now an ensign and still serving under Browne in northern Italy, Lacy began to make a professional name for himself. In Europe during the seventeenth and eighteenth centuries the Irish often faced their fellow Irish in combat and sometimes even their own relatives. This time in Italy was no different. Yet the Irish on Austria's side were individual soldiers whereas those who served Spain and France were in Irish formations. At Velletri the Spanish regiments of Irlanda and Hibernia faced Browne and others, including Lacy. There were many other Irish on both sides, including O'Donnell, O'Reilly, MacGuire and MacDonnell, to name just a very few. The Irish seem always to have been in the forefront of battles and high up on the casualty list, and by the mid-eighteenth century, Irish names in the ranks were no longer numerous.

At the Battle of Velletri, Lacy led the Austrian Hussars in a desperate attack at the Nettuno Gate, but Captain Slattery and his detachment from Hibernia prevented their entry by managing to close the gate. Lacy had three horses shot out from under him and was wounded during the fight. The wound wasn't serious and in a second attack, Slattery's Irish were wiped out. During the 1740s, Spanish, French and Austrian soldiers, many of whom were Irish, were busy killing each other in northern Italy to gain a modest advantage there, but not for themselves. As Patrick Sarsfield is said to have lamented as he lay dying: 'Oh, that this was for Ireland.' For those soldiers, it never was. It was every cause but their own.

In the Second Silesian War, 1744–1745, Lacy was still with Browne in an unsuccessful Austrian attempt to regain the lost territory of Silesia. Meanwhile, Browne was subordinate to the Hungarian General, later Field Marshal, Carl Batthyány. He was then a very ill man whose task it was to drive the French out of Bavaria and secure that nation for the Empress. Browne had been sent to give some jolt to the normally hesitant Batthyány. During the course of an assault upon the village of Vilshofen on the Danube, Browne was wounded and sent to Passau to recover. When peace was signed with Prussia on Christmas Day 1746, Browne and his forces were reassigned to northern Italy. Meanwhile, with a modicum of free time available, Lacy was in the position to study tactics and strategy while on field service. He was a perpetual student and strategy became a special interest which he studied carefully for years.

On 15 June 1747, at the Battle of Piacenza in northern Italy, Browne and his ally, Prince Liechtenstein, defeated the French armies, driving them towards their own territories. Captain Lacy once again distinguished himself when he led a cavalry regiment directly into the heart of the French camp and collected a hundred prisoners for which he was again cited and promoted to major.

The French, with the allies closely following, were heading for their own territory in Provence. In November, Browne arrived near Nice at the camp of his ally, King Charles Emmanuel of Sardinia. The combined armies of Browne and the King laid siege to the great Italian port city of Genoa. Their actions during the siege and interactions with the inhabitants of that city were less than congenial. The Genoese rose in rebellion and a French army under Marshal Charles Louis Auguste Belle-Isle raised the siege in July 1747. It wasn't the best of times for the Austrians. They fell back into the plains of Lombardy, but when the war ended that year they still held most of the duchy of Milan. By now the Austrian relationship with the King of Sardinia was becoming difficult. Charles Emmanuel demanded the northern territory promised to him at Worms as his share in the spoils of the recent campaign. He didn't get it. As a fairly young officer Lacy must have learned a lot about the pros and cons of coalition warfare during this period.

In 1749 Lacy was promoted to lieutenant-colonel and in 1750 given command of the regiment then known as Alt-Colloredo. It had been organised and formed at Diesbach in 1740. Later its name was changed to Jung-Colloredo. For the following six years he continued to command it while on service in Bohemia.

Meanwhile, one of the greatest of political administrators of Austrian history arrived upon the scene. On 13 May 1753, Wenzel Anton Kaunitz-Rietberg, former Austrian ambassador to Louis XV's court at Versailles, was appointed to the most important post in Austria, Chancellor of State. For twenty-seven years Kaunitz-Rietberg greatly affected matters pertaining to that nation until he retired in 1780. Lacy would have many occasions to bump heads with Kaunitz-Rietberg during those years, they were on opposite sides on most issues concerning the military. Kaunitz-Rietberg was in favour of a modest budget achieved by cutting military costs, while Lacy was always for enlarging the military, with corresponding increases in the budget. Kaunitz-Rietberg had minimal support from a vacillating Maria Theresa while Lacy was strongly supported by her son and co-regent, Emperor Joseph II.

By invading Saxony on 29 August 1756 Prussia, led by Frederick II, made the opening move in the Seven Years' War. The movement of over 60,000 Prussian troops was a pre-emptive strike against the new coalition formed around Austria. When the Prussian King took Dresden, the capital of Saxony, the modest Saxon forces fell back upon a fortified camp at Pirna on the Elbe River. By September Maximilian von Browne, in total command of the Austrian armies, began collecting his own dispersed forces as well as trying to save from annihilation the 15,000-man Saxon army at Pirna. Browne's primary move was to find the Prussians and dislodge them from wherever they were. Colonel Lacy now marched north along the east bank of

Maximilian von Browne

the river with a small force towards Leitmeritz where he would be reinforced, and the plan was that he would then march to meet the Saxons who were assumed to have escaped from Pirna, crossing the Elbe at Schandau. This move northward put Lacy almost directly east of Lobositz, a village on the west bank of the Elbe. In the meantime Browne came across the main Prussian army on the west bank of the Elbe. Lacy was ordered to return to Browne with his two regiments.

By 1 October, the two Austrian forces had merged near Lobositz and were preparing to meet the Prussian army. An imposing physical feature near Lobositz was a piece of high ground called Lobosch, which Browne recognised immediately as the key to the whole area. He loaded it up with Croats, his always effective light infantry, and backed them up with a hidden supporting force of Grenadier infantry. Browne placed five supplementary regiments at the north side of the village with their backs to the river. Lacy's Colloredo, one of those regiments, was situated just west of the village of Lobositz. These five regiments were closest to Lobosch and played a prominent part in the ensuing action.

At Lobositz, Frederick's army was slightly smaller than Browne's, about 28,000 to 34,000, but he was much stronger in cavalry and guns. For some reason the King was convinced that he was opposing a much smaller force than his own, in fact, just a rearguard. When the battle began, Frederick launched two separate cavalry actions straight across open ground towards Browne's positions in and around the village. Both times the cavalry was badly mauled by well-posted guns. Then the Austrian artillery opened up on the closely packed Prussian infantry located on the open ground. Frederick's army was not doing well and the extensive casualties soured his disposition. Accordingly he left the field early in the day and assigned his army to a subordinate, Field Marshal James Keith, a Scotsman and superior soldier, who was a friend of many of the Jacobites on the opposite side.

The fighting was most bitter on that hill which was wanted by both armies. After much slaughter, the Duke of Bevern chased the Croats off Lobosch. But Bevern and his men crashed into Lacy who, with added infantry, was rushing up the hillside to support the Croats. Later, Prussian Hussar General, K.E. Warnery, commented in his memoirs:

> The Austrian regiment of Jung-Colloredo fought very well on this occasion. It was formed, arranged and commanded on that day by Count Lacy. If the other regiments had done the same, the victory might have been with the Austrians.[5]

Lacy was once again wounded. His infantry in the attack was repulsed and pressed back down the hill by additional Prussian battalions. The Austrian infantry broke and many fled into the Elbe to escape the now out-of-control Prussians. This was the first time in the Prussians' memory that the Austrian army had fought them to a stand-still and caused many more casualties than they had expected.[6] Browne managed to pull the majority of his army out of this maelstrom and, covered by his cavalry, retained the ground between Lobositz and Sullowitz. However, Keith was in no condition to do any more that day and he halted all action.

The battle was over and the Austrians had once again lost, but this time they forced Frederick to pay an expensive bill for the day's events. Frederick himself realised that this was not the same Austrian army he had been using as a doormat during the past few years.

Browne, now proving to be Frederick's equal, was unhappily, and very unluckily for Austria, seriously wounded by a cannon ball during his defence of Prague on 6 May 1757. With his wife at his bedside, the great soldier died on 26 June 1757. Field Marshal Leopold von Daun, who was then in eastern Bohemia, assumed the role that Browne had relinquished. He never achieved Browne's level of competence but was considered for the time and place to be as good a leader as Austria then had.

By great good fortune, at Kolin on 18 June 1757, von Daun defeated Prussian forces led by the King. So complete was the victory that von Daun was immediately hailed as the greatest soldier of Austria next to the Empress' son Prince Charles. After Kolin, the prince assumed command of the armies in the field and proceeded to wreak havoc, but invariably on the Austrian army rather than the enemy. At Leuthen on 5 December 1757, losses including prisoners taken, totalled nearly 30,000. Von Daun was there but had little control over Prince Charles' terrible disposition of forces.

Even after the catastrophe of Leuthen Charles failed to resign, though his brother, the Emperor, Maria Theresa's husband, hinted twice that he should do so. On 16 January 1758 he received a letter from his sister-in-law, the Empress, strongly suggesting that he remove himself from her sight sooner rather than later, which he finally understood. Charles was finally out, and von Daun was in.

Von Daun, whom everybody was claiming as the greatest soldier of Austria, proved to be an innovator of substance. As the new commander-in-chief, he was Lacy's new mentor. The better officers realised that the Austrian army lacked a staff of substance. To successfully compete against Frederick , the Austrians would need to create a more effective army. They realised that Austria would continue to be in conflict with that aggressive King with his huge appetite for additional territory, usually Austrian, for some time to come.

Accordingly Lacy, strong in administration, was directed to establish a school for staff officers, with emphasis on planning, training and organisation. On 20 February 1758, Lacy was simultaneously promoted to lieutenant-general and to the post of *general-quartiermeister*. He replaced General Peter Guasco who, since occupying it, had done little with the post. The role was, among other things, to plan movements of the army and their places of encampment. As a sweetener, Lacy was shortly afterward given the proprietorship of an infantry regiment, named Lacy (also spelled Lascy). Like most Austrian 'German' infantry regiments, the uniform was white. Ownership of a regiment not only added honour to his name but, perhaps more importantly, also provided a steady income. Another formation was inaugurated called Kompanie Lacy (or Lascy), clothed in white with yellow facings, Lacy's favourite colour. This unit wore a grenadier-style cap with a brass plate upon which the double headed eagle was embossed in black. It was probably used as a training unit for the various pioneer and *jäger* (light infantry) troops he formed and trained.

Just planning road movements or encampments in his new role wasn't exactly what Lacy had in mind. He began at once to form what he conceived as a staff, by recruiting officers whom he had noticed as being above average in aptitude, intelligence and diligence. At that time there had never been a functioning staff anywhere within the Austrian army. Everyone played the game on his own terms, without serious input or control from Vienna. Foreign military people had severely criticised Austria's lack of proficient senior officers and a general staff. The first campaigns of the latest war had exposed the great deficiencies caused by lack of staff and Maria Theresa had readily consented to von Daun's plan to set up a staff and school under the direction of Lacy.

He was now Lieutenant-General Lacy, and he acquired two major-generals as his direct assistants. Under them he brought in a staff of colonels down through to captains, whose main tasks were to plan marches, compile statistical surveys, prepare maps and accumulate a small corps of useful troops to assign to any needful formation. Lacy trained these officers himself and they in turn trained others. From this time forward, Austria could boast of a central staff of excellence, whose expertise and advice filtered down to each commanding general. The great Austrian soldier, Archduke Charles, 'graduated' from this same training ground and later gave Bonaparte trouble.

Lacy assembled for his corps, troops, pioneers, bridge-making engineers, dragoons and *jägers* for a myriad of duties. These formed two regiments of infantry, one of dragoons, and a battalion of pioneers with an attached force of *jägers*, men with skills in hunting and scouting, to be used by a field commander as needed. Lacy also reorganised non-combat services such as supply and medical care. Eventually the Habsburg army's organisation would become the envy of even their foremost opponent, Frederick.

By May 1758, Lacy's staff work had already made differences

in the training and organisation of the army. When von Daun had managed to move 1,200 new troops into the fortress of Olmütz, then under siege, Frederick was heard to utter 'I can hardly believe that these are Austrians! They must have learned to march.'[7] A Prussian supply train, headed for those besieging the fortress, was waylaid by Generals Gideon Ernst Loudon and Joseph Siskovics on 30 June and demolished near Domstadt. Meanwhile, during late June, Lacy and his staff reconnoitred the area around the besieged town. They found tracks that allowed a large relief force to approach very close to Olmütz, nearly unseen. This forced Frederick to raise the siege on 2 July. These were badly needed victories in the Austrian column.

The next major effort took place at Hochkirch on 14 October 1758. Frederick had just repulsed a serious Russian attack at Zorndorf on 25 August and then rushed to the assistance of his brother, Prince Henry, whom he had left in command in Saxony. Von Daun was, as always, agonisingly slow. He had the perfect opportunity to badly hurt Henry but let the opportunity slip away while he spent a day honouring a visit by Count Friedrich Wilhelm Haugwitz.[8] Von Daun and Frederick manoeuvred for the next month or so until 7 October, when von Daun slipped into a better position near Kittlitz with his army of 80,000. Frederick followed three days later and assembled his army near the village of Hochkirch, but the King was careless. He failed to provide protection for his rear, which Lacy spotted and subsequently urged von Daun to take the offensive. However, Von Daun delayed for another three days.

By this date von Daun was thoroughly convinced that Lacy could plan anything and allowed the younger man to create what should have been the ultimate insult against the all-conquering King, a fully-fledged disaster. Lacy's plan was for seven main columns to converge on the Prussian position running northward from the village. Lacy had been exercising his skills in planning movements and was now capable of manoeuvring numerous separate columns to approach any given field and arrive on time. The Austrians left their tents up, smoke from burning cook fires continued to curl upwards and soldiers maintained a talking sound level that convinced Frederick that there was no movement amongst the Austrians on the morning of 14 October.

At exactly 5 a.m., as the church bells rang, the Austrians broke into the Prussian outpost just south of the village. Just as quickly they took the Prussian heavy artillery lying before the village of Hochkirch and pointed the captured field guns at their former owners. The King was absent, but Field Marshal James Keith managed to organise a series of counter-attacks to recover ground already lost. At this crucial moment, Lacy, son of Keith's great good friend from his Russian army days, gathered together three companies of mounted grenadiers and charged the Prussian flank. General Hans J. von Ziethen tried to repel Lacy's attack but he was in turn taken in flank by Loudon whose forces had come within striking distance. At this point the Austrian right flank, led by Arenberg and Buccow, took the towns of Koditz and Laussig while Loudon and his large force punched their way into the rear of the Prussian lines from the west. To Loudon's left and farther to the rear, Karl O'Donnell and his heavy cavalry fell on Ziethen's Hussars and Prussian dragoon and *kürassier* regiments. If some of the Austrian field commanders had been a bit more aggressive, they would have captured many more of Frederick's army than they did. Later reports blamed the right wing for its dilatory behaviour.

Most historians have agreed that the early attack by Lacy with his mounted grenadiers finished any chance the Prussians might have had to recover. The battle was costly for both sides. The Austrians counted a loss of 7,000 men, while the Prussians

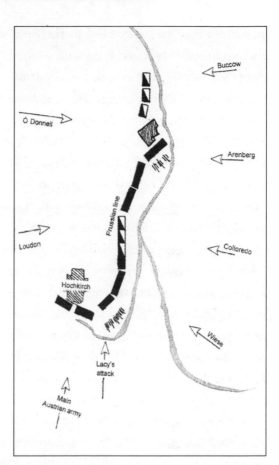

Battle of Hochkirch,
14 October 1758

lost 9,000. Particularly important was the Austrian's capture of over a hundred Prussian guns. In addition to the death of Keith during this battle, Frederick also suffered the loss of Prince Francis of Brunswick, and two generals, von Krockow and von Geist.[9] Frederick did manage to extract his army but was forced to leave the field in order not to lose more than he already had.

Lacy's plan to launch a new attack upon the King on 26 October, was rejected by von Daun. The latter was always cautious, many times to an extreme, and this gave Frederick space and time he badly needed. The King was free to hasten to the relief of his Silesian fortress at Neisse, then under siege by Austrian forces. This forced the Austrian commander to raise the siege and Frederick was back in Saxony before von Daun managed to do anything constructive. It was now commonly known that even though von Daun was less than aggressive, his armies had a new edge. Lacy has been credited for much of the improvement and he believed and stated that the Prussians were no longer the great scourge they had once been.

In November, Frederick regained the initiative and by the end of the year was in control of Saxony and Silesia, while Austria's allies, the Russians and Swedes, had evacuated Prussia. All the contestants then went into winter quarters. The year had been good for Frederick's enemies and very bad for him. He had lost about 100,000 of his superbly trained troops during this war and though he could still field 150,000 men, they were not of the quality of those he had lost. The troops required a long gestation period before they could be considered thoroughly trained. During most of 1759, Lacy added many more staff officers to the pool.

Meanwhile Frederick, who had been temporarily bed-ridden and out of action, regained his health and rejoined the war. He sent General Frederick von Finck to Maxen where he could interrupt Austrian baggage trains. Finck was purposely directed by the King to avoid any general action. Somehow Lacy learned of Finck's position on the Maxen plateau and went after him.

On the morning of 21 November, with Lacy in command, the Austrians launched an attack from all sides and Finck discovered that his forces were completely surrounded. Within a few hours Finck was in considerable trouble so he took the only path open to him; he surrendered his entire army to Lacy. Sixteen battalions, thirty-six squadrons, eight generals and over 500 officers (totalling ten per cent of the King's officer corps) were taken; a grand total of 12,000 troops, the worst loss for any Prussian army up to that time.

Fortunately for Frederick and the Prussians, they soon went into winter quarters, but this victory kept the Austro-Franco and Russian alliance alive for another year. Von Daun needed that victory to continue to enhance his position at court and the Battle of Maxen glorified and strengthened Lacy's reputation as a field soldier. This and his successful undertaking at Berlin in October 1760 with a small force of about 15,000 troops, ensured his place as a winner in Austrian military history.

But even his brilliant coup at Maxen failed to rescue Lacy from a period of deepening depression. Among other disheartening news he learned of his mother's death in far-away Russia. He was also well aware that some of the public and his peers held him responsible, however unjustly, for the procrastination and vacillations of the last campaigns. In a move to eradicate his depression, the well-meaning Maria Theresa advanced him to full general. It was a move that is questioned by some of today's historians, who believe that Lacy was not yet worthy of that high rank.

Loudon was a problem for the army command. He was generally disliked by nearly everyone at the top, including a fellow Russian Balt, Lacy. (A Balt was a person of Russian blood or ancestry who was born or lived in the lands along the Baltic Sea.) As chief-of-staff at von Daun's headquarters, Lacy was accused of having poured forth a stream of criticism about Loudon's accomplishments, or lack thereof. But it must be remembered that they were competitors for rank and preferment, so that must be weighed carefully in Loudon's favour. Philip Beck and Joseph d'Ayasasa, two of the capable lieutenant-generals in Austria's service, refused to serve under him, and Karl O'Donnell declined to lead reinforcements to him because he suspected that he would fall under his command should he do so.

Kaunitz-Rietberg, who was a Loudon supporter, knew the latter had a serious problem, so he sent Grechtler, a competent supply officer, to check out Loudon. Grechtler reported back that Loudon was unequivocally a good, substantial field commander, but also noted that there were few competent generals in the service of Austria, and those who were, Lacy, O'Donnell, Macguire and Beck, would refuse to serve under Loudon simply because he lacked the status of higher birth that they would insist upon as a requirement. In other words, they were all snobs. Unfortunately, this was the cause of many less than satisfactory military actions. Indeed, because of this attitude, Christopher Duffy has accused the von Daun-Lacy anti-Loudon faction of having caused Austria to lose the Seven Years' War.[10]

In 1760 von Daun should have made his way towards Dresden to relieve his commander within the city, General Johann Maguire von Inniskillin. Instead von Daun sat on his laurels and watched. On 29 July Frederick raised his siege, not under von Daun's pressure but to rescue his garrison at Glatz, which was under attack by Loudon.

During this period Lacy lost his personal baggage to a Prussian patrol. Frederick immediately sent back his personal effects but retained the many maps that Lacy had prepared while chief-of-staff. Lacy wrote to the King requesting their return and 'Old Fritz' responded:

[It is my ambition to] introduce more urbanity and politeness to a trade which is inherently hard and cruel. As soon as the pace of the campaigns begins to slacken, my topographical engineers will set to work to copy your maps, and I shall be delighted to send them back to you as soon as they have finished.[11]

Von Daun blundered once again when he planned to catch

Frederick in a giant 'Maxen-style' trap near Liegnitz. Loudon was to cross the Katzbach, come up from the south and hit Frederick while von Daun brought the main army across and made a frontal assault. This was to be on the morning of 15 August 1760, and Loudon, who followed Daun's instructions to the letter, found himself in deep trouble. Frederick withdrew to a nearby plateau which caused von Daun to reconsider his plans. Meanwhile Loudon, unaware that von Daun had second thoughts, entered into the fray with the Prussians and was soon overwhelmed. Von Daun had come up just south of the Katzbach where he was soon joined by Lacy's corps, but when he realised what had happened to Loudon, he ordered a withdrawal. Loudon was badly defeated and barely managed to limp away with a very reduced force. He, understandably, never forgave von Daun (or probably Lacy) for leaving him in the lurch.

In October 1760 von Daun, then being pressed hard by the court in Vienna to do something, agreed to meet the Russians in Berlin. Lacy was given 15,000 men to penetrate deep into Prussia. On 28 September he left on a northward path from Lagenwaltersdorf with his modest force to seize Frederick's capital. At about the same time the Russians, about 20,000 strong and under three generals, Tottleben, Chernyshev and Panin, began their journey westward to Berlin. This two-pronged advance was a great success. A small advance force under Tottleben was almost at the capital but was forced to retire upon the approach of the corps of Prince Eugene of Württemburg. On 9 October 1760, Lacy and his Austrians entered the city and a few hours later were reinforced by the Russians who had finally pushed aside Eugene's corps.

Lacy made sure that previously captured Austrian trophies, flags and standards snatched in earlier days, were soon in his possession. The Russians were mostly rushing about destroying private and public property, something the Austrians had been warned against doing. Esterházy, Lacy's Hungarian subordinate, placed the Kaiser's Regiment on guard against looting of the palaces in Potsdam. The Cossacks, and even some Austrian Hussars, managed to ransack several palaces and were soon 'knee-deep in broken porcelain'. There were now over 30,000 of the enemy destroying Frederick's capital, something that he wouldn't tolerate for very long. Obtaining information that Frederick was hurrying home, the Austrians and Russians departed on 12 October. This 'invasion' greatly angered Frederick and he never forgot, nor did he forgive the players. While nothing of strategic importance happened, it was an excellent example of what could be achieved in warfare when the forces did not have to worry about guarding their flanks or resupplying the army. It was certainly one of the boldest strokes of that and many another war.

Although by occupying Berlin for a week, the Austrians and their Russian allies had successfully humiliated Frederick, they needed a clear-cut victory to regain Silesia. Making surprise moves and occupying a capital was not really very productive. Overall the Prussian King had been having a bad year and was reluctant to get his greatly reduced army in too deep.[12] The season was just about over when Frederick finally offered von Daun his chance. On a cold windy day, 3 November 1760, he attacked von Daun in his protected position near Torgau in Saxony. Their armies, at approximately 56,000 each, were comparable in strength.

The Austrian forces were facing in a generally southerly direction with a stream to their rear and another to their front. Lacy's corps of 26,000 was on the extreme left of their position with his left nearly on the fortress of Torgau and a large pond to his left front.[13] General Karl Claudius O'Donnell was to his right rear with his formation of heavy cavalry. The main body of the army lay to their right with the village of Süptitz directly to their southerly front. The Prussians were coming across the Austrian front in a column formation from the south-east going in a north-westerly direction. Early that morning a large formation of approximately 18,000 Prussians under the command of Ziethen, halted and faced right, directly at Lacy's formation.[14] Von Daun issued orders for Lacy to remain where he was and to face Ziethen, tying up half of his army.

In the meantime the wily Frederick took the balance of his forces and continued in his original direction. Von Daun remained where he was on the high ground when perhaps he should have launched an attack on the moving columns. Frederick made a wide berth up, turned to the right and came around and to the rear of the Austrian army, forcing von Daun to realign his army. Some regiments to his right faced westward and a large contingent faced to the rear. Ziethen remained facing Lacy and contrary to Frederick's wishes remained there through most of the day. Lacy's corps continually beat back Ziethen's advance forces. His heavy artillery fire forced the Prussian to move more towards the centre of the Austrian line, towards the village of Süptitz. In the north, Frederick then hurled his best formations towards Arenburg's front – but ten battalions of Prussian grenadiers were mowed down by Major-General Walter Waldenau's 275 pieces of artillery.

It was at this time that three new Austrian regiments took it upon themselves to counter-attack, which in turn led the Prussian King to send sixteen more battalions into the fray. They too were repulsed with heavy losses but during this period von Daun received a severe musket wound to his foot. He kept his painful wound secret for two hours, even as the blood flowed quite freely. His army gave much more than they were taking. Von Daun desperately wanted to see a victory before leaving the field.

*Franz Moritz
Lacy*

A third suicidal attack by eleven battalions was launched by the King, but that was also beaten back with more heavy Prussian losses. Then the Prince of Holstein launched a cavalry attack upon Lieutenant General Adolph Nikolaus Bucow's line and O'Donnell reversed his position and charged Holstein. This badly hurt the Prussians even though they had made some progress into the Austrian infantry lines. They were hurled back northward and von Daun was convinced that the Prussians were defeated, but then realised that the firing he heard from Süptitz meant that fighting there persisted, so he ordered Lacy to continue to give support to the western flank. He then relinquished the command of the main

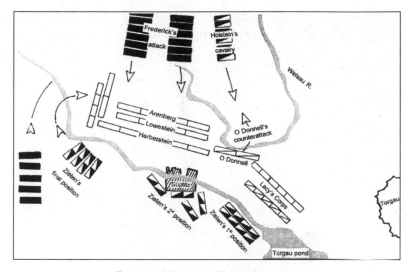

Battle of Torgau, 3 November 1760

army and at 6 p.m. had himself removed to a dressing station in Torgau. There he composed reports describing his victory and had them sent to Vienna.

Meanwhile, a restless Ziethen decided to move his force westward to rejoin his King. He had several battalions detached from the main body to attack Süptitz, which was the firing that von Daun had heard. The Austrian response was less than adequate. Lacy's corps did attack the King but were twice repulsed. With Ziethen's assistance the Prussians took the high ground which the Austrians had held so well all day. The Austrian army then fell apart, though their actual losses were only 9,000 compared to Frederick's 13,000 (some sources quote as high as 17,000). Led by Lacy, the bulk of the Austrian army managed to withdraw to safety. It was a loss for them and a victory for Frederick but not a rout. Nonetheless, Lacy was blamed for failing to continue von Daun's work after he left.

When von Daun learned of this completely unexpected reversal, he was flabbergasted. Both Lacy and O'Donnell had to bear the responsibility for the loss, for the former did little to counter Ziethen's manoeuvre, which he could plainly see, and the latter failed to attack Holstein.[15]

On 15 February 1763 at the Peace Treaty of Hubertusburg, the Seven Years' War came to an end. The boundary lines were finalised and were exactly as they had been seven years before. Neither Austria, Prussia nor Saxony had gained one iota from the bloodletting. France lost and Britain gained, in Canada and India among other places. Russia had made an impact upon the western Europeans. From now on they would all regret asking the Russians to 'come and give us a hand'. They came easily enough, but they didn't want to leave.

Austria may not have lost or gained ground but she did lose 120,000 men to death or wounds. She also lost heavily in horses, over 82,000, and much expensive equipment. But she had certainly gained in prestige. Her armies, once Prussia's doormat, won nearly as many battles as they lost. Austria was no longer the weak nation that she had been when Maria Theresa first ascended her throne in 1740. Her army had been greatly reformed and the primary person behind this was Lacy. His staff school and training of competent officers helped him to develop a first class organisation which Austria badly needed. It gave the Austrian army faith in themselves for the long-term future. Many of the infantry and cavalry regiments, especially *kürassiers* and light Hungarian Hussars, were superb. Their artillery was often considerably better than that of the Prussian army. Austria's army was finally considered to be 'professional' even by her enemies.

Von Daun, now Minister for War, turned to his still most efficient general to bring the armies home from their scattered positions all over Bohemia. Lacy began at once to arrange the march patterns. Soon the roads everywhere were crowded with columns on foot, on horse-back and in wagons. Within a few weeks the regiments had all been returned to their regular garrisons and the army settled down to its normal routines. When the war was over Lacy felt the let-down as much as anyone could who had been so very active those last seven years. In the form of a complaint, as much as an explanation of his daily routine, in a letter to a friend he explained:

> It is an invariable round. I get up when the sun already stands high over the city. I yawn, get dressed in a leisurely fashion, make a few visits, eat somewhere or other, attend the theatre, go for a stroll, dine and lastly find myself totally exhausted in bed, having really done nothing all day long. We occasionally go out hunting, and come back just as tired and pleased with ourselves as we once did when we returned from campaign.[16]

At war's end, Kaunitz-Rietberg immediately began trimming the military budget. He reduced the budget below what it had been before the war with the result that the size of the peacetime standing army had to be reduced considerably. His position, which he well articulated, was that military expenditures had to be seen in the context of the whole fiscal and credit picture of the monarchy and could not be allowed to undermine its economic foundations.

Naturally von Daun, and the other senior military leaders, including Lacy, worried that extreme budgetary reductions would cause the army to be entirely unprepared for the next war and in the face of possible enemy assault. Frederick II was still out there, always ready, willing and able to attack Austria, and still her primary threat.

In 1762 von Daun succeeded to the presidency of the Hofkriegsrat, which had been put into the hands of generals rather than of civilians. Later, in 1765, Joseph II took charge and had three inspector-generals appointed to oversee the main branches of the army. Plans were being prepared by Lacy for introducing conscription and the canton system, whereby each canton (province) provided a certain number of soldiers for a defined period to the army. During his four years as president, von Daun, tried to straighten out the mess in the army. He regained control of the General-Kriegs-Commissariat, but when he stepped down there was still much more to be done. Von Daun's right-hand man in all these efforts was General Count Franz Moritz Lacy.[17] In a 1761 memorandum, Joseph had argued, like von Daun, Lacy and other generals, against the Kaunitz-Rietberg army reduction.[18] Joseph had also argued for a substantial financial provision of 22 million gulden for the army during peace-time – 17,000,000 to be spent each year and another 5,000,000 to be saved for possible future war-time needs. These facts and figures came to Joseph from the generals who knew what was going on, namely von Daun and Lacy.

In the many debates that followed, civilian proponents of fiscal restraint fought and eventually lost out to the military advocates of an expanded military budget. Von Daun, Lacy and Joseph II, who soon became co-regent, obtained an independent investigation into the probability of a renewed Prussian attack and Austrian preparation for it. From the study, their conclusion was that security requirements demanded an increase in the permanent military establishment to 140,000 men, at an estimated cost increase of 2,000,000 gulden. The proposals also raised the issue of recruitment, for the war ministry had grave doubts that the recruitment practices in effect since 1748 could meet the regimental quotas of a greatly enlarged standing army. This introduced the concept of an army recruited or conscripted in the cantonal manner of, among other nations, Prussia and Switzerland, conceptualised and put forward by Lacy through von Daun and approved by Joseph.

On 19 July 1764, at the request of von Daun and Joseph, General Lacy presented a devastating critique of the recruitment programme.[19] Lacy's position recommended the creation of a viable well-trained reserve through conscription. Kaunitz-Rietberg agreed that Austria had to increase her military size but in such a way that wouldn't crush taxpayers and destroy the very source of all revenue. He recommended a redistribution of various garrisons, but he opposed the proposed budget increases on the grounds that armies were there to protect countries not to drain their resources. This also applied to conscription.[20] The military might find the process convenient, but the draftees would hardly share that sentiment. The fear of conscription, as in Prussia, where everyone was a soldier, would have 'the most dangerous consequences'. It would give military authorities far too much power over the civilian populace, and the great possibility of 'unending oppression and extortion after the Prussian example'.

In 1765, upon the death of Francis Stephen, the Holy Roman Emperor and consort husband of Maria Theresa, his son Joseph II replaced him on the imperial throne and was named as co-regent of Austria with his mother. Joseph was a strong, dominant type who had already and would repeatedly clash with the Empress for many years. Joseph as co-regent was not the easiest of men to get along with. He has been described as vain and commanding in most of his relationships. He felt most comfortable among military men. With women he was barely tolerant. He was married twice and neither time seemed to have brought forth more than a cordial relationship, though he is recorded as being genuinely depressed when his first wife, Isabella, died. The same was true when his very young daughter, Maria Theresa, died. He had mistresses but they appear to have been merely conveniences rather than persons with whom he communicated. His two close friends were von Daun and Lacy. With them he felt at ease. When von Daun died, for many years Lacy and Joseph were inseparable. Joseph was a great traveller and for years after Lacy retired, he would accompany the Emperor on various trips. Joseph seemed to need the guidance of a father-like figure, and both soldiers filled that void.

Joseph strongly supported Lacy's plan to introduce conscription and the cantonal system. When von Daun died in February 1766, Maria Theresa allowed Joseph to select his replacement. The Emperor's first and only choice was Lacy, who had also been von Daun's acknowledged first choice. At Joseph's recommendation, Lacy was made president of the Hofkriegsrat, the War Council.[21] With Lacy's advancement to the council, came his baton as marshal.

Field Marshal Lacy's selection to the presidency, the leading soldier of the empire, caused great indignation and dissatisfaction amongst the nobility. First, because he was a foreigner of Irish extraction and Russian by birth. But that wasn't entirely unheard of during the Habsburgs' reign. The Irish, among other foreigners, were usually well-received and esteemed. Secondly, because he was the youngest man to have filled that post (forty-one).[22] The new marshal was junior to many generals who considered themselves equally competent, though most weren't. Married to one of them, Princess Eleonore Liechtenstein thought Lacy 'a horrible man'.[23] The new president's zeal for economy, efficiency and professionalism was bound to offend the old guard. In many nations of that period holding military appointments often meant sizable increases in annual income and Austria was no different.[24] Lacy brought much of the 'skimming' to a rapid end.

Lacy asked whether, like von Daun, he could be a member of the Staatsrat as well as president of the Hofkriegsrat. Joseph replied that it was against the rules and that, although the rules were bad, it would be better to let matters ride until people came to recognise:

... the bad composition of the whole machine. Yet more confusion will clarify their minds. To overwhelm them with muddles, and to reduce them to the point when they don't know what's to be done, are better ways of curing and convincing them than the best-posed dilemmas. This is between ourselves.[25]

When Lacy took office in 1766, he found that despite von Daun's efforts, army affairs were still badly muddled. He at once began to make changes. He reincorporated the Commissariat under the control of the war minister and very importantly, moved many scattered offices into a single building where he could keep an eye on their daily operations. Soon after his appointment, Lacy had his hands in nearly everything related to army organisation, including services and supplies. He imposed a new system whereby colonels could no longer order their supplies directly. They were to provide him with accurate monthly returns, whereupon their needs were dispensed directly by his new organisation. This created a huge well of bad feeling against him:

[Lacy] lost the love of the officers, for he robbed them of the power to deceive their sovereign. Hitherto the captains supplied the needs of their companies, and they had become accustomed to making at least twice as much as their entitlement on the cost of cloth, hats, shoes and the like. The senior officers were usually in a conspiracy with the paymasters to appropriate part of the military chests for themselves. All this has now ceased. Everything that the soldier needs is supplied from huge magazines at the imperial expense. The Austrian soldier receives his full pay on the minute, he is better dressed than any soldier in Europe, and he is maintained in a way that is most beneficial to his health and bodily strength. The great field-marshal has been rewarded for his masterly arrangement by scorn and contempt.[26]

In other words, Lacy stopped them from cheating Maria Theresa and the people of Austria, so naturally they hated him.

He also became involved in the problem of supply in the field. Lacy organised a new, permanent, state-funded transport corps of 821 men and 448 horses which expanded into over 21,000 men and nearly 38,000 horses during the War of the Bavarian Succession, 1778–1779. About half of the new organisation was destined to transport artillery.[27]

Not long thereafter Lacy turned again to plans for increased military spending. Here he was in his element, and his calculations were nothing if not precise, urging an increase in the military establishment of 64,022 men at an annual cost of exactly 16,352,055 gulden and 25-5 kreutzer.

Kaunitz-Rietberg's lack of influence on this appointment was clearly demonstrated by Joseph's enthusiastic endorsement of von Daun's candidate for the job. Kaunitz-Rietberg's opinion of Lacy was extremely critical. His bias reduced Lacy to a non-talented and politically naïve soldier, fit only for dogmatic implementation of details. On the other hand, Lacy had the full confidence of both Joseph and Maria Theresa, with whom he was on increasingly intimate personal terms. Among other major issues that Kaunitz-Rietberg criticised was Lacy's 1764 objection to the old recruiting system. It is perhaps not surprising that one of Joseph's first acts, after Lacy became war minister, was to send him a confidential copy of Kaunitz-Rietberg's 1765 critique of the memorandum for refutation.

Maria Theresa claimed to have surrendered the direction of the army to Joseph. However, although the Empress had given control of military matters to her son she regularly corresponded with Lacy behind her son's back. The problem for Lacy, and undoubtedly other servants of the crown, was the tightrope they had to walk to placate two rulers, but Joseph had to be treated as

the official head. An incident in November 1766 illustrates the
position. Lacy had prepared a statement of what needed to be
done before an army could be put into the field. He submitted it
first to the Empress, asking her whether he should even show it to
Joseph. She thanked him:

> ... this is an admirable but also frightening survey. Everything that is
> pointed out is incontestably true ... Nothing is so necessary as to take
> measures against the misfortunes that threaten us, but where are we
> to find the funds for all that? I've been thinking about it the whole
> night, and I see no remedy, if you can't suggest one. You are the only
> man who can grasp the scale of the enterprise ... With your aid I am
> still hopeful of recovering my old [courage] – or rather the courage
> that I had in my youth, which has been destroyed by the defeats and
> the cruel losses of all kinds that I have suffered ... Give this paper
> to my son and indicate to me what is needed, and I shall willingly
> and as a duty support the only man in my Monarchy and perhaps in
> Europe who can undertake and carry through this task.[28]

With all the statistical information now available, Joseph gave the
proposal all the support he could muster in one of the most forceful
memoranda of his reign, which he submitted to his mother on 28
December 1766.

Joseph began his memorandum with the famous Roman
adage, *Si vis pacem, para bellum.*[29] And war, in his opinion, was
something for which the Habsburg monarchy was not prepared.
The previous war had shown that, even when the entire empire
wasn't entirely protected, the military strength of the monarchy
was still not enough to meet its requirements.[30] Increases were
therefore imperative, and the creation of a Prussian-style canton
system was 'the only true, efficacious and inexpensive way' to secure
them. Such a system, Joseph noted, would make every citizen a

soldier and every soldier a citizen, which, in turn, would lead to a more efficient society and the 'assurance that all orders will be carried out militarily, that is to say to the letter'.

With Lacy's support Joseph provided the state with a comprehensive and highly detailed report. He informed them how every man, regardless of disabilities, could be used in the new Austrian army. How they would improve training, intensify the fortifications programme and improve the cavalry branch. He desired an annual inventory of horses, stockpiling of arms, equipment and grain supplies, and a large increase in the officers corps. He urged an expansion as follows: Lacy's figures suggested augmentation by 65,000 men, 14,000 cavalry horses, 3,000 supply wagons, 1,900 pack horses or mules, 14,000 artillery horses, 3,000 pontoon horses, 100,000 new firearms and other equipment. While supporting these increases, Joseph made no mention of costs.

Joseph insisted that if his efforts to increase the army should fail, when the next war came along it would be disastrous for an unprepared Austrian army. Austria would once again be on the defensive and all that would entail:

> It is probable that the Austrian Monarchy will once again, before the end of time, face a war, and in consequence we must make all arrangements, even if only for the sake of our great-grandchildren, so that it can defend itself worthily. To this end we must choose, here and now, suitable places for fortresses; we must train men to replace the dead; secure horses both for fighting and to transport everything needful; have weapons to fire; and finally be sure of having bread for the men and oats for the horses.[31]

While Kaunitz-Rietberg supported some parts of the position paper he came down on the opposite side and said 'what Austria needs is better generalship, and no more expenses'. He was also right, but as the old saying goes, 'God is on the side of the big battalions.'

Maria Theresa maintained a modicum of support for Lacy's and Joseph's demands, but also agreed with much that Kaunitz-Rietberg said. Her major concern was the reaction of her subjects. Would they tolerate the full range of her son's proposals?

> It is well known how resentfully and unwillingly our peasants enter the army, and how they detest priests, lords and officials. Such deeply ingrained prejudices cannot be removed at a stroke. It will need much patience and time.[32]

She feared Joseph's scheme would lead to mass emigration. Her counter-argument was to keep trained soldiers in the army; why not let them marry, have children for her armies and by all means care for those children. But Lacy continued to press the case that he and Joseph had argued, while Kaunitz-Rietberg as steadily opposed it. The Empress finally submitted the question regarding the new cantonal system to a committee. The Emperor presided and the members included Generals Starhemberg, Lacy and Blümegen.

In 1767 Joseph started a project he titled 'The General Picture of the Affairs of the Monarchy'. It was a compilation of all the important things that concerned the crown and it was lengthy, factual, well organised and sombre in tone. He submitted copies to important persons whom he respected and who would contribute to its final version. Lacy was one of those and his suggestions were included in the final copy sent to the Empress.

Lacy was good at flattery, almost as good as Kaunitz-Rietberg, though somewhat succinct. His praise of the Emperor's 'General Picture' is an example: 'it shows the industrious, vigilant and sagacious spirit characteristic of Your Majesty, which will one day command the admiration of the universe'. In reality, Joseph comes across in it not as a wild, unrealistic extremist, nor a brutal despot, but more as a reforming statesman working conscientiously, knowledgeably and rationally, within the existing system, to strengthen the state and to benefit its people. It was probably the foremost production of his earlier co-regent years.

In 1769 Joseph was trying to rid Austria of the Jesuit order, who were attempting to interfere in the politics of the Empire. When he was preparing to travel to Rome to vote on who would be the next pope, Lacy wrote the following to him:

> Provided that YM [your majesty] causes the anti-Jesuit party to triumph at the conclave, we shall have gained enough in securing the immediate prospect of seeing YM's treasuries enriched by the immense spoils of the religious usurers of the Society of Jesus who swarm in your states. This, Sire, is not all. These ecclesiastical bankers have also very fine and very large buildings in every town of your Monarchy, especially in Prague and Vienna.[33]

Lacy continued to explain that such edifices were exactly what the army needed and the one in Vienna would make perfect offices for the Hofkriegsrat. His proposal was realised when the Jesuit building in Vienna, the Am Hof, became the offices of the Hofkriegsrat during the suppression of that order in the 1770s.

Implementation of conscription proved somewhat more difficult. Lacy was directed to prepare a draft proclamation in conjunction with Blümegen, the one Council of State member who tended to support conscription. Both were concerned to make the right impression. Despite this, resistance to conscription and the canton system persisted at all levels. Even after the formal decree, the necessary census proceeded very slowly. It was not until

March 1772 that the war ministry reported that conscription lists had been completed and regimental districts could be established. Thirty-seven regimental conscription districts were accordingly set up, though they were not in full operation until 1781, and they remained one of the most unpopular measures taken by the monarchy. A full Prussian military tone could never take hold in the Habsburg monarchy, but it was with some justice that Frederick II could now say of the Austrian army that they were 'Prussians in white uniform'.

During a war with Turkey in 1770, Russia conquered and occupied most of Moldavia and Wallachia. Maria Theresa had long stood for an independent and relatively strong southern balance to a continually encroaching Russian threat. Matters between Austria and Russia were beginning to deteriorate and Joseph and his mother were at odds as to how the matter should be resolved. Maria Theresa felt some degree of amiability towards the Turks, partly a result of their quasi-support when she was having problems with Prussia. Now Russia was at war with the Turks (1768–1772) and although she felt sympathy towards another Christian nation she was also strongly in favour of war with Russia to protect Turkey. Kaunitz-Rietberg also favoured that path, even if Austria had to take on Russia single-handed.[34] This was the Minister who was continually aiming to reduce the Austrian army's effectiveness by cutting costs wherever possible.

Lacy's role in this business must have been crucial. Born in Russia, though not merely sympathetic to his native country, he was convinced of its strength and impregnability.[35] On seeing Joseph's memorandum of 23 November, the marshal composed letters and a long paper of his own for both Maria Theresa and the Emperor. He contended that war against Russia would be fatal. Instead, 'wouldn't it be possible for YM [your majesty] to join this triple alliance to crush the Turks in Europe and share the spoils between us, Russia, Prussia and Poland?'

The Empress, now of a different mind, replied: 'I think you're both inclined to go to war, though in different ways, and I, who have been too much buffeted by war, intend to have no more of it.' She insisted that Lacy must not spur Joseph on to war. She would never fight against 'my Moslems' (Maria Theresa was concerned for the safety of her Muslim subjects in the Balkans). In February 1771 she used Lacy to tell the Russian ambassador of her regrets at the dispatch of troops to Hungary (an apparent threat) and of her otherwise peaceful intentions. But she said, 'inviolable secrecy is necessary here'. To further placate Lacy, who was concerned about Russia's greater strength, she also made pleasant overtures to Russia to reassure them of her peaceful intentions, but weakening the deterrent effect of the troop movements to which Kaunitz-Rietberg and Joseph attached so much importance.

Meanwhile, Prussia and Russia had mended many fences and became allies of a sort. Rather than allow his foremost enemy, Austria, to continue holding the Russian knife to his throat, Frederick found a way to become agreeable to Russia, which worried Austria's leadership. The 'Eastern Question' of how to divide Poland was of concern to all three countries and in 1772, they co-operated in partly dismantling the country. Most of these problems occurred while Lacy headed up the war ministry, so he was heavily engaged in these events.

In March 1772 Lacy reported that the conscription, or census, had been completed in the central provinces and was on-going elsewhere. But that was by no means the limit of his army reforms. New drill and exercise manuals had been created and issued; there were refinements and order in supplying the army. Professionalism continued to be the most important element in the training and assignment of officers. Regiments were now managed by professionals. Individuals of wealth were no longer allowed independence in the management of 'their' regiments. This also curtailed their 'automatic' promotion.[36] Foreign envoys marvelled at the results achieved and Frederick II admired the exercises he saw at Wiener Neustadt.

When, in late 1773, Kaunitz-Rietberg once again advised Maria Theresa that he intended to retire, she was fearful and exclaimed 'by whom can Kaunitz be replaced?' She wrote to Lacy and asked the same question, answering herself with: 'In my confidence, no one.' Since Joseph had provided much of the pressure which was forcing Kaunitz-Rietberg to leave, which, if any, of his protégés could be induced to replace him? Lacy appeared to be the obvious choice. Joseph had accepted him as his teacher in military matters and most likely would accept him in this new role. The two had attained some victories in the years they had worked and fought together.

Yet in October 1773 Lacy was given permission to take an extended holiday in France for the sake of his health. This journey provoked massive speculation both at home and abroad. It was known to a few that Joseph had been critical of Lacy's handling of the state supply magazines. Unpublished documents, however, make the true position reasonably clear. The marshal claimed that his workload was too great. He was coughing up blood, but his doctors would not declare that a trip abroad was essential. His desire to travel was plainly not a product of ill health alone. It was also a matter of disputes and misunderstandings with the man he had been working so closely with – Joseph. As early as December 1770, Lacy had complained of his lack of credit with the Emperor. Maria Theresa had replied that hers with her son was infinitely lower than Lacy's.

Early in 1772 Joseph, saying he was often 'under-employed and at a loss to pass his time at all usefully', asked to see all the minutes of the Hofkriegsrat, while protesting that he had no intention of challenging them or delaying the orders based on them. To maintain her personal influence in military affairs, the Empress resorted to ever more elaborate ploys and subterfuges in her contacts with Lacy, borrowing documents from him for a couple of hours, returning his letters to him, urging him to burn all hers, telling him what to say to the Emperor, letting the marshal know exactly how much she had told Joseph, writing ostensible letters for Lacy to show to her son, and paying secret pensions to officers whom the Emperor refused to promote.

Lacy's situation, despite his great skill as administrator and courtier, must have grown progressively more difficult. In April 1773 Joseph and he seriously disagreed about the peacetime deployment of the army and about promotions. In July, when the Emperor was in Galicia, Lacy asked for a short leave on grounds of health, but Joseph refused. Yet at the end of August he was telling Lacy not to take their differences of opinion 'tragically'. That Joseph was 'feeling the yoke' that Lacy tried to impose on him is quite evident from all of the Emperor's changes of mood towards his old friend. Later, when Lacy had travelled abroad to recuperate, the Emperor was thought to have agreed with unflattering alacrity that the services of the marshal could be dispensed with. The Emperor's friendships with General Nostitz and the Liechtensteins also threatened the marshal's authority over the army. Lacy was a fanatical worker, dictatorial and sensitive to criticism, a man of independent means rendered wealthier by the generosity of the Empress. He told his mistress, Princess Frances Liechtenstein, that he was 'cutting the thread of a thorny career'.[37]

Joseph's treatment of Lacy had terrified other officials, though many soldiers were glad to see the marshal go. But Kaunitz-Rietberg had seen his opportunity. In 1771 Lacy had contracted a 'diplomatic illness' in an effort to frustrate the chancellor's foreign policy towards Russia. But this time they were on the same side. With the marshal abroad and discontented, there was no one left in high office to whom the Emperor could turn for support. Maria Theresa evidently rubbed in the point as well. In his letter of 9 December 1771 Joseph spoke of having 'alienated from her men a hundred times more useful and capable' than himself. His mother was much cleverer, politically, than he. She used every device to interfere in military affairs behind his back, and to keep Lacy her servant rather than his.

In 1774 Lacy was forced to reduce his workload due to illness. He gave way to a comrade, Field Marshal Andreas Hadik. But, even outside the council, Lacy and Joseph II still retained tight control of the army. It was said that Lacy, while in his post, worked fourteen hours a day, and that he was a man of detail and precision, ingenious, resolute and indefatigable. Another Austrian called him 'one of the greatest men of genius of this century'. Regardless of illness and 'retirement', he still 'maintained a predominant influence over the Theresian army for more than one-third of its existence'. Among numerous European soldiers of distinction Frederick the Great continued to hold him in the highest regard as later so did Archduke Charles, a great Habsburg soldier. It was the latter who said, 'Field-Marshal Lacy was the first man who brought the essential branches of military administration into a coherent system, designed for both war and peace'.[38]

Lacy left for France and the welfare of the army remained entirely Joseph's responsibility. The exhausted Lacy stayed abroad for more than six months and during this time both Maria Theresa and her son wrote him a stream of flattering and confidential letters. She told him the Emperor had never been 'so consistent as in his actions relative to your absence. He refuses to permit any change in your arrangements.' Joseph, still not entirely sure of himself, kept sending Lacy documents from the Hofkriegsrat, asking his opinion about them. He also described the arrangements for taking over the Jesuits' building which he and Lacy had earlier discussed. 'We were made for one another,' Joseph wrote. Joseph claimed he was 'a friend … who sincerely respects and loves you, and who would not tell you so if he did not'.

Without advising Joseph, Maria Theresa had promised Lacy that if after some months of rest he was still inclined to resign as President of the War Council she wouldn't try to hold him. There was no question that Lacy had decided upon retirement and eventually in May 1774 Joseph faced up to that fact. He wrote:

> However much pain it gives me to see my life made gloomy by exceptional ill fortune, I nonetheless confine myself to expressing the hope that, although I no longer have the best president of war, good management and a quiet manner of life will at least preserve to me for many years a useful friend, who is not only willing to offer his life to help me to win glory on the day of battle, but will also assist me with his good advice and his talents to win it during the sad days which I spend, worn out by my responsibilities, working for the general good.[39]

Because of the recently concluded Russo-Turkish war, Field Marshal Andreas Hadik determined that further military increases were necessary. He argued that the growing strength of Russia and Prussia, coupled with the feebleness of Austria's ally, France, as well as the territorial expansion of the Habsburg monarchy all made such increases imperative. Lacy, who was still acting as the Emperor's adviser, agreed with Hadik and Joseph that the increases were indeed required. He suggested that instead of creating new regiments, every company in the army be strengthened by the addition of nine men.

The Queen and Emperor decided to sweeten Lacy's retiring years. He at last became a member of the Staatsrat, but without the full burden of duties normally associated with membership. He continued to advise the two rulers on military matters. With the change of personnel, Hadik for Lacy permanently, a review of military policy was undertaken. It was decided that, while great improvements had taken place, it was not nearly enough. Conscription should be expanded through the many national kingdoms, including reluctant Hungary, always the most difficult of the 'loyal territories'. The Empress wrote to Lacy on 20 December:

> I'm going to make one final attempt more to get the Emperor to work within the system ... He grumbles only too often about his critical situation, and that he would like to be Prime Minister. There's nothing I should like better, and I shall insist that he organise business himself, as and with whom he wishes. We shall see what emerges. I have no great hopes, but I shall try. There would be nothing for me to do but give in and cheerfully align myself with you two [Lacy and Joseph?] if I did not love my states and did not believe that I ought to try everything else before taking this course.[40]

Lacy was less than enthusiastic about the irresolution and vacillation of mother and son, and the evident threats towards Russia. Accordingly in 1776, instead of continuing his no longer strong position as the 'loyal opposition', he instead claimed illness and a desire to adjourn to Spa for his health. However, he later returned and continued in his role of adviser and confidant of both mother and son until she died and Joseph assumed the title of Emperor of the Holy Roman Empire and King of Austria, and until Joseph died in 1790.

Lacy had a philosophy of life that included wine, women

and song, but perhaps the latter was least important in his busy schedule. Lacy was especially fond of the ambience of Spa and the Ardennes, and after the Seven Years' War he begged his friend Count James Robert Nugent,[41] envoy to Berlin, to meet him there so as 'to live, to eat, to drink, and let ourselves go a little … In Spa we can admire the great rocks, the peculiar beasts of the mountains and all sorts of other things which are well worth seeing.'[42] Lacy continued to visit Spa for many years. He was noted as a wine connoisseur, with a special affinity for French burgundy, which he bought in prodigious volume and laid down in a famous cellar. Michael Kelly, an Irish tenor then travelling on the continent, later recalled in his memoir that he was well received by the marshal. His described meeting Lacy and the marshal's seeming lack of interest in Ireland but mentioned his hospitality and that he was 'a fine-looking man, free, convivial and communicative'.[43]

Lacy was a man with a low boiling point. He was especially touchy when individuals or groups questioned him about his opinions, which he expressed easily. Often he was heard to charge the questioners with personal attacks upon himself. He seemed, on occasion, to suffer from deep depression, which may have been a family malady. Certainly his brother Peter suffered from it, and Franz was 'down in the dumps' when his mother died and following the battle at Torgau.

Lacy somehow managed the almost impossible feat of developing an extremely close personal relationship with the rulers of one of the most powerful nations in the world. How that happened is difficult to answer. His only possible important contact in Austria initially was with Maximilian von Browne. His own father, certainly a capable general in Russia, had little contact with Austria, and his mother's family were Baltic Germans. It is true that the Irish managed to do quite well in Austria but, here again, he was only partly Irish and was considered by his hosts to be Russian.

He was a smart, forceful, conscientious, honest soldier who excelled in military administration. His position was always clear – to protect his adopted homeland. When relations between Austria and Russia began to fray, he frequently seemed to side with Russia, or at least not against Russia. But those appeared to the monarchy to be honest disagreements about power rather than disloyalty. He recognised the various weaknesses in the Habsburg monarchy and truly feared for Austria's safety.

Long after Lacy retired from active service within the monarchy, he was still their man at court. Whenever the Empress, or later the Emperor, wanted facts, considered opinions or honest dispute, they continued to call upon Lacy until he was quite elderly. For many years, Joseph would not make a move without invoking his 'friend's opinion'. Nor would he travel, which is something that Joseph often did, without including his close friend in his trip.

When friends or acquaintances were in difficulty with either monarch, they sometimes referred their problems to Lacy. He usually found some way to soften the monarch's displeasure. In one instance, de Ligne, a fine field general, made some critical remarks about the monarchy. He hadn't been promoted and had ended a letter to some official with 'I can always look elsewhere for a position!' Joseph's immediate reaction was to demand that he be banished. A member of the court recommended that he be imprisoned. But Lacy suggested that Maria Theresa not speak with him for three months. She readily agreed, as she was fond of her Belgian subject, and consequently didn't look at de Ligne once during the period. He was properly subdued and chagrined, but saved.

Another time, in 1775, Lacy recommended that Maria Theresa import a French theatrical company to entertain visiting royalty. But she replied that she couldn't do that while Joseph was away. He believed that entertainment was his own prerogative and within his realm of responsibility. She responded: 'You know the sensitivity of the Emperor on this subject.' And though usually Lacy did know what the Emperor was thinking, this time he slipped up, and since Joseph was a difficult man, it was just as well that his suggestion was turned down.

Dornbach, Lacy's home, was visited regularly by both Joseph and Maria Theresa. When Joseph's daughter, Maria Theresa, fell seriously ill, her grandmother wrote to Lacy about how it was affecting Joseph, and when the child died she wrote:

> After this cruel blow, take care of my son. Try to see him every day, even twice a day, so that he may share his grief with you whom he knows to be his friend. No one can distract him better than you with your business, the only sort where he does not find fault.[44]

For many years, with his 'ups and downs', Lacy continued to be part of the decision-making cabal in Vienna. He was seriously engaged in the so-called 'Potato-War' between Austria and Prussia over who would dominate Bavaria. In 1777 the Elector of Bavaria died leaving no direct descendants. Joseph decided to annex the nation and Frederick opened hostilities in July 1778. Fortunately for Austria, she had been busy making arrangements for war and was reasonably well-prepared, certainly more so than Prussia was at that time. Frederick's forces suffered from the climate in the Bavarian Alps but Lacy's preparations were sufficient to keep Austria's army well fed and clad. Duffy quotes Richter:

> The campaign of 1778 was a masterpiece in this respect. No army has ever known such admirable arrangements, and everything was available in superfluity. Although the large and powerful army in Bohemia grew from day to day, the price of all kinds of provisions had fallen by the end of the campaign, and actually stood lower in

Bohemia than in the provinces which were distant from the theatre of war.[45]

Joseph wrote to Lacy telling him:

> We owe everything to you, uniquely and exclusively – to your knowledge of the ground, and to your gift for devising schemes that were capable of frustrating everything the enemy could undertake.[46]

Lacy returned to the centre of Austrian military affairs as a result of the disaster before Belgrade in 1788. At the request of Joseph he had reluctantly accepted the post of commander of the Austrian armies in the war against Turkey, as part of which the army besieged Belgrade. Lacy's part in the siege was not all that it could have been and he was subsequently recalled. Between June 1788 and May 1789, 33,000 men from the garrison at Belgrade died of disease in various epidemics. The following year the Austrians did take the city but the alliance with the Russians was beginning to fray and in 1790 peace negotiations ended that war.

That same year Joseph died at the age of forty-eight. This left Lacy less powerful, and though he was only sixty-five years of age, he was an exhausted old man. He had survived his two friends, Maria Theresa, who died in 1780, and her son Joseph who perished ten years later. In 1794, Lacy was made Chancellor of the Order of Maria Theresa, probably the final honour that he received. For the next seven years he was fully retired and lived a quiet life on his estate, enjoying his 'English' gardens and drinking his French Burgundy. In 1801, at seventy-one, he too made his quiet exit.

Franz Moritz Lacy died without having married, and left no known issue. It is said that he 'courted in vain' the beautiful daughter of the old Field Marshal Reinhard Wilhelm Neipperg, and failing to win her, remained unwed for the rest of his life. He was a perennial bachelor whom his Empress, Maria Theresa, once jokingly threatened to marry herself to end his 'freedom'.[47]

He now rests at his former estate, Neuwaldegg, which is located in the western part of Vienna.[48] As described by Edith Kotasek, 'within the young forest stands a small temple with neat walls under the green dome of slender beeches over head'. In bold letters over the entrance to this mausoleum the words read: 'Count Lacy's tomb'. That is all – not one additional word to denote his distinction and impact upon those most glorious years in the history of Austria. Unlike some of his contemporaries, he was never known during his lifetime as a vainglorious man. We must assume the simple inscription was his own composition.

CHAPTER 11

THE IRISH IN DENMARK, POLAND, SWEDEN AND RUSSIA

DENMARK

Denmark and Sweden were at each other's throats continually for many years, especially during the seventeenth and eighteenth centuries. Denmark was a Protestant nation and like its enemy, Sweden, not likely to easily accept Roman Catholics as subjects or soldiers. However, there are records indicating that a few of note found homes there.

As early as 1657 Colonel Philip O'Sullivan Mor (or Moore) agreed to supply an infantry regiment of ten companies of a hundred men each. His offer was accepted and he received 1,000 rigsdalers for his trouble. At least one battalion of Irish appeared at Glückstadt in March 1658 and were assigned to Hamburg, then a Danish possession. The commanding officer was apparently not Irish; his name was Jacob de Leon (although that may have originally been Lyon), but other officers included Captains John Brinan and Diarmaid O'Sullivan, Lieutenant James O'Sullivan, ensigns named Egan and Murphy and a sergeant named Patricio O'Kennedy.

Several names appear as independent soldiers during Denmark's war with Sweden, 1675–1678. Among them are Oliver FitzHarris, Jan Kennedy and David Magennis. Lieutenant James Kennedy fought for Denmark in the same war with Sweden and was part of the assault on Landskrona Castle, and on 4 October 1676 was wounded in the head at the Battle of Lund. Undoubtedly Protestant Irish served Denmark, especially after Danish troops had fought with them in Ireland during the War of Three Kings 1688–1690.

Other Irish names found in Denmark's military forces include Anthony O'Neill and Michael O'Carroll in the 1675–1678 war with Sweden. In 1679 Michael O'Carroll served in the Marine Regiment of Norway, that nation being part of Denmark at the time. In the 1690s Irish-born James Butler was appointed a page at the Royal Danish Court and in 1694 joined the army as a captain. He retired, still a captain, in 1722 but the King promoted him to lieutenant-colonel in 1748 when he was seventy-seven years of age. One of his daughters petitioned the King for support for his family in 1758 – it seems that he had perished leaving twenty-eight children unsupported.

Hugh O'Kelly was captured by the Danes at Aughrim in 1691, along with his brother and twenty other Irishmen. They were compelled to fight for the Danish King. They were inducted into the Danish Foot Guards and Hugh was promoted to sergeant, then lieutenant, captain and commander of the company, finally retiring on 4 September 1716. Felix O'Neill and his friend, a Lt Maggenis, joined the Danes in 1689, just before the War of Three Kings began in Ireland. O'Neill was made a half-pay officer, 'laid-off' until his recall to active service, and attached to Prince Frederick's Regiment. He never received a regular appointment and in fact, though he begged for it, was never paid for his eight months' service. He disappeared and was apparently never recompensed.

POLAND

The King of Poland also wanted some Irishmen, especially for his personal guard, and in 1619 entered into an agreement with the English government for Captain James Butler to secure some men. Butler, an officer in Polish service at the time, went to Ireland and found 'nine idle gentlemen' for service in Poland. Butler seems to have been in the Polish service of King Sigismund for a short period of time, approximately 1627 to 1632, in which he fought in Germany. In 1636 he was a general and commanded on the Polish-Silesian border. He became a naturalised Polish citizen and his descendants may be living in that country today.

SWEDEN

In the early part of the seventeenth century many Irish, Scots and English were shipped to Sweden, as part of an agreement between the governments of King James I of England and Charles IX of Sweden. Sir Robert Jacobs, England's solicitor general, wrote to Salisbury in 1609 stating that there were 12,000 idle men feeding on the gentry of the land.[1] He complained that many were lately returned from the Low Countries and that there was trouble brewing 'underfoot'.

During this period Sweden was engaged in conflict with Poland. The genuine King of Sweden, Sigismund, was a Roman Catholic and his Swedish relatives and subjects refused to allow him to remain on the throne. He was, however, king of Roman Catholic Poland.

In 1614 Sir Arthur Chichester, the Lord Deputy of Ireland, claimed credit for having shipped many Irish to Sweden, mostly from Ulster. He boasted that 'besides the cutting off of many bad and disloyal offenders within the land I have sent away 6,000 of the same inclination and profession to the wars in Sweden'.[2] Most had been in rebellion during the risings of Hugh O'Neill and Sir Cahir O'Doherty against English rule in the late sixteenth and early seventeenth centuries respectively. John Jordan mentions locating Irish names such as Brian Fferrall (O'Farrell) and Lieutenants Edmont Bourke and Arthur McMahon who served in Swedish forces in 1629. He also found other Burkes and some Butlers.

It wasn't long after the first Irish arrived that Irish priests in military costumes found their way to Sweden and spread defamatory tales about the nation and its leaders.[3] 'It is unlawful to go to such a war, where they [Irish] should fight for a heretic and usurper against a Catholic and rightful King.'[4] This created unrest in regiments in which the Irish were serving, thus making retention and further recruitment of Irishmen for Swedish service very difficult. The matter came to a head when in 1631, Gustavus Adolphus declined to accept any more Irish, as they were not considered trustworthy.[5]

Yet in later years there are numerous Irish names still on the rolls. These include a number of undoubtedly Protestant Irish and others who may or may not have converted, including an ensign named Thomas MacNamara who served in the Foot Guards after 1679. Actually, it was the Protestant Irish who made a fine career soldiering for Sweden.

The Hamiltons, many descended from Malcolm Hamilton, Protestant Archbishop of Cashel, including his son, Hugh, were sent to Sweden. He arrived in 1624 and joined the army as a private soldier. He returned to Ireland in 1662 after the restoration of the Stuarts to the English throne, as a master-general of artillery and ennobled baron of Deserf and Ljung. His nephew, Malcolm, also became a major-general and Baron Hamilton of Hageby, dying at Göteborg in 1699. The family continued its relationship with Sweden and provided numerous soldiers over the next century.

RUSSIA

Peter Lacy's (see Chapter 12) son-in-law, George Browne, served in nearly every army and everywhere in Europe, including Russia. His Russian name was Yuri Yurivitch Browne and he became a full general and governor of Riga in Estonia. He was born at Castle Mahan, Moyne, County Limerick, on 15 June 1698, the son of George and Honoura de Lacy Browne, descendants of Norman families on both sides who had arrived in Ireland in the twelfth century.[6] One researcher claims that his mother was the sister of Peter Lacy and that his uncle was Marshal Maximilian von Browne of Austria.[7] He was said to have married an Irish woman, first name Eileen, when he was very young. Of that union there was one son (who left no issue) and possibly a daughter. Leaving Ireland for the usual reason that there were no prospects for him there, he enlisted in the army of the Elector Palatine of west Hungary, serving briefly. He left that post and joined the Russian army in 1725 as a lieutenant-captain.[8] His first regiment was the Ismailovsky Lifeguards. Then, in the same year and at his own request, he transferred as a major to the Narvasky Regiment, a regular infantry unit of the line.

With the outbreak of the War of the Polish Succession, Browne served with his regiment in the army of Peter Lacy. Lacy laid siege to Danzig but Stanislas, the Polish 'pretender', managed to escape to Prussia when a fleet from his ally France arrived. During the siege Browne was wounded in his left arm and consequently did not fight in much of the campaign.

With the outbreak of war with the Turks and Tartars in 1736, now a colonel, Browne was once again with Lacy at the siege of Azov (see Chapter 12) and was wounded twice and again disabled for a period of time.

In 1737 he was assigned to the army of Marshal Münnich at the siege and capture of Ochakov on the Bug River, where he was again wounded and for a while detached from active campaigning. In 1739, by special request of the Austrian army, allies of Russia who were fighting Turkey, Browne was sent to serve in the Balkans. At the Battle of Kroszka, Colonel Browne was serving under another Irishman, General Count Georg O. von Wallis. The Austrians were overwhelmed by a huge Turkish army and forced within the walls of Belgrade, which was then besieged.

During the battle Browne was captured by the Turks and subsequently sold as a slave, three different times. While in captivity, Browne managed to steal some secret plans which described in detail Turkey's plans for future wars with Russia. During the following year, de Villeneuve, the French ambassador to Turkey, managed to buy him out of slavery. With the plans secretly hidden Browne made his way back to St Petersburg on foot to deliver them. For this, in 1740 the Empress Anna promoted him to major-general.

Having returned to Russia he once again served under Lacy in the war with Sweden, successfully commanding the forces between Narva and St Petersburg. Following this war, Browne, now a lieutenant-general, was once again assigned to the Austrian army. This was the period of the Seven Years' War and he was, like all Austrian officers, fighting Frederick the Great and his Prussian army.

He was at the first major battle of the war on 1 October 1756 at Lobositz where he was once again wounded, this time in the thigh. Frederick defeated the Austrians, but not easily. In fact Browne's kinsman, Maximilian von Browne, commanded and his cousin Franz Moritz Lacy (see Chapter 10) was credited with severely damaging Frederick's army. For this battle he received the coveted Russian medal of Alexander Nevsky. Browne was at the siege of Prague beginning on 6 May 1757 where Maximilian von Browne was mortally wounded.

On 18 June 1757 Browne fought at the Battle of Kolin in which Frederick was decisively defeated. For those services the new Empress, Elizabeth, awarded him a snuff box on which her picture was encircled with diamonds. Augustus, the Polish King, awarded him the Order of the White Eagle and it is said that Louis XV assumed the care of his son.[9] He was with von Daun and Charles of Lorraine at the Battle of Gross Ebersgorf. There Browne was general-in-chief and once again wounded, this time in the leg.[10]

Lastly he fought at Zorndorf on 25 August 1758 with the Russian army. The battle was indecisive – the Russians left the field but the Prussians were too exhausted to pursue them. Browne commanded a corps on the army's left wing. His horse was shot from under him and he was severely wounded by numerous Prussian cavalry sabre cuts, one of which cut off his scalp. He was lying on the field and considered dead when someone looked closely enough at this high-ranking officer to discover that he was still alive. Medical care was supplied, his scalp was covered by a silver plate and he survived the ordeal.

However, his days of war were over. He was returned to St Petersburg where Czar Peter III awarded him the Order of St Andrew and the post of governor of Riga. He remained at that post for thirty years, from 1762 to 1792, until his death at the advanced age of ninety-four. While governor his record was one of useful reforms, which included improved communications and the founding of schools and hospitals. In 1774 he was raised to the rank of count and in 1782 received the award of St Vladimir in the first degree. Empress Catherine the Great gave him a large estate in Finland. In the last years of his life when his health was failing, he offered his Empress, Catherine, his resignation, which she refused. Her words to him were: 'I do not want to lose such a gifted representative, only death can separate us.' Count George

Browne was buried on an estate at Shemberg in the Russian Duchy of Courland.

The O'Rourkes of County Leitrim sent several soldiers to Russia who earned distinction. The first, Count John O'Rourke, wrote a famous treatise on warfare while he and his brother served Catherine II very well as soldiers. His nephew, Major-General Count Iosiph Kornilovich O'Rourke made quite a reputation leading much of the Russian cavalry against Napoleon I. His Irish name was Joseph Cornelius O'Rourke.

Last, but perhaps not least, an Irish officer in the Russian army named Charles Barry entered Romania with the Russian army in 1915.[11] Barry was better known later in life as the author of a series of adventure novels.

Several Irishmen distinguished themselves while serving in the Russian navy. The first seems to have been John Delap (also known as Delapp) and, according to Richard Hayes, the name was originally O'Lapain. In fact he identifies the man's name as 'Peter' Delap, but according to the General Naval List published in St Petersburg in 1885, the name was John.[12]

Delap 'may very well have reached Russia as a member of the crew' of one of the ships built in England for Peter the Great.[13] He was recruited by Captain Naum Sinyavin, promoted to lieutenant on 18 May 1714 and in September, by a courageous act, brought himself to the attention of Czar Peter. The Czar was riding on board the *Katharina* off Biörkö Island in the midst of a great gale. Tides were pushing down from the Neva River into the already turbulent waters of the Biörkö Sound. Peter wanted to leave the ship, perhaps due to sea-sickness, and asked if any officer would put him ashore. Delap volunteered and safely set him ashore on the island, receiving a hundred roubles for his troubles which Delap shared with his enlisted crew. The storm was so vicious that several of the warships were damaged.

The following June, Delap was selected by the Czar to take dispatches to the Admiral Aparaksyn, who was with his fleet at Odensholm in the Gulf of Finland, Russia then being at war with Sweden. On 3 November 1715, he was promoted by the Czar to commander, and in 1717 Delap was engaged in a successful raid on the Swedish island of Gotland. The following year he was given command of the *Prince Alexander* and took part in the blockade of Danzig. A British colleague of his claimed that later the same year Delap commanded the seventy-gun ship, the *Marlborough*. That seems questionable because he was still only a commander.

On 18 May 1719, now in command of the fifty-two gun ship, the *Yagudiel*, he sailed from Reval (now Tallinn) with the fleet commanded by Naum Sinyavin. Six days later they encountered a Swedish fleet between Oesel and the island of Gotska-Sandö. There Delap attacked the Swedish flagship with forty-four guns and compelled its commander to strike his colours. His promotion to captain, third class, came a month later. In June another fleet left Reval to assist Peter Lacy during a raid upon Sweden's coast. John Delap commanded a ship during this period. He then became captain of the fifty-two-gun ship *Randolph* in 1721.

The Treaty of Nystadt was signed in September 1721 and ended the long war with Sweden. Delap continued serving in the Baltic aboard his ship, was promoted to captain, second class, in 1725 and was a part of several administrative commissions. Then in 1726 he assumed command of the sixty-four-gun *Moskva*. He commanded the ninety-gun *Fridemaker* in 1728 and the *Schluesselburg* during a summer cruise in 1729.

After Czar Peter the Great's death it became evident that the Russian fleet was being allowed to disintegrate. Not wishing to be a part of that, Delap and several other non-Russian officers resigned their commissions on 14 July 1729, Delap having completed sixteen years' service.

Christopher O'Brien was an Irish seaman who had been a captain in the British navy and in 1737 took service with the Russians as a vice-admiral. He commanded the second division of the Russian fleet but spent most of the following three years in training and reorganisation of a fleet that had been allowed to fall on hard times. In 1741 he was appointed commander-in-chief of the Kronstadt naval base but found that there were never enough sailors to man the fine ships he was producing. In 1742 Admiral O'Brien terminated his service with the Russian navy.

CHAPTER 12

COUNT PETER LACY
FIELD MARSHAL OF RUSSIA

'The Prinz Eugèn of Muscovy'
Frederick the Great about Peter Lacy

At Kileedy in County Limerick, Maria Courtney Lacy gave birth to a boy on 9 October 1678. His parents, Peter and Maria, named him Peter. Five hundred years earlier the de Lacys had arrived in Ireland with the Normans. Peter hadn't a drop of Russian blood in his veins but he was to 'shed much blood for Mother Russia'. In Peter the Great's Russian army a foreign soldier could attain any eminence – only competence was the measuring rod and Peter Lacy had a large measure of competence.[1]

Lacy, his father and his uncle John were three of the many thousands of Irishmen who had followed Patrick Sarsfield to France in December 1691. In Ireland, at age thirteen he had been an ensign in the Prince of Wales' Regiment of Infantry. But when the *émigrés* arrived at Brest, France, he switched and joined the Regiment of Athlone as a lieutenant. Most of those soldier *émigrés* had already served in Ireland as members of 'King James'

Irish Army'.[2] Louis XIV always needed effective soldiers and he certainly kept them busy for the many years of his reign. Lacy and some of his kinsmen served the French monarch for several years, first in Italy during 1696 and the following year on the Rhine. When the War of the League of Augsburg ended in 1697 many soldiers from all the nations engaged were out of work. Usually they were without family or friends to help, and forced to find employment further afield. Some of the Irish made their way to other parts of Europe; many to Spain or Austria, but Catholics weren't generally welcome in the Lutheran nations, so they went where there were job opportunities.

During this period, Lacy and many other Irish officers joined the famous Prince Eugène of Savoy in his battles, fighting the Turks for Austria. Less than two years later they were again without a job and Lacy took up with a soldier of fortune, the Duke of Croy. Croy was engaged in hiring a hundred officers to train the newly raised Polish army of King Augustus II, who was also the Elector of Saxony.[3] Augustus planned an expedition to Latvia and Estonia to expel the occupying forces of King Charles XII of Sweden.

The Great Northern War began in April 1700 and was to last for twenty-one years. Sweden had taken lands in the Baltic from Russia in the seventeenth century, when the country was weak, but on his accession Peter the Great decided to re-establish a Baltic presence. Having allied with Denmark and Poland-Saxony he began the campaign. In the spring of 1700, young Peter Lacy began his campaign with the Saxon army besieging Riga, while the Russian army assaulted the nearby Swedish fortress of Narva in Ingria. The Russian ruler had obtained the loan of a number of officers from the Saxon army for this siege, one of which was Lacy. Soon Lacy became a captain in the Russian infantry regiment, commanded by a Scotsman named Colonel James Bruce.

Charles XII swiftly approached Narva to relieve it of the besieging Russian forces. He arrived on 20 November with his superbly trained 8,000-man army. Peter lost his nerve and retired to Russia, ostensibly to 'gather together reinforcements', leaving Croy in command.[4] The Swedes attacked in a blinding snowstorm, and Croy witnessed his foreign officers being battered and some killed by Peter's unsoldierly mobs. Needless to state, the Swedes had a somewhat easy time overcoming the defenders. Croy himself fell captive to the Swedes, as did much of his army. Lacy, the exception, managed to pull his company out, leaving torn-up roads in his wake to hinder any attempts to capture him and his command. This type of action would continue to be Lacy's signature. He never surrendered his command throughout his long career. He was in the thick of the voluminous fighting during this period – always showing himself to be a consummate soldier and leader. This was noticed by the Czar, even though he may not have been on the scene.

It was during this period that Czar Peter the Great began to revamp his existing armed forces. While campaigning in Poland and on the Baltic his primary military force in Russia were the *strelzi* ('shooters'), using either muskets or bows and arrows. A sort of local militia, they were practically a law unto themselves, and were then (and often) in revolt. Shortly after his return Peter overcame that impediment. Realising that he required a professional military force if Russia and he were to impress and awe his enemies, Peter set to work developing an army of consequence. Lacy was an important cog in this transformation.

Czar Peter's initial plan was to make his army the equal of any other in Europe. During the next few years he transformed an un-military peasantry into a major military force to be reckoned with by his real and potential enemies. In the space of three months he raised twenty-nine regiments, two of which were mounted dragoons. Their apparel was uniform in style but the colour of the cloth was left up to the discretion of each colonel commanding, so the army was, for a time, very flamboyant. Within a few years the colours became green or red, with blue as a rare exception. The uniform consisted of a coat that reached to the soldier's mid-thigh, with a neckerchief and a cap with flaps which could be turned down to provide some small protection in the sometimes bitter cold of the northern clime. Even that was soon changed and infantry and cavalry began wearing a tricorne hat.

Peter invested huge sums in attracting foreign soldiers to Russia. His scouts were on the lookout everywhere for officers who had been cut adrift after Ryswick. Lacy was one of those recruited.

In 1703, Lacy was given command of a newly formed unit of a hundred gentlemen, styled the Grand Musketeers, composed of a group of Russian noblemen armed and mounted at their own expense. Two years later Lacy was promoted to major in Marshal Scheremetoff's regiment, in which he fought against the Swedish General Lowenhaupt. In 1706 Czar Peter promoted him to lieutenant-colonel of the Polotski Regiment and ordered him to train three newly raised regiments encamped nearby. The following year he and his regiment were sent to aid Lieutenant-General Bauer's corps, then blockading Bucko in Poland. He and his men repulsed a sally of the enemy with considerable loss to that force. After the reduction of the town he led his regiment into Lithuania, which they occupied and where they rested for a spell.

In 1708 he and his regiment rejoined the Czar's main army where he was soon promoted to colonel and given command of the Siberian Regiment of infantry. With Charles XII's army advancing in their direction from Saxony, Peter ordered his men to entrench themselves at Copaisch, along the River

Borysthenes, to await the Swedes. Charles rather easily defeated Prince Repnin's corps, which forced Peter to cross the river and retire to Gorigorhi. The Swedes continued their march towards the Ukraine where Charles intended to join up with Mazeppa and his famous Cossack band.

In October, the Swedish General Lowenhaupt was badly defeated at the River Lesna by Czar Peter. In the clash the Swedish supply wagon train, which Charles was eagerly awaiting, was destroyed by the accompanying Swedish army, to keep it from falling into the Czar's hands. Charles was also greatly disturbed because he had counted upon having most of that force to continue his offensive. In November 1708 Lacy was detached with two regiments to stop Charles XII at Peregova, where he was attempting to build a bridge across the Lesna. Lacy and his men repulsed the Swedes, who suffered significant losses. They tried to cross the river lower down, but Lacy had built a redoubt with a battery to defend that crossing point. Consequently, Charles couldn't cross there either. He made an attempt to force passage of the River Desna, where Lacy once again stopped him.[5] Regardless, as intended, Charles was successfully moving in an easterly direction towards Moscow.

The Swedes made another attempt, this time at Mishchin, which Lacy also stopped. He was then ordered to move further south because it was assumed that Charles XII would make another move to cross the river lower down. A general named Gordon was left to hold the redoubt and battery at Mishchin. That officer was not as fortunate as Lacy had been. The Swedes got across and routed Gordon's troops. At that time, it seemed that no one could defeat Charles XII in open warfare.

In December 1708 Lacy was given command of 15,000 troops and ordered to assault Romny, which lay part-way between Kiev and Kharkov. It was where Charles and his Swedes had taken up winter quarters and it was to be the worst European winter in memory. Russia was even colder than usual and everyone suffered because of it, especially the greatly exposed Swedish army. Though ostensibly resting in winter quarters, the Swedes were kept quite busy by Peter's army and forced many times to drive off attacks. Lacy took three battalions, a company of grenadiers, a regiment of dragoons and about 500 Cossacks, and made his way into the Swedish camp – a most dangerous place to be. They created massive upset and confusion for the Swedes and Lacy retired without serious losses. His reward this time was the command of a regiment of grenadiers. The young Irishman was continuing his climb up the ladder of success.

Next came Poltava, the most decisive battle in Russian history before the Second World War. If Peter's army had been defeated there, the road to Moscow would have been virtually wide open to Charles. Lacy was still a colonel but posted as a brigadier on Bauer's right wing of the army. Lacy's most important individual contribution to this battle was his insistence to Peter that all Russian troops follow the training he had given to his own units. In the past, Russian soldiers advanced, fired their muskets, then continued their advance never to fire again. Most frequently they fired from a distance which precluded any hits, let alone accuracy. Fifty to seventy-five yards was about the maximum distance from which any musket could be expected to hit its target, and then not necessarily with accuracy. Of course, the Russian troops took heavy musket fire from the enemy and by the time those who were still alive had reached the enemy, they were completely disoriented and in disarray, and frequently easily defeated.

This time the Russians followed Lacy's directions; to fire when they were only twenty-five paces before the enemy. The result left the enemy's ranks in disarray and was so successful that the Swedish army was practically destroyed. Charles was so badly defeated that he had great difficulty getting away from the victorious Russians. He escaped to Turkish territory, remaining away from Sweden for almost five years, a decision which was ruinous for him and Sweden.

Lacy served with the Russian forces throughout the aptly named Great Northern War from 1700 to 1721. He emerged as a lieutenant-general and was internationally known as a brave, skilful and resourceful officer. During this period Lacy was wounded three times at the Battle of Poltava, but not seriously enough to interfere with his career. He was credited with making many changes to Russian training and field tactics, all so successful that he was known far and wide as the 'man who had taught the Russian army to beat the King of Sweden's army'.[6]

During the next decade Lacy participated in several successful landings on Swedish soil, once landing within twelve miles of Stockholm. At a brief distance from the capital, he had his army disembarked from where their galleys were tied up and prepared to march directly to Stockholm. They were, however, repulsed by the depleted Swedes. The following year he again landed close to Stockholm and with 5,000 troops razed three towns, including Sundsvall. There he forced a Russian-dictated peace. In a brief engagement, the exhausted Swedes were barely able to hold their own. The battle was credited with forcing the Swedes to the bargaining table, which resulted in the 1721 Peace of Nystadt. The treaty gave Russia control of all the eastern Baltic. Sweden was a spent force, but that was largely a result of what had happened at Poltava, more than ten years before. The Russians were just beginning to realise the fact and to take advantage of it.

Coincidentally, another Irishman, General Hugh Hamilton, commanded the Swedish troops ashore which Lacy was fighting. Hamilton was one of those Protestant Irishmen who were also serving as 'Wild Geese', mostly for economic reasons not related to religion, and were esteemed by Sweden as they were in other Scandinavian countries. Many achieved great reputations as did their descendants.

Lacy's rise in rank and prestige continued long after the Peace of Nystadt. In July 1723 Czar Peter called Lacy to St Petersburg, to take a seat among his peers at the College of War. While in residence there and until 1725, Lacy gave his advice and opinions on matters pertaining to war, often to the Czar or Czarina. In June 1725, at the ceremonies connected with the coronation of Catherine I, as a mark of honour, he followed the Czarina's carriage on horseback, tossing gold and silver coins (provided by his sovereign) to the onlookers. Additionally, in 1725, following the termination of his position at the College of War he received the prestigious Order of Alexander Nevsky medal. That same year he was made general-in-chief of infantry, and given command of the troops in St Petersburg, Ingria and Novogorod. In 1726 the troops in Estonia and Karelia were added to his command.

In 1727 Menshikov, the power behind the Russian throne, assigned Lacy a task to eliminate a problem for the Czarina Catherine I. [7] Maurice de Saxe, a soldier then gaining a reputation in Europe, and incidentally an illegitimate son of Augustus the Strong (Elector of Saxony 1697–1704 and King of Poland 1709–1733), laid claim to the Duchy of Courland. Courland is a peninsula jutting into the Baltic from land that is part of Lithuania. Maurice had asked for the hand in marriage of the Duchess Anna of Courland, which she accepted. Unfortunately for both, the Czarina Catherine I had already refused Anna permission to marry anyone, as she wished to retain some control over Courland. Besides, the Czarina had promised the dukedom to her adviser, Menshikov, the man who had ensured that Catherine would become the first non-Russian woman to rule Russia. [8]

With the little bit of money he had, Maurice had made every

effort to gather together men from all over Europe to serve his cause. Unfortunately the future marshal of France could only gather fewer than 500 soldiers, which would not be anywhere near enough for the job at hand. Lacy was given orders to expel the usurper forever from the Czarina's domain. He sent a message to Maurice, suggesting that he leave 'before he was transported to a landscape with a wider horizon'. Maurice ignored it, whereupon Lacy showed up in Courland with an army of 8,000 and Maurice soon fled. Maurice took his small force to an island in a lake near Windau, and there they dug themselves in. As Lacy and his forces encircled the little band, Maurice requested a ten-day period of grace which was immediately refused. He then made the only decision that circumstances allowed. The future marshal advised his small command that he, with a price on his head, would have to flee. He gave them permission to surrender knowing that Lacy was a man of honour and would be lenient with them. He managed to escape and his troops surrendered, and as Maurice surmised, no harm came to the prisoners.

During the balance of the 1720s Lacy continued his rise within the army and in the early 1730s was appointed governor of the large province of Livonia (now Latvia). While so engaged, he was confronted with several extremely difficult problems which he managed to overcome with his usual consummate skill. He was charged with governing a Lutheran population of German origins, who had been Swedish subjects as recently as 1710. To add to the distress, they hated both the Roman Catholics and Russian rule. Somehow he managed quite well, regardless of the differences. In 1733 when he was recalled for military service in Russia during the War of the Polish Succession, he left behind in Livonia a reputation as a kind, tactful, benevolent and popular administrator. He had gained the populace's appreciation, even though he was a Roman Catholic.

The war for the Polish throne, popularly known as the War of the Polish Succession, 1733–1738, was between two claimants: the French supported Stanislas Leszczynski and the Austro-Russians supported the son of Augustus II, Augustus III of Saxony.[9] Stanislas was Polish and the father-in-law of the French King Louis XV, while Augustus III was in the pockets of both Austria and Russia. Interestingly, Poland was then a Republic; the Poles didn't want a King and refused to accept one.[10] Regardless, both outside groups insisted that Poland needed a King, therefore her people 'must' accept the man chosen for her. In 1733, Count Lacy was ordered by the Czarina to enter Lithuania at the head of 20,000 men.[11] He at once advanced by forced marches to interrupt any proclamations 'King' Stanislas might issue, and captured Warsaw in October. He very nearly captured Stanislas himself, who barely made his way to Danzig and temporary safety. In the winter of 1734, the Russians and Saxons then turned upon Danzig but Lacy could not assemble more than 12,000 men at this stage. On 16 January 1734, Lacy took the Polish-Prussian town of Thorn, leaving a Russian garrison behind when he moved on. He also established magazines there which he and other Russian forces would be able to use for supplies during that winter. On 6 February they arrived in the territory of Danzig and by the 22 February were approaching the town and occupied houses in the neighbouring villages. Lacy established his quarters at Prust, a few hundred yards from the city of Danzig. He sent a messenger to the town to give the populace an opportunity to abandon Stanislas and accept their 'lawful' King. The Danzigers had the assurances of the Marquis de Monti, representative of Louis XV, that France would never let them down. They raised several new regiments and made arrangements for an anticipated lengthy siege. Sweden sent a hundred officers and muskets plus other munitions. France sent several professional military engineers and promises of additional infantry regiments. The residents were very encouraged, especially when they learned that Lacy had only about one-third their number of military forces. Had the besieged shown any real aptitude for warfare they would have attacked the scattered Russian forces and easily overthrown them. Lacy was so badly extended that one aggressive move would have destroyed any further immediate operations of the Russian forces in the Danzig area.

The month of February passed without Lacy making any overt moves towards the town. He so thoroughly lacked everything needed and the season was all wrong for an extended siege. But he and his men made life as unpleasant for the Danzigers as they could. They interfered with the operation of the only mill grinding wheat by diverting the river water which powered the grindstones. Supplies were stopped from arriving and the increasingly reduced sustenance began to make bellies growl. There were occasional sorties and scarcely a day went by when skirmishes with the Russian forces didn't occur. All this time there was a Polish army of 50,000 in the field but it was doing nothing for Stanislas. They were too busy plundering and ruining the Polish countryside.

Back in Moscow, Count Biron, who was suspicious of Marshal Münnich, had managed to have him removed from Moscow and put in command of all Russian troops in Poland.[12] Biron gave him orders to 'act vigorously' for the reduction of Danzig, without truly wanting him to succeed. In addition to those orders he also gave Münnich several regiments of infantry. Upon arrival in the vicinity, Münnich issued a directive to the people of Danzig to 'renounce Stanislas, submit to Augustus III and receive a Russian garrison'. He gave them twenty-four hours to accept. He might just as well have given them an hour for all the good it did. Meanwhile, now subordinate to Münnich, Lacy and his men were constructing trenches and a redoubt at one side of the village of Zigankenberg.

On the night of 19 March, Lacy's men attacked Fort Ohra. Two hours later resistance ceased and Lacy was master of the position. The following day the first artillery fire against the town took place. The Russian forces were limited to a few field pieces and two mortars taken at Ohra, but it kept the besiegers busy and the besieged on their toes.

Learning that a large force of Polish supporters of Stanislas were headed in his direction, Münnich sent several generals with modest forces to intercept them. The Russians were barely able to keep the force from interfering with the siege. A few weeks later, however, Münnich learned that another force under Count Tarlo, numbering 15,000 men, was forcing its way towards Danzig. Tarlo had pushed aside General Segraiski with his few Russian troops. Münnich sent General Lacy, his top man, with 1,500 dragoons to join Segraiski. Making a forced march, Lacy joined Segraiski the same day and took command of the combined forces.

They marched for three days and at a village named Wuicezina, found their adversaries. The Poles were drawn up behind two deep trenches in parallel, with a third directly behind them. It was a very good defensive position for an army of mainly non-professionals. Both gullies had to be passed before they could even get to the Poles. Lacy and his men would have their work cut out for them in taking the position.

Two regiments of Russian dragoons dismounted and drove forward through the first defile. To deceive the Poles into thinking that they faced infantry, Lacy had the infantry march beat on the drums. Through and over the second trench they went and the dragoons finally met the enemy. In the meantime, hundreds of Cossacks were sent to harass the Poles to give the dragoons time to deploy. At first the Russians were repulsed but soon Cossacks and dragoons merged and advanced again. Deserting their followers, the Polish nobles were the first to depart. Then the men followed the example of their leaders. The defending Poles comprised at least 15,000 men while the Russians totalled about 3,000 dragoons and another 1,000 Cossacks. This was the final effort the Poles made to succour Danzig and Stanislas. The city and its populace were now entirely isolated and on their own. It was time to begin the physical assault.

Having constructed trenches before the city, Lacy then took 2,000 of his men and attacked Fort Sommerschantz, driving all before him. Meanwhile, an attack upon the city proper was stalled by the Russians' very meagre manpower resources. On 8 April Lacy took a few officers to a height overlooking the town and a decision was made to attack the main defences. On 9 April Lacy mounted an attack with 8,000 men, 3,000 in the front ranks with the balance in support. In the meantime three other attacks were launched to divert attention from the main strike and although the main advance was going very well, the diversion wasn't. The primary leaders were all killed by a single cannon shot, while their forces were being bombarded by seven artillery pieces. The troops were soon intermixed and confusion reigned. Yet they maintained the position taken as best they could and refused to be pushed out or accept an order recalling them. Lacy's men, who called him Batyyushka or 'Daddy', would, according to all reports, follow any order he gave them. The troops refused to retire until he went forward and personally issued the order.

The siege continued for many more days. The French fleet landed three regiments of infantry which, being only 2,400 in number, were unable to lift the siege. On 25 April eight battalions and twenty-two squadrons of Saxons finally arrived. Two days later the three French regiments launched an attack in collaboration with an attack by the besieged, which hit the Russians very hard.

But success remained with Russian arms and both the French and the townspeople retired.

By the end of April the besiegers had finally obtained mortars to begin a serious bombardment. They came by way of Saxony through Prussia and on to Danzig. The Prussian King, Frederick William, had refused entreaties to allow passage of contraband through his country. Someone managed to get them through in covered wagons described as carrying the Duke of Weissenfel's baggage. They arrived before Danzig on 29 April and on the following day were throwing the first shot over the walls. Soon several fires were raging but otherwise there were no great results.

On 12 June the Russian fleet finally showed its colours, bringing artillery and ammunition for the continued siege. The French were forced to surrender on honourable terms. This effectively cut Danzig off from any outside support. The noose was getting tighter but still wasn't tight enough to cancel out the stubborn Danzigers.

The firmness of the next Russian attack drove the defenders off the walls and the Russians over and through them. Just before the capitulation, the elusive Stanislas again made his escape, this time to Prussia.

Lacy's losses are not known, but the assault on that defended town caused enormous casualties for both sides. Between Lacy and Münnich's forces, over 8,200 Russians were lost during the 135-day siege, which began on 22 February and didn't end until 30 June 1734. In acknowledgement of Lacy's services, Augustus presented him with his portrait set in diamonds, then valued at 25,000 crowns, and proclaimed him a Knight of the Order of the White Eagle of Poland. Lacy was detained in Poland because of the Russians' continued support for Augustus. At Busawitza, with 1,500 dragoons, 80 Hussars and 500 Cossacks, Lacy managed the almost impossible feat of defeating the 20,000-man pro-Stanislas army then commanded by the Palatine Lublin. With the surrender of Czerski Castle in April 1735, Augustus was without enemies either at home or abroad and was now certifiably King of Poland. Lacy had been vital in bringing that about.[13]

Having held a suitable reception for the victor at Warsaw, the Czarina ordered Lacy to take sixteen regiments and march to the aid of Austria. He led them to the frontiers of Silesia where they took up winter quarters and were maintained in fine condition. Early that next spring, Lacy with 10,000 infantry marched to the aid of Austria, then allied with Russia in a contest against France. This was part of the lesser-known Austro-Russian and Turkish War, 1735–1739, in which Lacy would eventually be heavily engaged. French forces, having overrun Lorraine between April and September, had captured the German fortress of Philippsburg. Meanwhile, Lacy arrived at Mannheim in June to join the imperial forces led by Prince Eugène. Eugène was agreeably impressed with the Russian army and its leader. However, the Russians didn't arrive until the campaigning was over and consequently had nothing important to do. This was the farthest west any Russian army had ever penetrated in Europe. There was no future Russian egress into western Europe until 1814, when, in the closing days of the Napoleonic Wars, Russian forces would get as far as France. Eugène and FitzJames, Duke of Berwick, both died at this time: Eugène, a Savoyard, served Austria all his life and Berwick, an English illegitimate son of James Stuart, had served France faithfully for most of his.

Lacy and his army then went into winter quarters in Bohemia. On 5 February 1736 he arrived in Vienna, probably to meet his son Franz, but certainly to meet in a private audience the following day with Emperor Joseph II and the Empress Maria Theresa. He was to meet with them both again on 10 February, but, in the meantime, met with several other members of the royal family. The Emperor also gave him his portrait set in diamonds and 5,000 ducats. In his journal Lacy wrote: 'The 11th, I quitted Vienna. On the road, I met a courier from Petersburg, who brought me the patent of field-marshal.'[14]

Meanwhile, beginning in 1735–1736, Turkey and Russia were at each others throats once again. Official causes for the war from the Russian perspective included the depredations of the Turk-supported Tartars upon Russians and their land. Having been defeated in 1711 the Turks had managed to regain much of the former Russian access to the Crimea, the Sea of Azov and the area surrounding the Black Sea. Romania and Bulgaria were both still within the Turkish empire as was the estuary of both the Dnieper and Bug Rivers and Yeni-Kalé guarded the very narrow entrance to the Sea of Azov at the Strait of Kerch. Russian trade southward depended on the goodwill of Turkey, which was lacking, especially where Russia was concerned. A Russian attempt to break that stalemate was made in 1735, but was a disaster. Now in 1736 a second attempt was to be made by the two heavy-hitters of the Russian army, Field Marshal Count Burkhardt C. von Münnich and Field Marshal Peter Lacy.[15]

On 2 May, while Lacy was travelling in his carriage to join his forces, about 2,000 Tartar marauders unexpectedly assailed him and his escort. Twenty-one of his thirty-six dragoons were captured along with his carriage but Lacy managed to jump on a horse and escape while the Tartars were plundering the carriage. They evidently paid little attention to the occupant because no Tartars followed him as he made off to safety. Having arrived where his army was encamped, Lacy began making his own plans for the forthcoming campaign.

Münnich commanded a 40,000-man army with which to invade the Crimean peninsula.[16] They took the Tartar

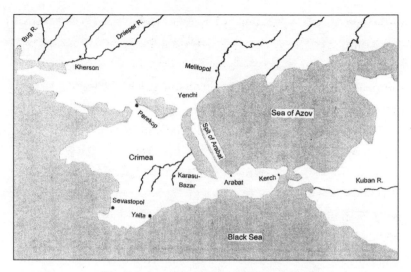

The Crimean Campaigns, 1737 and 1738

capital, Karasu-Bazar, but lost over 30,000 men to the battles, exhaustion, starvation and diseases, and Münnich was forced to retire. Meanwhile, during May and June, Marshal Count Lacy besieged Azov 'with great spirit'.[17] With a somewhat smaller force than Münnich (numbers not known), he captured the important fortress after a bitter struggle, but with comparatively few casualties. Lacy had taken reasonable precautions to ensure his men's safety by having trenches dug to protect them. Then he had his guns pulverise the interior of the fortress, making life for the Turks appalling and dangerous. To stifle the guns, the Turks made constant unsuccessful sallies against his lines. Having sailed down the River Don on 19 May, Vice Admiral Bredal arrived near Azov with twenty-four large boats and many smaller ones. The biggest asset was the battering train he brought Lacy, which was immediately unloaded and brought into action. Lacy had Bredal sail further downstream to position himself so as to batter the town on the side towards the river. On 14 June, 3,000 Turks attacked the Russian trenches and drove back the 600 men guarding that stretch of the line. Lacy rallied his troops and hurried forward with a force of reserve and other unattached troops and then quickly made his way to the area. After a costly encounter he beat them back into their fortress. While so engaged, Lacy had gone too far forward himself and had received a gunshot wound just below one knee. He was nearly enveloped by the Turks and most likely would have been taken or killed if his men, energised by their leader, hadn't fought desperately to gain his side. Except for the unsparing devotion and exertion of those soldiers 'who he knew how to spare and preserve on every opportunity; to guard against their over-fatigue and want of subsistence' his story would have ended there.

On 18 June a bomb-shell fell on one of the largest powder-magazines in the middle of the town. Five mosques and more than a hundred houses were destroyed, and over 300 people were killed. Provisions were drastically lacking and the complete destruction of the town made a severe impact on the besieged. By the beginning of July the town was 'nothing but a heap of ruins' resulting in the surrender of the Turkish Basha, but not without certain conditions, otherwise he would destroy everything, including all the Christian slaves within. Lacy agreed with the limitations: no honours of war. Instead the Turks were conducted, without arms, to the town of Abskouk under the condition of not serving for one year against the Russian army. Inside the devastated town the Russians found 200 to 300 brass or iron cannon, a great quantity of ammunition plus 291 Christian slaves who were immediately liberated.

In August Lacy marched to Münnich's support with 7,000 men. During the course of their march, three Cossacks were discovered on the banks of the River Kalmius. These three insisted that they belonged to General Spiegel's Russian corps and had lost their way. Lacy didn't believe that story and had them put in chains. The next day four more Cossacks were brought in and they

confirmed the previous story. Without notifying Lacy, Marshal
Münnich had left and was on his way back to the Ukraine. Lacy
was understandably furious to have made such a great effort to
help his colleague and not been considered worthy of notice. He
went back to his forces at Azov. This may have been the initial
cause of enmity between the two, but it is clear from many other
incidents that Münnich, the senior in rank, was jealous of Lacy
during the ensuing years.

In October Lacy decided to go into winter quarters near
Kharkov in the Ukraine. But even in the winter the people of the
Ukraine weren't safe from the various raids made upon them by
the Tartars. Everyone had to be on constant alert as the swiftly
moving, mounted detachments managed to penetrate and pass
the Russian outpost defences. The most common occurrences were
the sweeping away of cattle, destruction of villages and capture of
country people as slaves. But it wasn't all one way. For example,
Lacy's patrols surprised a band of 800 marauders, including a
number of Turks led by the brother of the Khan of Crimea, and
killed 300 while capturing fifty others. They also took 400 horses
and rescued over 3,000 Russian citizens who had been reduced to
slavery.

The year 1736 finally ended and both Lacy and Münnich made
plans for the coming season. In February 1737, both assembled
their men at Glukhov. Renewal of the attempt upon the Crimea
was entrusted entirely to Lacy who had twenty regiments of foot
soldiers and thirteen of dragoons. Additionally he had 12,000
Ukrainian and Don Cossacks plus a substantial number of
Kalmuck irregulars. Factoring in illness and guard detachments to
protect his lines of communications, Lacy still had about 40,000
men for the campaigning season. During the wintering at Kharkov
a Tartar and Turkish force, variously estimated at between 20,000
to 100,000 strong, made a five-pronged raid into the Ukraine. This

served to underline the necessity for quick and drastic reaction by both Russian armies in bitterly cold weather.

In early April, as the ice in the rivers was beginning to break up, Lacy's army concentrated at the mouth of the Mius River which lies north and west of the Sea of Azov. To co-ordinate a campaign against the Crimean fortress town of Perekop, he then rendezvoused with Vice Admiral Bredal at the mouth of the Kalmius River.[18] Bredal commanded the flotilla, which had been built that winter, and he exercised control over his part of the combined operations. By mid-June both Lacy and Bredal were at the Yenichi Strait, ready for whatever was to be their fortune that year.

The stronghold of Perekop was situated on the narrow connecting land link, blocking the only land approach from the west. There the Tartar khan waited behind powerful man-made positions for the anticipated attack. Because of the emplacements, the attack had to be a frontal assault. His lines ran completely across the isthmus and it would require very extensive casualties to breach. Unfortunately for the khan, Lacy didn't like frontal attacks; some other place had to be found that would not render his infantry and cavalry cannon-fodder.

Miles to the east, at the Yenichi Strait, there was a land formation which delved deeply into that body of water known variously as the Putrid Sea, or today as the Ozero Sivaš. At this point, a sixty-mile long narrow strip of land, the Spit of Arabat, and the Putrid Sea separated the Sea of Azov from the mainland of Crimea. Using a bridge of boats Lacy managed to get enough dragoon regiments and 3,000 or 4,000 Cossacks across to form and secure a bridgehead. Two days later, on 29 June 1737, his entire army was across without the loss of a single man and was on the march south on the narrow Spit of Arabat to the town of the same name. At Perekop, far to the north-west, the khan was taken completely by surprise by Lacy's outrageous flanking of his stronghold. But he recovered sufficiently to send some of his fast-moving irregular cavalry in an attempt to intercept Lacy at Arabat. The town was at the narrow exit of the Spit and the khan was convinced that he would only have to occupy that position to stop the egress of the Russians onto the Crimean mainland.

It was at this time that Lacy's natural flair for audacity came to the fore. Reaching a point on the Spit that was just opposite the Salghir River, and at the narrowest point to the mainland, he had the depth of the Putrid Sea tested and found that though deep, the cavalry and Cossacks would be able to ford at that point. Taking all the water casks and wooden *chevaux-de-frise* plus other materials available, rafts were constructed to ferry the infantry across. They all made it and upon arrival on the mainland of Crimea, turned south-east towards their main objective, Karasu-Bazar.

This success broke the khan's nerve. It had also affected Lacy's generals in somewhat the same manner. In the beginning his generals had tried to change Lacy's plan, insisting that to turn back was the proper movement. Lacy, in his usual courteous fashion, had explained what he was doing and that he wouldn't back down, and then ordered his secretary to prepare the general's passports so that they could leave and return home. He even detailed 200 dragoons to accompany them back to the Ukraine. It took the generals three days to convince Lacy they really were willing to do what he ordered before he finally accepted their contrite apology and cancelled the directions to his secretary.

Lacy was now heading for the town of Karasu-Bazar, the major arms depot of the Tartar army. On 22 July, the khan's cavalry attacked Lacy's army, which was then within fifteen miles of the town. Within an hour's fighting the Russian infantry and artillery had beaten them off. Lacy at once counter-attacked with his Cossacks and Kalmucks. The rapidly retreating Tartars were caught within a dozen miles and killed.

Two days later his advance guard attacked an entrenched Turkish army of 12,000 in their positions on the heights above Karasu-Bazar. The Turks were driven out of their entrenchments and forced to fall back in disorder towards the south. Lacy's army destroyed the town. That same afternoon the Russians moved some miles away to camp for the night. At nightfall some of the advance guard, those who had pursued the Turks, returned to camp loaded with cattle and about 600 prisoners. The next morning as the Russian army was again on the march, the Tartars attacked. Lacy sent Lieutenant-General Douglas forward with dragoons and several regiments of foot and light infantry to counter-attack.[19] Crossing the Karas River, Douglas marched directly to the enemy. The action was heavy and both sides were taking a beating when Lacy ordered the Kalmucks to attack the Tartars in their rear. Though hard-pressed Lacy and his men managed to defeat them with a double envelopment and the Tartars fled with the Kalmucks close behind them. Two days later the Kalmucks returned to Lacy with over 1,000 prisoners.

At their main camp Lacy and his generals sat down to a council of war. It was decided that they had accomplished all that was set out for them to do in 1737. Soon the weather would begin making trouble for their army before they could get to winter quarters. Recognising that he was over 150 miles from his base in the Ukraine and that the grass upon which the animals fed was dried out from the summer sun, Lacy made the decision to march his army back to the Shungar channel which was not far from the Yenichi Strait. But first he sent his irregular cavalry out to harass and destroy various Tartar settlements along his route.[20] His successful raiders brought back over 30,000 oxen and more than 100,000 sheep. Meanwhile the Tartars continued harassing the marching army, including the taking of horses in any way they could. At one point the Tartars, reinforced by thousands of Turks, attacked the army as it was crossing the Shungar. They attacked several times but their losses to cannon fire soon made them wary of continued and fruitless offensives.

Crossing back over the strait on 4 August, Lacy and his army marched towards their winter quarters. There they covered the line of the Donets and Don Rivers, from Izyum to Azov. During the winter of 1737–1738 the Tartars didn't try any largescale raids but there were a few alarms. In the meantime, Münnich took the important town of Ochakov on the Black Sea, but failing to first reconnoitre, he lost well over 11,000 troops.

In the new year, 1738, the Russian forces were again divided. This time Münnich was tasked with invading Romania from the north-east while Lacy's mission was once again to keep the Tartars busy in Crimea. Lacy was to direct his main effort at Feodosija, the important port and major slave-market on the eastern coast of the peninsula. Because a plague was raging at Ochakov, an enormous amount of supplies from the main base at Kizi-Kerman on the Dnieper had to be carried overland through the Steppes. To support this major invasion, many of the supplies had to be transported by Bredal down the Don River.

Lacy started early in the year, before the snows had completely melted and there was plenty of forage. The Tartars, who had elected to make a stand in the Steppes rather than be forced back to Crimea as before, almost immediately pressed him with attacks. With some hard fighting, the Russians prevailed. Lacy beat off the Tartars, who suffered heavy casualties as well as losing 15,000 prisoners of war to Russia.

It was decided to eliminate the obstruction leading into Crimea, the fortress town of Perekop, instead of bypassing it. By 6 July 1738, Lacy was once again within sight of Perekop. The

Tartars, all 40,000 of them, were formed up before their lines, but right behind them the entrenchments were still there. Not much had changed from the previous year. Nor had Lacy. If those lines were to be successfully taken by direct assault, Lacy had to come up with a viable plan and a direct assault wouldn't be part of it. He had his army form up in three columns in which every dragoon was to carry an infantryman behind him on his horse. That night he forced the enemy to fall back within their works by continuous deceptive attacks.

The Cossacks had been regularly bringing Lacy reports that the waters surrounding the isthmus were 'bottomless'. Lacy didn't trust the reports but on 6 July a furious westerly gale arose and within two days had lowered the waters around the isthmus considerably. Lacy took soundings of the shallows himself and made his decision. According to his Scots physician, Dr John Cook, Lacy covered himself with the cloak of God by having the priests administer the sacraments to him, which he invariably did before every action. He had his regimental bands play as loudly as they could and at the same time opened up with his artillery on the enemy lines. The volume of noise and the fire upon their front lines forced the Tartars to prepare for the coming assault.

But Lacy didn't launch an attack, not yet at least. Instead, he and his dragoons forded the shallows. Leaving his dragoons and the accompanying infantrymen to face the Tartar lines, he brought his main force through the shallows and within hours was on the southern face of the Tartar lines. Seeing themselves completely surrounded, the Tartars surrendered. The slender Russian force took impassable Perekop with few casualties.[21]

Lacy penetrated further into Crimea but found desolation everywhere, 'almost a desert' one contemporary account called it. On 20 July his forces engaged in a sharp action, when a force of some 20,000 Tartars attacked the Ukrainian Cossacks who constituted Lacy's rear-guard. It was a long and bloody battle with 1,000 Tartars and 600 Russians and Cossacks dead and 2,000 Russians and 3,000 Tartars wounded. The Tartars could tolerate the losses, Lacy could not.

Although Lacy had performed a near military miracle at Perekop, fate was unkind to everyone else. Admiral Bredal's fleet of provision-bearing boats was destroyed in a storm. The ravaging of the entire peninsula for many years had left little forage for Lacy's army, leaving him without the means to take Feodosjia. In addition, poor planning by the Board of War had left him no alternative but to retire to the Ukraine for the balance of the season. Meanwhile Münnich had been badly defeated in an attempt to cross the Dniester River, leaving half of his army dead or dying, while abandoning all his artillery. As a result the First Crimean War ended in 1739 without appreciable results for Russia, though with Lacy's reputation firmly intact.

The relationship between Münnich and Lacy continued to deteriorate. The former, a Baltic German, was senior to Lacy though both were field marshals, and he was the product of the heavily German-influenced court of Russian Empress Anna. Therefore Münnich invariably drew the most prestigious and spectacular missions. To make matters worse he invariably demeaned Lacy in his dispatches. But his operations towards the west were not as productive as Lacy's and were conducted with far less skill, as evidenced by the Dniester River debacle. Lacy's good management of his soldiers and their lives contrasted greatly with Münnich's. In four campaigns the latter's losses to were calculated at over 90,000, not counting those slain in combat. In the same period Lacy's losses were certainly much less and caused solely by the enemy rather than mismanagement.

Because of the extent of those losses Empress Anna charged Lacy with investigating Münnich. Lacy delicately refused the honour knowing full well that his report on Münnich would be taken in the worst possible manner by the latter's many adherents at court. Münnich soon uncovered the information that Lacy had the commission to investigate his performance and, not knowing that Lacy had already refused, approached him. Lacy did not tell his opponent that he had refused the task. There was a serious altercation between them. The ringing of their swords clashing was soon heard in the corridors and their weapons were taken from them by cooler heads. One general threatened to place both of them under arrest and to advise the Empress of what they had been up to. Nothing further was heard of the matter and Münnich retained his post and honours as did Lacy.

At this time Russia's army was in bad shape overall, mainly because of serious deficiencies in the headquarters staff. The army had fallen far below the standards set by Czar Peter the Great, mostly because of interference from politicians and courtiers. Russian officers and men had proved, as they always had and would in the future, to be excellent soldiers when they were properly led. Lacy's men had accomplished their missions and during that ill-fated war with Turkey and the Tartars, were the only shining success in an otherwise drab era in Russian military history.

Czarina Anna died in October 1740 leaving no heir. The infant Grand Duke Ivan succeeded her, but the baby's Russian parents were powerless to protect their child. The Germans at court still controlled the throne. Meanwhile, various European nations were working overtime to control or at least dominate the continent. The intriguers of France, always eager to dominate Europe, made many plans to that end. Because Russia was allied with Austria she too was an enemy to be kept weak. France had one more ally and that was Russia's always implacable enemy to the north, Sweden. Following the Battle of Poltava, Sweden was just another small nation with more winter than summer but it took a while before they became aware of that fact. As the Swedes were heard to boast, 'One Swede was enough to drive ten Russians before him!' Unfortunately they should have paid more attention to the Athenian orator Phocion who said, when that city was chanting for war against Alexander the Great, 'you should either have the sharpest sword, or keep upon good terms with those who have'.

But Sweden could still cause Russia problems. On 28 July 1741 she declared war on Russia once again. Sweden had a total army of 25,000, so was not in a very strong position relative to a nation like Russia, which could field two armies of 50–70,000 men each. Finland, a Swedish possession, was where the first land battles took place. There were 9,500 Finnish infantry and dragoons, 6,000 Swedish-born regulars, 1,600 German mercenaries and possibly 750 artillerymen there. All told nearly 18,000 warriors were available to meet whatever force Russia could send against them. The Finnish were very good, but the regular Swedish army was the main force to be reckoned with – and was justifiably feared. More importantly, the Swedes planned to attack rather than to defend. Lacy wasn't the only audacious soldier in the north. Actually another, probably more important reason for the planned attack was because they didn't have enough food to provide for a fortress defence. For Sweden it had to be a short and glorious war.

Finland's main line of defence against Russia was the great lake district in the south and from Lake Ladoga north and westward. One Finno-Swedish force was gathered on a road between Turku and Willmanstrand with Tavastehus between them. Just south of that was another force on a road from Helsingfors and along the coast to Frederikshamn.[22]

General Henrik Magnus Buddenbrock, who commanded the Swedish forces in Finland, had constructed two entrenched camps connecting the two forces at Viborg and Frederikshamn. He was located at the village of Kvarnby and Major-General Wrangel at Martila. Meanwhile a Swedish fleet of eleven men-of-war was stationed off Frederikshamn and a flotilla of galleys guarded the channel between the multitude of islands and the shore along the coast. But none of these played any part in the forthcoming drama.

By the spring of 1741 the Russian forces, totalling 100,000, were spread out between Riga in the south and St Petersburg in the north. The Russians had expected a Swedish attempt to land near the latter city, which the fleet would have been powerless to prevent, as the Swedish fleet was stronger and more efficient than their own. Münnich was in command in that area and had been busily examining the Russian fortresses. Lacy, who had spent much of the winter at his home in St Petersburg, had also been busy planning the forthcoming campaign. In early May, having received court approval, he held a conference at his home to discuss his plan for the campaign. His second-in-command was a Scot named James Keith.[23] Keith's orders were to take three regiments of dragoons and five of infantry to concentrate at a point twelve miles north-east of St Petersburg. In addition, two smaller reconnaissance groups were to form on both the east and west sides of Lake Ladoga to observe any movement by the Finno-Swedish forces.

In July, Keith moved his forces up the Karelian Isthmus and established a defensive position between two lakes at the village of Muolaa, some thirty plus miles south-east of Viborg. Meanwhile, Lacy was forced to wait for Russia's declaration of war, which wasn't issued until 11 August 1741. Then he moved cautiously, remaining mostly in a defensive posture. He ordered Keith forward to Viborg, where five more infantry regiments joined him, and then moved closer to the frontier. Lacy met Keith at Viborg on the 18 August and assumed overall command of the army. Many spies, both Russian and Finns, kept Lacy well informed of Swedish dispositions and movements.

Lacy planned to assault the defences around Willmanstrand because they were a serious threat to his northern flank. His spies had convinced him that there were upwards of 10,000 Swedes in the town, and he had only 11,000 troops immediately available. However, he later learned from two deserters that in fact the garrison included only six companies of infantry, six companies of dragoons and a company of artillery. This information prompted him to attack as soon as possible and on 21 August he began his advance.

Wrangel had 3,500 men at Martila and Buddenbrock had another 4,000 at Kvarnby. But Lacy reckoned that neither would be able to interfere with him because of his speed and the resultant surprise. His army only took five days' rations and no cumbersome wagons or baggage. Movement through the wilderness was slow and Lacy had to continually concern himself with a potential ambush. Even if the enemy was slow they could still get between him and his base at Viborg. But as always Lacy was an opportunist, an optimist and audacious. The risks were great but a lightning thrust would overcome any enemy force as well as any doubts he may have had.

On 21 August the troops moved forward through forest tracks which were hemmed in by bog or granite boulders. That night they halted at the village of Airmail, located just five miles from their objective. During the bivouac, Russian sentries fired wildly upon a Swedish reconnaissance force and nearly killed Lacy and Keith, both of whom were sleeping between the lines.

Dragoon horses bolted and sped off towards Willmanstrand. Swedish outpost forces assumed that a night attack had been launched and took off in panic, infecting the Swedish garrison when they reached it with the same emotion. Wrangel, twenty miles away, heard the firing and assumed that the Russians were attacking their target. He then sent word to Buddenbrock that he would march to relieve the town and after midnight he set forth towards Willmanstrand.

Early the next morning the Russians resumed their march towards Willmanstrand but a broken bridge forced them to halt for three hours until it was repaired. Lacy had three redoubts built to cover the crossing so as to delay any Swedish force that might happen along. It took until late afternoon for Lacy's army to reach within a mile of his objective. In his report he stated:

> As soon as I left the convoy at the foot of the hill situated in front of the fortress I reconnoitred the fortress at such close range that the enemy were able to fire on me with pistols and other small arms.[24]

From a hill overlooking the town, Lacy could see that a palisade defended it with a dragoon regiment drawn up in between the glacis at the front and a lake just beyond. At the top of another hill between the Russians and the Swedes, lay a windmill. An officer who had reconnoitred that hill reported to Lacy that it was defended by two artillery pieces and that a large formation of infantry was marching towards the town. The hour grew late and soon dusk fell upon the area. Lacy decided to wait for the following day before resuming his mission, but before leaving the hill he assaulted the Swedish forces in and about the town with his artillery.

The main Swedish army had arrived and the odds were now less in Russia's favour. Lacy had to wait upon the arrival of the balance of his army to equalise the numbers. Even then, the defending Swedes within the fortress and with fortress guns, held a definite advantage in any assault. Lacy decided that with only three days' rations left they must fight the following day, return to camp or

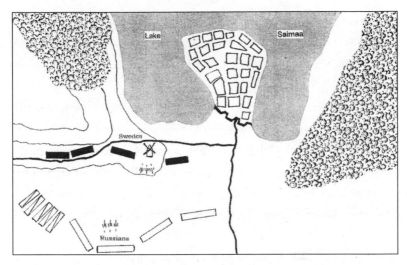

Battle of Willmanstrand, 23 August 1741

starve. Hopefully the Swedes would attack them the following day. If not Lacy decided that they would return to Viborg on 24 August. To make the possible withdrawal slightly easier Lacy had his heavy guns sent back to Viborg that night. Only three six-pounders, plus the regimental three-pounders, remained. No walls were going to be battered with those pieces. These changed circumstances under a lesser man might have ruined his chances for a successful outcome but Lacy's luck held.

Next morning Lacy made another reconnaissance. The fortress occupied most of an isthmus which was about 600 yards long by 400 yards wide and jutted into Lake Saimaa. Its front was defended by a shallow ditch behind which lay a palisaded, covered way on a steep glacis. Immediately to its front was a valley a hundred yards wide which ran across the isthmus. At the southern side there rose a height of land with a crest located about 800 yards from the fortress. Wrangel had taken the Mill Ridge with the windmill, and had positioned his infantry upon it and down on the flat land between the hill and fortress. He held about a one-mile length of ground with the fortress to his left rear. The actual dispositions were three dragoon squadrons on his right flank, two Swedish foot regiments and six guns on the ridge, and on his left, in the valley, one Swedish and two Finnish regiments. The mercenary German regiment, which was the permanent guard of the fortress, plus the three additional dragoon regiments which had joined them in the defence, occupied his left-most flank to the lake. It would have been very defensible except that Wrangel had only 4,500 men to cover so vast a position. As a consequence, he could not hold it with any strength and an attempt to do so would be very costly for Sweden.

A Russian occupant of the town led one of Lacy's officers to a point close to the Swedes. From that point their formation could be easily seen. What the observer saw was a formation which totalled three regiments and what appeared to be a nearly deserted town. Upon receipt of this information Lacy placed his infantry in two ranks with two grenadier and five regular infantry regiments forward. Six dragoon squadrons were on the right flank and three dragoon squadrons on the left. He positioned his three six-pounders right behind the front rank and his remaining five regiments in the second line. Lacy gave the order to advance.

Because of the broken ground on the right, Lacy's advancing dragoons had to move over to the left. The Swedish guns opened up and soon holes began to appear in the advancing Russian formation. Lacy got all three six-pounders up on the high ground facing the Mill Ridge and as soon as they were established they engaged their opposites. He then ordered one of his regimental commanders, Colonel von Manstein, to take the two grenadier and two regular infantry regiments forward to capture the Swedish guns. As they went forward Lacy brought up his second line to the left, making it a continuous line.

Meanwhile, the thick wooded area they were going through

forced the grenadiers to form a two-company column which was then badly mauled by the Swedish guns and quickly fell into disarray. The men of the two Swedish regiments on the hill facing them, Dalarna and Södermanland, were of the highest quality but their officers were sub-standard. Lacking the necessary discipline, the Swedish line broke formation and attacked the Russian left. They saw what seemed to be irreparable disorder from the on-coming Russians. As Lacy later stated: 'with such fury they [the Russians] found themselves compelled to fall back in some degree'.

When the Finnish units of the Swedish force on the left saw the Russians giving way, they attacked their enemy's right. But in doing so they too lost formation. This was Manstein's opportunity. His men were already rallying and now they opened a steady musketry fire and swept the Finns away. The Finnish regiments, Savolax and Tavastehus, gave way and retired to the fortress with the Russians following closely behind.

Although the Russian right was giving the Swedes a hard time, their left was taking some great heat. Full of vim and vigour the Swedes advanced against the retiring Russian formation. They far exceeded the forward line that Wrangel had allotted them. Their guns, which until now had worked splendidly, were covered by Swedish troops and could no longer be used. Lacy swung his dragoons to his left forward against the Swedish flank and drove them down the hill in confusion and with no chance to reform. With all speed Lacy launched his remaining infantry against the lone Swedish infantry formation still on Mill Ridge. The six Russian battalions went up the hill against the Västerbotten Regiment. There the Swedes continued holding their own for a period but were soon surrounded. In addition Wrangel had been wounded, which wasn't yet known to Lacy. Rather than finish off men who had fought so well, Keith gave the Swedes the opportunity to march away, which they did and with a Russian salute for the bravery of the men. That was the way most gentlemen fought in the eighteenth century.

By late afternoon the Russians controlled Mill Ridge and the captured guns. With those they were soon in the process of firing at the fortress and its occupants. Two failed attempts were made by the Russians to take the palisades but as they were forming up for a third attempt the Swedes raised a white flag. Unfortunately not all were gentlemen on that day. As a three-member party of Russian senior officers went forward to deliver the terms, unruly soldiers within the fortress killed them. This time the orders were to take the fortress and with 'no quarter' given. As the Russians went over the walls the Swedish commander again raised the white flag. Even then some posts continued firing and the assault continued. The Russians were finally successful and at 7 p.m. held the entire fortress.

Lacy, who had been wounded in the hand-to-hand fighting on Mill Ridge, stopped the slaughter by withdrawing his front-line regiments and replacing them with two fresh regiments. Wrangel was found wounded in a cellar where he formally surrendered the 1,500 remaining survivors. About 500 defenders escaped to the nearby woods but they too were rounded up the following day. Reports state that over 3,300 Swedes and Finns were lying dead on the field but others say 2,700 of the Finno-Swedish army died in battle or in the taking of the town. Among items captured were four standards, twelve colours, twelve guns, one mortar and a chest containing the payroll. Russian losses were 529 killed and 1,837 wounded, enlisted and officers. Buddenbrock made a half-hearted attempt to come to the assistance of Wrangel but upon learning of the disaster he wisely retired to Kvarnby. Lacy destroyed the fortress, burned the town of Willmanstrand and then retired to Viborg. Some complainers at court, none of whom were with the army in the field, believed that Lacy should have continued after Buddenbrock and taken Frederikshamn. But his report clearly stated that his losses of over 2,300 killed and wounded, along with the soldiers assigned to convey the wounded and prisoners to Viborg, precluded any more actions at that time. As it was, he only had two days' rations – it was fifty miles to Frederikshamn and he had no siege artillery – and then, if successful, he would have to march another seventy miles to safety in very disagreeable weather.

As it was, Lacy had 'cleared the decks'. It would be another year before it was evident even to his critics that what he had accomplished in his short campaign had paralysed the Swedish high command. In 1742 Lacy kept the Swedish commander, Levenhaupt, on the move from one position to another.[25] The former would never stand and fight and when finally trapped in the fortress city of Helsingfors, Levenhaupt surrendered his entire army, which numbered only 1,000 men less than Lacy's. Finally, in 1743, Lacy's amphibious campaigns against Finland ended the war in Russia's favour. In the meantime his captive, Wrangel, wounded in the arm and forced to remain in Russia until terms were agreed, found a safe and hospitable residence with Lacy at his home.[26]

At the close of May 1742 Lacy reviewed his military forces at Viborg in preparation for his next campaign against Sweden. It was a 36,000-man army of which upwards of 10,000 would go to Sweden in galleys to make an amphibious landing on its shores. Among Lacy's generals were Keith and Count Ulrich F.V. de Lowendahl, who later made a brilliant name for himself serving the French in the Netherlands. He also had several major-generals amongst whom was George Browne and Count Maurice Lacy, a relative who was also born in Limerick.[27]

In late June of that year Lacy and his army ventured forth

into Finland once again travelling over the worst imaginable roads to Helsingfors, the capital of Swedish Finland. Five days later they approached Mendolax, where the Swedes had established a 'strong point by nature, and rendered still stronger by art'. After some desultory fighting the Swedes withdrew. It was just as well because the place was so strong it was decided later that the Russian infantry storming it would have been decimated and probably failed to take it.

By 6 July the marshal and his generals reconnoitred Frederikshamn. By 9 or 10 July he was going to open trenches and establish his battery positions when the Swedes once again made it all unnecessary – they abandoned the town. To render the town useless to the Russians, the Swedes had made a booby trap of the entire town by filling houses with powder, bombs, grenades and anything else that would explode and cause death and destruction. One after another they went off, making the Russian entry slow and difficult and consequently diverting them from putting out the resulting fires. Lacy entered the town on 10 July without the loss of even one man and in thanks a *Te Deum* was sung for him in St Petersburg.

On 12 July the Russians arrived on the east bank of the Kymen River. Swedish batteries were on the opposite shore and immediately began pounding at the forming Russian cavalry. Lacy had them withdrawn into some woods nearby for protection. His guns came forward and with a few well-placed shots, silenced the enemy's artillery. The following day when most of his army had crossed the river, Lacy received orders from St Petersburg to hold the Kymen River line, but conclude the campaign.

Lacy immediately held a council of war with his generals. All the native Russian generals elected to submit to the orders; all the foreigners including Lacy decided to push forward and take Helsingfors while the momentum was still with them. After several unspectacular skirmishes the Russian army lay before Helsingfors but the Swedes once again elected to retire, this time to Turku which lay about a hundred miles west of Helsingfors. Unless Lacy could catch them he couldn't defeat them and they were always one or two steps ahead of him as they retreated.

As so often, his 'Irish luck' overcame many obstacles. A Finnish peasant came forward and offered to show Lacy how he could overtake the retreating Swedish army. The Finn took him and his staff to a place where, thirty years before, Peter the Great had built a road through what was now an impassable tangle of bushes and small trees. If cleared of the entanglements this roadway would allow the Russians to bypass any Swedish forces left to hold them at Helsingfors and obtain access to the road the Swedes would use on their way westward. Lacy's engineering officers concluded that the peasant was correct. Lacy had Lowendahl proceed with sixty-four companies of grenadiers and four battalions of regular infantry to recreate a passageway. By four in the morning the entire army was underway and by six o'clock, Lowendahl and his men had rejoined them.

When the Russians arrived at the road junction they saw in the near distance the van of the Swedish army. The Swedes were very surprised and retreated towards Helsingfors with Lacy chasing them. Upon their re-arrival the Swedes tried to create as strong a position as they possibly could before the expected Russian assault. Soon a Russian fleet blockaded the Swedes, effectively cutting off any possibility of provision or succour by land or sea. Lacy offered terms and the 17,000-man Swedish army submitted. Lacy's army's strength did not exceed the Swedes by more than 500 men. Because of the odds against the attacking force, it has been theorised that if Lacy had assaulted the fortress he most likely would have been decisively defeated. Once again victorious Lacy left behind a holding force and returned to Russia.[28]

A mutiny broke out among the Russian guards on Easter Sunday 1742 in St Petersburg. The mutineers were brutal to several foreign officers and indeed assaulted and badly handled a man named Sautron, Lacy's aide-de-camp. When Lacy had put down the mutiny the miscreants were placed in irons and punished. Lacy then had a picquet of loyal troops continuously on the streets with constant patrols, walking everywhere for the following five or six days and nights. The trouble finally quieted down and the inhabitants of that city were once again safe in their homes. Due credit was conveyed to Lacy for protecting 'Petersburg, and, perhaps, the whole empire'.

In 1743 the Russians used amphibious operations against Sweden. Most of the Russian army was carried by a great fleet of large vessels, ships of the line and frigates, and small galleys. Before Lacy and the fleet left St Petersburg, the Czarina Elizabeth came aboard Lacy's galley and assisted the priests at divine service. She then made Lacy a present of a 'ring of great value, and of a small golden cross containing some relics'. She returned to her palace and, watching from the windows, received a royal salute from Lacy as the fleet left the harbour. The Russian fleet of galleys made straight for Kronstadt where the large men of war lay in wait.

Lacy's force consisted of over a hundred galleys, many of which were built after the large Turkish style, capable of carrying eighty men plus provisions for a month. Besides the marshal there was one general, two lieutenant-generals, three major-generals, nine regiments of infantry, eight companies of grenadiers and 200 Don Cossacks and their horses. His galley fleet followed the ships of the line as far as Hanko which lay about a hundred miles beyond Helsingfors and, regardless of ice and late winter storms, they arrived intact on 6 June 1743.

Lacy decided he wanted to be victorious not only upon the

land but also on the sea. He directed Admiral Gollowin to attack the Swedish ships lying before them. Gollowin refused stating that Peter the Great had once given his fleet instructions that they were never to attack unless they had the advantage in numbers by at least three to two – and his ranking was only seventeen ships against twelve. Lacy went into a rage. As he entered in his memoirs: 'Nothing was done.' Aggravated, Lacy sent Gollowin seething messages when, finally, the admiral responded by requesting some of the large Turkish-style galleys to off-set what he perceived to be a deficiency between his and the larger Swedish fleet. Lacy sent him fourteen galleys as reinforcements.

When the Swedes saw Gollowin and his fleet finally making an aggressive move they weighed anchor. Both squadrons passed each other cannonading the other, neither having any advantage. Lacy and his fourteen galleys went after two Swedish ships of the line. The ships had been positioned so as to defeat any attempt Lacy would make to affect a passage to the city. He eventually made his way past them as his galleys drove them away. Lacy would have followed up on his success but a thick fog descended making observation nearly impossible. The Russian fleet had driven off the Swedes and on 23 June, Keith joined Lacy with his galleys.

At this point Lacy decided to take his entire fleet and descend upon the Swedish coast. The rendezvous was to be the island of Degerby, one of the Aland group of islands, which would put them within fifty miles of the coast, just north of Stockholm. On 29 June they arrived and the marshal signalled to get under way for the proposed descent upon Sweden. The whole plan fell apart when he received notice that preliminary agreements of peace had been signed between Russia and Sweden. Lacy and his disappointed force were ordered to return to St Petersburg.

The Empress Elizabeth had her own personal yacht sent to

pick up Lacy and hurry him to her court. Great rejoicing and celebrations were made in response to the treaty, and continued for several days. Lacy was the man of the hour but his hour was finally drawing to a close. As soon as he decently could, Lacy retired to his estates in Livonia, and officially took over the reins as governor of that state, remaining so until the day he died.

Lacy was truly a man of outstanding ability in an age when many of Russia's military men were primarily courtiers. One story told is that when another revolt occurred, which put Princess Elizabeth on the throne, the old man's sleep was shattered by a group of officers of the Guards. When he barely had his eyes open they demanded, 'Which sovereign do you support?' Quick as any Irish wit he responded: 'Why, the sovereign now sitting on the throne, of course.' Everyone had a laugh and with apologies they left him to continue his interrupted sleep. True to his word he did support whichever monarch sat on the throne. Lacy seems to have been entirely apolitical.

The balance of that story is told as follows: Lestock, Elizabeth's closest adviser, suggested that a number of individuals be arrested. Included amongst those were Marshal Münnich and his son, Lord Steward to the Grand Duchess, the other claimant to the throne. Before Lacy could hear from other sources that she had ascended the throne in a coup, she sent Lestock to Lacy to advise him that he was completely secure and safe, and was told to appear before her at once. That he did and was personally assured by Elizabeth of her affection.

According to his personal physician, Dr John Cook, Lacy caught a chill in 1750 while supervising the extinguishing of a severe fire in Riga. He made a last public appearance on New Year's Day, 1751, and was very ill from 19 April until his death on 30 April 1751. He was buried with great honours as befitted his great victories and position.

Lacy wasn't the only Irishman who found success in Czarist Russia, but he was the most eminent. He has been described, in the manner of that time, as 'tall and well made'. We know that in 1711 he married a widow, the countess Martha Philippina Frölich von Funken, a German Balt of the von Loeser family. Through her deceased husband von Funken, she had estates in southern Livonia. Since German was the language of the nobility of Livonia it is fairly certain that Lacy used it in his everyday conversations and other communications.

Three of his daughters married into the Livonian nobility while two married other expatriate officers in the Russian army, one an Irishman, Major-General George Browne of Limerick, and the other a Scotsman named Stuart. Lacy had three sons: the eldest, Michael, took service with Austria under Prince Eugène and was mortally wounded in 1735. The second son, Peter Andreas, served with the Polish-Saxon army. The younger, Franz Moritz Lacy (see Chapter 10) earned a reputation as famous his father's in the imperial service under both Maria Theresa and her son the Emperor Joseph II.

Lacy did very well for Russia and its rulers considering that he started with nothing but his name, honour and ability. His son, Franz Moritz, carried on the tradition and ensured that the name would never be forgotten, at least in the Austro-Hungarian Empire.

In 1891, 140 years after his death, this remarkable Irishman was commemorated with the naming of a division of the Russian army after him. But perhaps the highest accolade appeared in S.M. Soloviev's *Istoriia Rossii s drevnei-shikh vremen*: 'Soldiers expressed their feelings thus: "Even though he was a foreigner, he was a good man."'

DATES OF THE REIGNS OF THE RELEVANT HEADS OF STATE IN ENGLAND, FRANCE AND RUSSIA

ENGLAND

Stuart Dynasty
James I (1603–1625)
Charles I (1625–1649)

Commonwealth (Lord Protectors)
Oliver Cromwell (1653–1658)
Richard Cromwell (1658–1659)

Stuart Dynasty (restored)
Charles II (1649–1685)
James II (1685–1688)
Mary II (1689–1702)
William III of Orange (1702–1714, co-regent with Mary during her lifetime)
James III (The Pretender, 1701–1766, lived in exile for the entire duration of his 'reign')

RUSSIA

Romanov Dynasty
Peter I (the Great) (1682–1725)
Catherine I (1725–1727)
Peter II (1727–1730)
Anna (1730–1740)
Ivan VI (1740–1741)
Elizabeth (1741–1762)
Peter III (1762)
Catherine II (the Great) (1762–1796)
Paul I (1796–1801)
Alexander I (1801–1825)
Nicholas I (1825–1855)

FRANCE

Capetian Dynasty
Louis XIV (1643–1715)
Louis XV (1715–1774)
Louis XVI (1774–1792)

First Republic (1794–1804)
(Louis XVII titular head 1793–1795)

Bonaparte Dynasty
Napoleon I (1804–1814)

Capetian Dynasty (restored)
Louis XVIII (1814–1815)

Bonaparte Dynasty (restored)
Napoleon I (the Hundred Days) (March–June 1815)

Capetian Dynasty (restored)
Louis XVIII (1815–1824)
Charles X (1824–1830)

Bourbon-Orleans Dynasty
Louis Philippe I (1830–1848)

Bonaparte Dynasty (restored)
Napoleon III (1852–1870)

Endnotes

Preface

1   When the revolutionaries overthrew the monarchy, the reactionary Franco-Irish left France and some even went so far as to volunteer their services to the British King, an offer that was accepted.

Chapter 1

1   The non-conformers were just as cruel and inhuman, when they had their chance, as those who obeyed the rules.
2   So as not to lose their meagre holdings, this forced many an eldest son to convert to the Protestant faith.

Chapter 2

1   Louis renounced the limited freedom that certain, but not all, Protestants were allowed in France.
2   A descendent of the Irish family of Wallis that had established itself in Austria more than a hundred years earlier.
3   Cumberland was known in Scotland as 'The Butcher' for his slaughter of defeated Scots after Culloden in 1746.
4   The main British support on the continent was money, and they now cut all subsidies.
5   The Empress Elizabeth of Russia hated Frederick with a passion. Her death and the accession of her nephew Peter to the throne was what saved Frederick. His admiration for Frederick was

incomprehensible to everyone. His German wife, Catherine II, overthrew Peter and ascended the throne but did not re-enter the war on either side.

Chapter 3

1 Parker (1972), pp. 271–272

2 Although this move eventually led to the creation of an Irish Brigade in Spain as well as in France, many more Irish soldiers were set adrift than could be accommodated in both nations and other European armies benefited from the wanderers. Many went to central Europe and others to northern Europe and Russia.

3 Some have questioned why a relative youngster was awarded command of the regiment. It has been suggested that Daniel O'Mahoney was responsible, or perhaps even the Duke of Berwick.

4 See G.B. Clark (forthcoming), *Irish Brigades of France and Spain* for full details.

5 A small three-masted schooner usually found in the Mediterranean.

Chapter 4

1 Some sources give the parental names as Dermod and Mary Moriarity O'Mahoney, and others as 'Joan', birth date unknown. See D. Carney, *The Irish Sword*, 1980, p. 95 for a detailed refutation. Another source is the application made in O'Mahoney's name for the Order of Calatrava, 17 May 1711. His grandfather is stated as being Cornelius O'Mahoney and grandmother, Catherine FitzGerald. See M.K. Walsh, *Spanish Knights of Irish Origin*, volume 1. The O'Mahoney's were well represented on the Dingle peninsula. Some of the kin from Clare even claimed descent from Brian Boru. I can find no information about his

early life except that his kinsmen claimed close relationship to most of the important people of Kerry.

2 This is according to O'Callaghan (1870). In the Chevalier Gaydon's memoir of the Regiment of Dillon he insists that Captain James Dillon commanded in the absence of other senior officers of the regiment. When he was wounded a 'Captain' MacDonagh assumed command. It appears that O'Mahoney, a 'reform captain', was an aide to Count Revel who took command of Cremona when Villeroi was captured. According to Revel he sent O'Mahoney to command both Bourke's and Dillon's Regiments which was why O'Mahoney became so well known.

3 O'Conor (1845), p. 245. Lieutenant-General Arthur Dillon, the colonel of the regiment, was somewhere else, perhaps even back in Paris.

4 He, according to O'Conor (1845), p. 246, was 'a great martinet' and had left orders for his unit to be up and ready to parade at daybreak.

5 O'Callaghan (1870), p. 216.

6 Named for King James II's illegitimate son by Arabella Churchill – she being the sister of John Churchill, Duke of Marlborough. The uncle and nephew fought against each other many times during this period. The major difference between them was that Berwick was always loyal to his father, the King, while Churchill betrayed James II.

7 Most likely Daniel O'Carroll, Colonel of Berwick's Regiment, in Italy from 1701–1706.

8 These figures are from O'Callaghan (1870). Other sources cite 4,000 French and 2,000 losses for the imperial army.

9 This meant that O'Mahoney was now proprietor of his own regiment, an income provider of no little substance for men of small means. He, of course, as was usually the case, was leading many other troops elsewhere.

10 O'Callaghan (1870), p. 235.

11 This wasn't the only time that Peterborough (Mordaunt) was guilty of less than honourable conduct. In later years his wife refused to allow his memoirs to be published after his death because 'he had confessed, he had been guilty of 3 CAPITAL CRIMES, before he was 21'. Quoted in O'Callaghan (1870), p. 241, note.

12 O'Callaghan (1870), p. 245.

13 Berwick's army units, it was claimed, weren't complete, with many companies badly understaffed. It also seems that the artillery wasn't taken into account; it was an uncertain number, and was little used during the forthcoming battle.

14 As in most armies of western Europe, the Irish officers were numerous but there were only two Irish regiments. However, they would both play a prominent part.

15 Churchill (1934), p. 259 as quoted by Petrie. But also seen in much earlier correspondence about an entirely different period and battle.

16 One of the battalions were of those Irish which had deserted Marlborough in 1702.

17 O'Mahoney was not supervising his regiment, he instead commanded the left wing of the second line.

18 O'Callaghan (1870), p. 250.

19 According to O'Callaghan (1870), p. 276, the *Fameux Mahoni* was also known as 'the Murat of his day'.

20 By this date, like France, Spain had established an Irish Brigade. The names of the regiments, as in France, changed over the years. But the Brigade in Spain lasted well over a hundred years and its regiments, like their French brethren, earned many laurels.

21 Regiments were given to outstanding soldiers and they 'owned' this regiment, which provided them with a source of income. The colonel-proprietor of a regiment could also negotiate all business

transactions within the regiment including but not limited to purchasing supplies, contracting for uniforms, transportation of goods and services, and recovery of soldiers' pay upon their death.

22 O'Callaghan (1870), p. 278. The names were slightly askew. They were, of course, MacDonnell, MacAuliffe and Comerford. It is somewhat difficult to track down Irish names in Europe when the names were frequently mangled.

23 *Ibid.*, p. 280.

24 *Ibid.*

25 The Regiment of Edinburgo was formerly a regiment of O'Mahoney's Dragoons.

26 O'Callaghan (1870), pp. 204–205; Hayes (1949), pp. 240–241.

27 O'Callaghan (1870), p. 205.

Chapter 5

1 The nickname credited to O'Reilly in later years, possibly because he studied that great man's work closely and even fought against him for a period of time.

2 Irlanda had been formed in France in 1699 as the Regiment of Bourke from disbanded Irish troops (Treaty of Ryswick) under the command of Colonel Walter Bourke and began their service in Italy. After the War of the Spanish Succession the regiment passed from the French to the Spanish army in 1715.

3 This war, which Britain declared in 1739, had the unusual title of 'The War of Jenkin's Ear'. Supposedly, a British seaman captured by the Spaniards had his ear cut off and Great Britain went to war because of it. The real reason, of course, was the trade rivalry between Spain and Britain, especially the slave trade. Although Britain had several successes in the Americas, the English admiral Edward Vernon was badly beaten at Cartagena on the Caribbean coast of Columbia.

4   This campaign was an off-shoot of the War of the Austrian Succession.

5   The Irish Brigade of Spain was heavily engaged in the Battle of Camposanto as were several notable Irish officers in the Austrian service.

6   Browne was born in Basel, Switzerland, in 1705, the son of Ulysses Brown and Anna FitzGerald who were passing through on their way to his post in the Austrian army. The Brownes were from an ancient Norman-Irish family, as were the FitzGeralds of Desmond. The 'von' was part of his ennoblement in the imperial service.

7   When he ascended the throne of Prussia, Frederick had the distinct good fortune to have a ready-made, first class, well disciplined army. But it was his audacity and skill that made it into the finest trained fighting machine in Europe and probably the world. Not many Catholics served in the Prussian army, but Austria openly welcomed Irishmen to their country.

8   During most of the century the Austrian army was engaged in warfare against, and sometimes with, the Prussians, French, Italians, Turks and Russians. Irish soldiers fought on every side (perhaps excluding the Turks) and earned notable reputations, plus high rank and wealth. The Irish were numerous in Austria and achieved great glories which their religion forbade them in their own country.

9   Nothing ever came of his suggestion but the Irish continued to go to Spain and its colonies for many years to come. One notable, Ambrosio O'Higgins, an Irish peddler who caught the crown's fancy, bred a son with one of Chile's most prominent daughters. His son was named Bernardo and, with a few other patriots, he later helped free South America of colonial domination by Spain. Unfortunately, O'Higgins senior was considered, by the Spanish crown, to be a Spanish noble and consequently not allowed to

marry a colonial, even one of high rank. Bernardo, therefore, was technically illegitimate.

10 There were a number of distinctive military orders in Spain. The Knights of Alcantara was one of the most desired and generally held for those whose services to Spain were superlative. A listing of some of his sponsors included a Jacobo MacSweeny, Antonio O'More, Edmundo O'Ryan, Daniel O'Sulivan, Daniel MacCarty and Phelipe Kearney.

11 Reported in J.D.L. Holmes (1965), p. 18.

12 For a more detailed account of Spain's influence in Louisiana and especially for O'Reilly's numerous administrative successes see J.F. McDermott (1974).

13 Their responses are listed in David K. Bjork (1924), pp. 20–39.

14 They were Augustin, Juan, Juan Bautista, Luis and Theodore, and they were possibly brothers.

15 The Corsairs had a long and bloody history. One historian claims they were the descendants of those Moors whom Spain had driven from the country in the late fifteenth century. They attacked Spain and her galleons in reprisal for their loss of lands and other valuables. The Corsairs also attacked anyone else in the Mediterranean that came with their grasp. They were a type of pirate.

16 In the sixteenth century many Moriscos, including those members of the Islamic faith who were forcibly converted to the Christian faith, clandestinely left Spain for North Africa. They were enemies of Spain and in the forefront of those who levelled attacks against her. This of course was another excuse that Spain used during its crusade – to bring the fallen back into the true faith.

17 The Creaghs originated in Ireland and this one was possibly from County Clare, the home of most of that ancient Irish family name.

18 A rather interesting alternative version of events to that of the

Algerians: the Duke of Gloucester, brother of George III, told a Neapolitan Minister that 'O'Reilly is going to take the Spanish fleet to his native land – Ireland I mean'. When the Neapolitan replied that Carlos III would never take advantage of any nation that was so engrossed with the war in the colonies (the American colonies) Gloucester responded: 'I can assure you that if Spain were in this position ... we should not hesitate to invade Cuba.'

19 Charles V, Holy Roman Emperor, landed on 20 October 1541 in spite of having been warned by Admiral Andrea Doria that the seas were troublesome. A storm erupted and destroyed much of the fleet; the Algerians attacked them with the result that of the 21,000-man force, one third was destroyed. The survivors managed to make their way back to Europe.

20 Well-trained, disciplined Irish troops from France accompanied Charles Stuart in his vainglorious attempts to win back the throne for the Stuarts in 1745–1746. After the defeat at Culloden, they held off the victorious English forces who were chasing the Scottish Highlanders, allowing many to get to safety before the 'Butcher' (Duke of Cumberland) could get them. The 'Butcher' boy and his lads slaughtered many more in the days following. Most of the victims were wounded and devoid of weapons and had little chance of defending themselves.

21 This seems more accurate.

22 This is a most senseless argument: the man in command on the ground had orders not to advance if drawn forward by the Algerians, and should have carried them out. He failed to do so.

23 This chapter has been greatly enhanced by two articles published in *The Irish Sword*, a general biographical article by Eric Beerman and another by John de Courcy Ireland. The many successes O'Reilly had in Louisiana were mainly of an administrative nature and have not been included.

Chapter 6

1 François Michel Le Tellier, Marquis de Louvois, French Minister of War, 1666–1672.

2 Monmouth was an illegitimate son of Charles II.

3 Sarsfield is too well known to be included here but it should be mentioned that his career, until cut short in French wars, included valuable service during the War of Three Kings in 1689 in Ireland. He was in command at Limerick when the Irish army surrendered and brought most of the army to France.

4 Drake, P., *Amiable Renegade: The Memoirs of Captain Peter Drake 1671–1753*.

5 Wogan was selected to find an appropriate princess for the Stuart pretender by James III himself. Travelling about Europe Wogan settled upon the dispossessed Sobieski heiress. She was pretty, her family had legitimate claims to the throne of Poland, and she was a Roman Catholic.

6 Peasants of Brittany who supported the Bourbons. They continued to oppose Napoleon as late as 1803.

7 Leader of the Royalist conspiracy who was eventually captured and executed in 1804.

Chapter 7

1 The name Jennings originated from the Norman-French Jenin, which became MacSeinin or MacJonin – son of Jenin (diminutive of Jean). The family was a branch of the Burkes of Connacht, the name being adopted by one of the latter called Seinín or little John (Burke).

2 The title, 'Baron of Kilmaine', was taking a liberty. Or as one note alluding to it states, it was 'a mythical one'. This wasn't unusual; most Irish on the continent, those who could get away with 'doctoring' their previous lives, did so. It helped them to advance.

3   At this time, Colonel Charles MacMahon was commanding the regiment. Because 'Kilmaine' was in common use as his name, I will use it.

4   Interestingly, in 1940 the Germans' armoured onslaught through those same woods caught the Allies completely unprepared and caused their defeat. It had 'never' been done before.

5   The documents quoted in this chapter are sourced from Hayes (1934).

6   During his period of incarceration, Kilmaine was moved at least four times to different places.

7   On St Patrick's Day 1798, Kilmaine was the chief guest at an Irish banquet in Paris and many notable Irishmen were present. Napper Tandy presided and had Kilmaine on his right hand and the revolutionary apostle, Thomas Paine, on his left. Many patriotic speeches were delivered and the toast of the Irish Republic was drunk on enthusiasm.

Chapter 8

1   More often than not young Irishmen were signed up in their father's or uncle's regiments almost at birth. This gave them precedence and opened doors for the future.

2   Anon., *Campaigns of the Armies of France*, Vol. 4, (1908) p. 209, note 2.

3   At the urging of the British authorities Theobald Wolfe Tone had left Ireland with his family in May 1795 and gone to the United States. Obtaining letters of introduction from the French Minister in Philadelphia to the Committee of Public Safety in Paris, he arrived in France in February 1796.

4   Paul François de Barras, a French revolutionary, had been Napoleon's patron and protector and introduced the younger man to his own mistress, Josephine de Beauharnais, whom Napoleon

later married. As Napoleon's star rose, Barras' went into decline, though they apparently remained friends for many years after.

5 Cronin (1972), pp. 122–123.

6 When discussing with Bonaparte the possibility of making Italy a republic, Clarke's response was 'the slavish Italians are not ripe for liberty', a proposition to which many Italians also assented. Cronin (1972), p. 139.

7 Castelot (1971), p. 89.

8 Louis Antoine Fauvelet Bourrienne, a school friend of Napoleon's who became his private secretary in 1797 but in 1804 was fired for theft or embezzlement. On 18 May 1804, Napoleon was proclaimed Emperor of France

9 General Armand Augustin Louis de Caulaincourt, the Marquis, Duke de Vinceza, became Napoleon's Master of Horse, and took part in a number of military campaigns. He wrote a memoir that is considered a vital source for the events of 1812–1814. General Jean-Baptiste Juvenal Corbineau, discoverer of the vital ford over the Beresina, which enabled the French to escape their Russian pursuers, also saved Napoleon's life at Brienne. General Geraud Christophe Michel Duroc, Duke de Frioul, served with Napoleon in Austria, Prussia and Poland and was mortally wounded in Silesia on 22 May 1813.

10 Anon., *Campaigns of the Armies of France*, Vol. 4, (1908) p. 209.

11 Marshal Louis-Alexandre Berthier, Prince de Neuchâtal et de Wagram, later chief-of-staff of the Grande Armée in Russia, amongst many other posts.

12 General Antoine Lavalette, Napoleon's military postmaster, quoted in Elting (1988), p. 57.

13 In 1809 he was created Duke of Feltre, named after a town in north-eastern Italy.

14 Joseph Fouché, Duke d'Otranto, supported Bonaparte at Brumaire and was placed in position as Minister of Police from

which he managed to silence most opposition to Napoleon. Then he reversed that position to become his enemy.

15 Marshal Jean-Baptiste Jules Bernadotte, Prince de Ponte Corvo, later a King of Sweden, married Napoleon's first love, Desirée Cleary (also Clary), a daughter of Irish parents, in 1798. He and Napoleon did not get along and he was a constant thorn in Bonaparte's side.

16 Charles Fagan, born in Killarney c. 1760, had been a captain in Dillon's Regiment until the revolution. He briefly left France and returned in 1802 after the Peace of Amiens. When hostilities with England broke out once again, Fagan was arrested and incarcerated as a prisoner of war. In 1809 Fouché had him brought to Paris where he entrusted Fagan with his proposal for peace negotiations with England.

Upon Fagan's return from England in 1810, he was promptly arrested and imprisoned on a charge of exceeding his instructions. Napoleon had the charges quashed and within twenty-four hours Fagan was at liberty with apologies from the Emperor and thanks for the distinguished manner in which he carried out his instructions. Fagan died of natural causes on 6 March 1813.

17 The Duke of Wellington's older brother.

18 Connelly (1968), pp. 147–149. Marshal Jean-Baptiste Jourdan had been transferred in 1807 to be chief-of-staff to Joseph Bonaparte in Spain. He later commanded a corps and suffered several major defeats. He was recalled to France and fired.

19 *Ibid.*, p. 154. It appears that with proper handling, Joseph's force was certainly in much better shape than any possible combined English force would be.

20 *Ibid.*, p. 159.

21 *Ibid.*, p. 159.

22 Marshal Jacques Etienne Joseph Alexandre MacDonald, son of Scottish Jacobites, born in France, like Clarke initially served

with an Irish regiment. His public defence of Marshal Moreau against charges of treason in 1804 angered Napoleon and he was dismissed.

23 Luvaas (1999), p. 21.

24 *Ibid.*, p. 17.

25 *Ibid.*, p. 16.

26 Castelot (1971), p. 397.

27 Alexander (1985), p. 58.

28 Schom (1997), p. 576.

29 Quoted in Elting, *Swords Around the Throne*, p. 355.

30 Daniel's twin brother, William, was in Clare's Regiment and later in Berwick's. He later joined the newly created Irish Legion and soon became aide-de-camp to Clarke. He had a good career, retiring as general of brigade.

31 General Claude François de Malet built a long career in opposition to everyone and anyone, especially Bonaparte. He was incarcerated numerous times and during the last imprisonment made an agreement to live in a private mental institution in Paris. He found ways to escape but was caught, tried and executed with his fourteen accomplices on 29 October 1812.

32 Second Consul Jean Jacques Regis Cambacérès, a lawyer who supported Napoleon at Brumaire, had made a large contribution to the development and enactment of the Civil Code. He became Prince, Arch-Chancellor and Duke of Parma until 1814 when he supported the Bourbons, then returned to Napoleon's side in 1815.

33 A Parisian newspaper, usually giving the government's position.

34 Connelly (1968), p. 220.

35 Alexander (1985), pp. 217–218.

36 Marshal Nicolas Jean de Dieu Soult, succeeded Jourdan as Joseph's chief-of-staff.

37 Lachouque (1961) claims the words were 'Joseph is an ass ...

Clarke an old woman ... where is my wife? My son? The enemy? The army?'

38 Marshal Laurent Gouvion Saint-Cyr held various commands. After joining the Bourbons he briefly became Minister of War. It is questionable whether Saint-Cyr ever held the post permanently or just on an interim basis.

39 Certainly as late as March, Clarke is quoted as having told Marie-Louise at Blois: 'As long as one village remains in the Emperor's hands it is there that I shall be found, rallying round me all the troops that are still faithful.'

40 Elting (1988) suggests that during this period, Clarke formed a spy ring to act against Napoleon but gives no evidence to support that theory.

41 Quoted in Stenger, *The Return of Louis XVIII*, p. 308.

42 If this was true Clarke certainly didn't tap the displaced King's treasury, for there was little enough money in those coffers. We have to assume that he made himself affluent while Napoleon's Minister of War, yet everyone noted that he was 'honest'. His family was comfortable but evidently not rich.

43 Stenger (1909), p. 381.

44 According to Hall, she and her sister waited for Clarke to make an appearance and as they attempted to beg his intercession 'he thrust them aside and continued on his way'.

45 Comte Charles Artois, Louis XVIII's younger brother.

46 When Saint-Cyr was appointed Minister of War he brought many of the old Bonaparte officers and soldiers into the new army. His successor was obliged to get rid of them for treasonable actions and utterances, proving that Clarke was harsh but correct.

47 France had, after all, been at war with its neighbours since early in Louis XIV's reign; more than 150 years. France, with the largest population in Europe, was still a threat.

48 I can't conceive of how that may have happened, Clarke being

definitely of Irish ancestry. Perhaps he knew of some Norman blood that modern records don't display.

Chapter 9

1   O'Callaghan, (1870), pp. 601–602.

2   With the possible exception of Butler's regiment.

3   Walter Butler's chaplain was a Thomas Carve. Carve may have originally been Garvey.

4   Butler had served Poland since at least 1619 when he recruited Irishmen for Polish service.

5   According to Henning, Deveroux, (as he spelled it) struck the fatal blow, but gave Wallenstein time to say an act of contrition.

6   Butler was the son of Peter Butler of Roscrea, County Tipperary. The family had been deprived of its estates by James I in 1616. The earliest record of Walter Butler's service on the continent is in 1620 when he fought at the Battle of White Hill, the opening battle of the Thirty Years' War. There were at least five other officers named Butler in imperial service during this period.

7   Monro (1999), p. 160.

8   *Ibid.*, p. 163. Monro also added in a letter that he wished to 'see his Armie [that of the Prince Elector of Palatine] should be all of Britaines, Dutch, and Irish ...', p. 50.

9   I believe that the other Butler the King was asking about was James Butler, his father or uncle.

10 Alexander Leslie gained a reputation fighting for the Swedes during this period. His only major defeat was in 1642 at the hands of Owen Roe O'Neill in Ireland while leading the Scottish forces. He turned his command over to his subordinate, Monro. Monro was thoroughly defeated at Benburb.

11 Monro (1999), p. 201.

12 Henning (1952), pp. 35–36.

13 The name Wallis is sometimes derived from Walsh but also from the Scottish name, Wallace; there were also some Irish-born bearing the same name.

14 The title 'Carlingford' was presented to his father, Theobald, after the restoration of Charles II because of his friendship and his help in several diplomatic endeavours in 1665–1666.

15 The proprietorship of a regiment was a social leveller as well as an income producer. Any and every income source was important to those who didn't have estates or a private income that would ensure comfort in their old age. With it a man, no matter how or where he was born, was a figure of some consequence in the Empire. There were only so many regiments to go around and the Irish, to the chagrin of many socialites who felt more deserving, eventually owned several of them. So if you see reference to the Regiment O'Donnell or Kelly or whatever, the rankers weren't necessarily Irish but the colonel proprietor was.

16 This information on Taaffe can be heavily attributed to an article by Harman Murtagh in *The Irish Sword*, Vol. XV, (1983), pp. 255–257.

17 Quoted in Duffy (1964), p. 6.

18 There is a story about him that deserves re-telling. It seems that he was cosy with the daughter of an enlisted soldier. He refused to marry the girl because he claimed to already have a wife in Dublin. The court was about to nail him when it was learned that the plaintiff's daughter was chasing another man. MacDonnell got away with paying a modest sum for his freedom.

19 That situation would change, especially during the Napoleonic Wars when England needed bodies to fill the ranks of units being sent all over the globe as well as to the continent. Later, in the nineteenth century, Irish Protestants absorbed command of the British army and the ranks were heavily populated with Irish Catholics.

20 *The Irish Sword*, Vol. XV, No. 61, Winter 1983, pp. 267–270. The title translated is 'The Irish, Scottish, and English element in the Imperial Army'. For this Schmidhofer was awarded a degree of Doctor of Philosophy in 1971.

21 *The Irish Sword*, Vol. XVII, No. 67, Winter 1987/Summer 1988, pp. 116–119. O'Neill's article gives a superb overview of the period insofar as the Irish in Austria are concerned.

22 *The Irish Sword*, Vol. III, No. 10, Summer 1957, 'Replies 33', 'Irish Units in the imperial Service', pp. 74–75. Dr Christopher Duffy added many names in later issues of the same journal as did Dr Micheline Kerney Walsh.

23 K.J. O'Malley, *The Irish Sword*, Winter 1998, pp. 220–221.

24 For a biography of Maximilian Browne see Duffy, (1964).

25 Count Andreas Hamilton, who in 1738 was the proprietor of the 7th Kürassier (Bohemian Dragoons).

26 I cannot locate a regiment with that name during the period. Probably it is the regiment formed in 1721 as the Spanish Kürassier Regiment Emanuel Sylva Mendoza de Galbes. Sometime after 1756 this became the O'Donell (5th) Kürassier Regiment.

27 There is a question as to who was left in command. Duffy states it was O'Donnell but other sources suggest either Franz Lacy or, worse, a combination of both. Whichever it was, Lacy took most of the heat for the eventual defeat.

28 R.S. O'Cochlain in *The Irish Sword*, Summer 1956, pp. 267–269.

29 G. Rothenberg, (1998).

30 J.E. de Courcy Ireland, *The Irish Sword*, Summer 1974.

31 Karl, the grand-nephew of Franz Joseph, succeeded him on his death on 21 November 1916.

Chapter 10

1   Now a part of Latvia and Estonia.

2   Translated it reads: 'For Maurice Lacy, Supreme Commander [General-in-Chief?] of the army, who, in the military knowledge of a teacher and friend, taught the army to conquer by means of the arts of war and peace and to return unconquered by virtue of these, his own arts. Joseph II, Emperor in gratitude ordered this monument to be erected.'

3   Kotasek (1956), p. 4. See also, O'Neill, J. and F. G. Thompson, *The Irish Sword*, Summer 1987.

4   Lacy's sister, Helene Marthe, married General George Browne, an Irish soldier also in Russian service who had considerable adventures. He and Maximilian Browne were cousins.

5   Quoted in Duffy, (1977) p. 172.

6   The Prussians lost over 3,000 but the Austrians, even in defeat and when routed, had 200 fewer casualties.

7   Quoted in Duffy, p. 188.

8   The Queen-Empress' chief financial adviser.

9   Wraxall, as quoted in Duffy (1977), tells of the genuine dismay amongst the senior Austrians over Keith's death. Especially Lacy who moaned 'Alas! Tis my father's best friend, 'tis Keith ... At so melancholy a piece of intelligence, von Daun burst into tears as did Lacy, and every person present.' Keith was the brother of the Earl Marshal of Scotland.

10 Frederick was almost always better than anyone the Austrians put up against him, including Loudon, Lacy and von Daun. Browne was the exception. In any other period, against almost anyone else, they would all have excelled on any battlefield.

11 Quoted in Duffy (1977), p. 198.

12 Frederick had continued the practice begun by his father. Enlisting men from other countries was the only way he could maintain his sizeable personnel. Service in the Prussian army

was severe and finding more men to die under harsh conditions was difficult.

13 Some say as small as 20,000 men.

14 Also known as Zieten.

15 Lacy has been blamed for the loss by some historians and also, according to Szabo, for 'divine stupidity'. Von Daun acknowledged that the entire army blamed Lacy. But was he, after all, the ground commander? O'Donnell was designated commander of von Daun's army but his main role in the battle was as leader of his heavy cavalry, which he was accused of not using when he should have. For this deleterious behaviour Lacy's reputation with military historians as a field commander has suffered dramatically and perhaps unfairly.

16 Quoted in Duffy (1977), p. 206.

17 See Kotasek (1956), pp. 24–70, for excellent coverage of this period.

18 Maria Theresa gave much of the credit for the establishment of the canton and conscription plans to Lacy. He requested that she give his mentor, von Daun, equal credit. It appears from the records that Lacy originated the ideas and plans for their implementation, while von Daun fully supported his concepts.

19 Kotasek (1956), pp. 78–79.

20 Up until the period under review, recruiting was entirely up to the regiment. It was obviously haphazard at best.

21 According to Kotasek (1956) pp. 246–249, Joseph greatly admired Lacy.

22 In order to cushion the outrageous shock of appointing a young foreigner, Maria Theresa retired the senior chief commissary, Count Rudolph Chotek, on full pay and Field Marshal Carl Colloredo was given the direction of the service academies. There were other rearrangements in order to make the appointment more palatable.

23 Eleonore was also not fond of Joseph whom she thought 'impenetrable' and cold though apparently he had little trouble with her since she was alluded to be his mistress, or at least so her husband believed. Perhaps Lacy, a notorious womaniser, found her cold, or vice versa. He is said to have had her, or her sister, or both, as mistresses.

24 The selling of commissions was an extremely lucrative business.

25 Quoted in Beales (1987), p. 184. The Staatsrat was an unofficial advisory body with no discernible power other than through the Emperor. Membership was seemingly important as a matter of prestige.

26 Quoted in Duffy (1977), p. 128.

27 Until this time obtaining transport, even during wartime, meant contracting for services with civilians who might own one or hundreds of wagons with horses. They in turn would hire drivers. Sometimes in battle zones supply wagons never made an appearance. Lacy changed all that for Austria.

28 Beales (1987), p. 185.

29 Roughly translated: 'If you desire peace, prepare for war.'

30 The empire consisted mainly of lands in the Germanic states. The heritage lands (the term for lands belonging to the Austrian crown) included the Austrian Netherlands, portions of northern Italy and Hungary.

31 Beales (1987), pp. 185–86.

32 *Ibid.*, p. 187.

33 *Ibid.*, p. 257.

34 This essentially was the same Austrian policy as on the eve of the First World War. War with Russia, regardless of the obvious suicidal consequences.

35 Lacy was right. Russia had finally, with the aid of foreign officers, created an extremely powerful military force that continued powerful until the early half of the nineteenth century. For details

on Russia's army see Duffy (1981).

36 Kotasek (1956), especially pp. 80–83, 92–95, 97–100.

37 A sister of Eleonore.

38 Kotasek (1956), p. 253.

39 Beales (1978), p. 227.

40 *Ibid.*, p. 228.

41 Field Marshal Count James Robert Nugent, born at Castlenugent, Ireland, in 1720.

42 Kotasek (1956), p. 220, also Duffy (1977), p. 41.

43 O'Neill and Thompson, *The Irish Sword*, Vol. XVII, No. 66, p. 2.

44 Beales (1978), p. 201.

45 Duffy (1977), p. 212.

46 *Ibid.*

47 Quoted in Duffy (1977), p. 208.

48 It is said to be located in the Vienna Woods. Possibly Lacy, like many of the upper classes of that time, had two residences, the second being named Dornbach. It is also possible that the two residences were really one. Kotasek makes several references to 'new forest' which she identifies as his resting place.

Chapter 11

1 Robert Cecil, First Earl of Salisbury, secretary of state, 1596–1608.

2 Modern historians find a great deal of fault with those numbers, generally conceding to no more than 2,000 over a great length of time.

3 This was because the 'legitimate' Roman Catholic King Sigismund was deposed from the Swedish throne because of his religion. The war was between Catholic reformers and those Protestants who didn't want to be reformed. The Irish were being persuaded to desert for service in Spain or other Catholic countries.

4   Bagwell (1963), Vol. 1, p. 100.

5   The trouble, as almost always, had to do with the differences in religion. By 1631 Sweden and its King were the defenders of Protestantism in Europe.

6   While engaged in research, the Reverend F. Winston Leyland determined that the Austrian and Russian Brownes were descended from a common ancestor, Ulysses Browne. *The Irish Sword*, Vol. VIII, No. 31, Winter 1967, pp. 146–147.

7   In later years he was said to have married 'a Baltic noblewoman', who happened to be Lacy's daughter. That would have been his first cousin. There was no known issue.

8   Polontsov, A. A., *Russian Biographical Dictionary*, states that 1725 was the year he left Ireland. I have accepted a different source, which gives the date he joined the Russian army, at the advanced age of twenty-seven.

9   Was this son from the first marriage to Eileen? He might have been married to Lacy's daughter long enough to have a child in that marriage, but it isn't clear what happened to his first wife.

10   The source (Jordon, 1954) isn't clear as to what that title meant but I have assumed it meant that he was actually chief-of-staff to von Daun or Lorraine. Therefore he issued orders from them to the field commanders.

11   Though the date 1915 is used by my source (McEntee, 1937, pp. 309–311), I believe that the correct date should be 1916.

12   Hayes, R., 'Irishmen in the Naval Services of Continental Europe', *The Irish Sword*, Vol. I, No. 4, 1952–1953, p. 315.

13   Jordon, J., *The Irish Sword*, 1954, pp. 54–61.

Chapter 12

1   Although, from the early eighteenth century until well into the nineteenth century, if a man wasn't a Baltic German he

had problems. During this time the Russian nation was, for all intents and purposes, run by the German Balts from the recently conquered territories along the southern coast of the Baltic Sea.

2   When the Irish army of James II was defeated in 1690, many if not most of the soldiers left Ireland for France.

3   He was frequently referred to as 'Augustus the Strong'. He was said to be the father of over 300 illegitimate children.

4   Croy had vast experience with the Austrian and Danish forces. Croy could speak no Russian, but was in command of an army of more than 40,000 largely composed of mercenary foreigners led by foreigners. The Russian 'army' was then composed of a primitive militia, and generally kept at home.

5   The Lesna was on the Polish-Ukrainian line near the modern Brest. The River Desna flowed south from a large lake near the city of Kiev. At least 300 miles separate the two.

6   Quoted in O'Callaghan (1870), p. 483.

7   Prince Aleksandr Danilovich Menshikov, soldier and statesman for Peter the Great.

8   She was born in Livonia of German Balt ancestry. Interestingly the second Catherine, also 'the Great', was not Russian either. She too was German.

9   The French had refused to accept the Austrian 'Pragmatic Sanction' while Russia and eventually Augustus, for Saxony, had both approved it. The sanction was arranged by Maria Theresa of Austria's father, Charles VI, to force the various 'important' heads of state in Europe to agree that his daughter would be his legitimate successor. Most, with reservations, did, but Frederick wanted Silesia as a prize for his approval and when refused, he invaded. Austria went with its supporters. The Czarina didn't like the way Louis XV oscillated in the matter of Courland, hence Russia's involvement against France.

10 At least the ruling Polish nobles didn't want a King chosen by

the Russians, which caused Lacy some real trouble. They were ruling the 'republic' themselves and wanted no interference.

11 Other sources make it 30,000 men. Lithuania and Poland were then combined into a republic. They had earlier been combined and were hampered by their inability to rule themselves. Each noble was 'King' and could veto any measure agreed to by everyone else.

12 Biron was a former stable-hand in the Czarina's employ. He hated everyone and it was reciprocated. The difference was, he was her lover.

13 Eventually, in November 1738, the Treaty of Vienna firmly established Augustus III as King of Poland.

14 With the promotion he also received orders to join the Russian force then assembling for an attack upon Azov, an extremely important fortress at the northern end of the Sea of Azov, a few miles west of the modern city of Rostov.

15 I have a 1737 list of the most important people in the Russian government and army, many of whom were German. Over half of the military leaders were foreigners but Lacy was the only Irishman.

16 The numbers have been variously stated as 58–60,000, but 40,000 seems more accurate. In those times a Russian regiment was composed of two battalions. The manpower of each regiment was supposed to total 1,280 rank and file plus an additional 295 officers and non-commissioned officers. A dragoon regiment numbered 1,231 rankers plus officers and non-commissioned officers as above.

17 Lacy had been especially ordered by the Empress to leave western Europe and to take charge of the siege which had been going badly under Münnich. The quote is from von Manstein's memoirs.

18 Both the Mius and Kalmius Rivers drained into the Sea of Azov.

They are about 100 miles apart with the former north-east of the latter.

19 Probably Count Otto Douglas, formerly in the Swedish army of Charles XII, who changed sides after Poltava.

20 Also known as the Scoungar. Neither name can be located on modern maps.

21 In the past, the stronghold had survived many Russian assaults with resulting enormous casualties. In fact, in Russian-style warfare heavy casualties were generally expected.

22 Turku is now Abo, Willmanstrand is Lappenranta, Tavastehus is Hämeenlinna, Helsingfors is Helsinki, and Frederikshamn is now Hamina.

23 Lieutenant-General James Keith was the brother of the Earl-Marischal of Scotland. He became a field marshal while serving under Frederick the Great until he fell at Hochkirch, in 1758. Keith's death greatly bothered those Irish in Maria Theresa's army, such as his friend, Franz Moritz Lacy, who were fighting opposite him on that field.

24 Quoted in John Jordan in *An Cosantóir*, June 1955, 'The Generalship of Peter Lacy' (Part II), p. 259.

25 My source (Jordon, 1955) reads as shown but was it possibly 'Loewenhaupt'? A Swedish general of that name was one of Charles XII's senior commanders. Perhaps this was a younger relative?

26 Various Wrangels appear in the Prussian, Swedish and Russian armies, in different periods.

27 I believe that this man was a close relative to Peter Lacy and that perhaps his youngest son, Franz Moritz, may have been named after this one. He fought against the Turks, the Swedes and under the great Suvorov in Italy, and died unmarried in 1820, according to the sources, though he would have been aged about 100 years. Therefore I have come to the conclusion that the first name was the father of the second who 'died unmarried'.

28 I haven't been able to find a single instance where Lacy was defeated when he was in command. In many other instances, when he was a subordinate, he was often the only successful officer in the Russian forces. This was notable in the early part of his career while serving under Peter the Great.

BIBLIOGRAPHY

Adlow, E., *Napoleon in Italy, 1796–1797* (William J. Rochfort, Boston, 1948)

Alexander, D.W., *Rod of Iron* (Scholarly Resources, Wilmington, DE, 1985)

Anon. [Peuchet?], translated by Samuel Mackay, *Campaigns of the Armies of France, in Prussia, Saxony, and Poland, under the command of his Majesty The Emperor and King, in MDCCCVI and VII. Etc.*, 4 volumes (Farrand, Mallory, and Co., Boston, 1808)

Anon., *The Attaché in Madrid or Sketches of the Court of Isabella II* (D. Appleton and Company, New York, 1856)

Anon., *The Irish Abroad and at Home, At the Court and in the Camp: With Souvenirs of 'The Brigade'. Reminiscences of an Emigrant Milesian* (D. Appleton and Company, New York, 1856)

Arnaud, R., *The Second Republic and Napoleon III* (G. P. Putnam's Sons, New York, 1933)

Asprey, R.B., *Frederick the Great: The Magnificent Enigma* (Ticknor & Fields, New York, 1986)

Aubry, O., *The Second Empire* (J. B. Lippincott Company, Philadelphia and New York, 1940)

Bagwell, R., *Ireland under the Stuarts*, 3 volumes (The Holland Press, London, 1963)

Bartlett, T. and K. Jeffery (editors), *A Military History of Ireland* (Cambridge University Press, Cambridge, 1996)

Beales, D., *Joseph II, In the Shadow of Maria Theresa 1741–1780*, Vol. 1 (Cambridge University Press, Cambridge, 1987)

Bengtsson, F.G., *The Sword Does Not Jest: The Heroic Life of King Charles XII of Sweden* (St Martin's Press, New York, 1960)

Bergamini, J.D., *The Spanish Bourbons: The History of a Tenacious Dynasty* (G. P. Putnam's Sons, New York, 1974)

Berkeley, G.F.H., *The Irish Battalion in the Papal Army of 1860* (The Talbot Press Ltd, Dublin and Cork, 1929)

Black, J. (editor), *The Origins of War in Early Modern Europe* (John Donald Publishers Ltd, Edinburgh, 1987)

Bredin, A.E.C., *A History of the Irish Soldier* (Century Books, Belfast, 1987)

Brockington, W.S. Jr. (editor), *Monro, His Expedition With the Worthy Scots Regiment Called Mac–Keys* (Praeger Publishers, Westport, Connecticut and London, 1999)

Browning, R., *The War of the Austrian Succession* (St Martin's Press, New York, 1993)

Castelot, A., *Napoleon* (Harper & Row, Publishers, New York, 1971)

Casway, J.I., *Owen Roe O'Neill and the struggle for Catholic Ireland* (University of Pennsylvania Press, Philadelphia, 1984)

Chandler, D. (editor), *Robert Parker and Comte de Mérode–Westerloo: The Marlborough Wars* (Archon Books, Hamden, CT, 1968)

(–) *Marlborough as Military Commander* (Charles Scribner's Sons, New York, 1973)

(–) *Dictionary of the Napoleonic Wars* (Macmillan Publishing Co. Inc., NY, 1979)

Childs, J., *The Army, James II, and the Glorious Revolution* (St Martin's Press, NY, 1980)

Christiansen, E., *The Origins of Military Power in Spain 1800–1854* (Oxford University Press, London, 1967)

Christiansen, R., *Paris Babylon: The Story of the Paris Commune* (Viking, New York, 1995)

Churchill, W.S., *Marlborough, His Life and Times*, 4 volumes (George G. Harrap & Co. Ltd, London, 1934)

Clarendon, E. [Hyde], Earl of, *The History of the Rebellion and Civil Wars in Ireland, etc.* (J. Wilford, London, 1720)

Clark, A., *The Old English in Ireland, 1625–42* (MacGibbon and Kee Ltd, Worcester and London, 1966)

Clark, G., *War and Society in the Seventeenth Century* (Cambridge University Press, Cambridge, 1958)

Clark, G.B., *Irish Brigades of France and Spain* (forthcoming)

Clarke, B., *Modern Spain, 1815–1898* (Cambridge University Press, Cambridge, 1906)

Clissold, S., *Bernardo O'Higgins and the Independence of Chile* (Frederick A. Praeger, Publishers, New York and Washington, 1969)

Colonie, M. de la., translated by W. C. Horsley, *The Chronicles of an Old Campaigner, 1692–1717* (E.P. Dutton and Company, New York, 1904)

Connelly, O., *The Gentle Bonaparte, A biography of Joseph, Napoleon's Older Brother* (The Macmillan Company, New York, 1968)

Connolly, S.J. (ed.), *The Oxford Companion to Irish History* (Oxford University Press, Oxford, 1998)

Crankshaw, E., *Maria Theresa* (The Viking Press, New York, 1969)

Crone, J.S., *A Concise Dictionary of Irish Biography* (Kraus Reprint, Nendeln, Liechtenstein, 1970)

Cronin, V., *Napoleon Bonaparte, An Intimate Biography* (William Morrow & Company, Inc., NY, 1972)

Curry, J., *An Historical and Critical Review of the Civil Wars in Ireland from the Reign of Queen Elizabeth, to the Settlement under King William*, 2 volumes (Luke White, Dublin, 1786)

D'Alton, J., *Illustrations, Historical and Genealogical, of King James's Irish Army List (1689)* (For the Subscribers, Dublin, 1855)

Defoe, D., *Life and Entertaining Adventures of Mrs Christian Davies commonly called Mother Ross* (Robert M. McBride & Company, New York, 1929)

[–] *The History of the most Remarkable Life, and Extraordinary Adventures, of the Truly Honourable Colonel Jaque, vulgarly call'd Colonel Jack, etc.* Vol. II (Basil Blackwell, Oxford, 1927)

De La Tour du Pin, Madame La Marquise, *Recollections of the Revolution and the Empire* (Brentano's, New York, 1920)

Detaille, E. and J. Richard, translated by M.C. Reinersten, *L'Armée Française, An Illustrated History of the French Army, 1790–1885* (Waxtel & Hasenauer, New York, 1992)

Drake, P., *Amiable Renegade: The Memoirs of Captain Peter Drake 1671–1753* (Stanford University Press and Oxford University Press, Stanford and London, 1960)

Duffy, C., *The Wild Goose and the Eagle: The Life of Marshal von Browne 1705–1757* (Chatto & Windus, London, 1964)

(–) *The Army of Frederick the Great* (David & Charles, London, 1974)

(–) *The Army of Maria Theresa: The Armed Forces of Imperial Austria 1740–1780* (Hippocrene Books, New York, 1977)

(–) *Russia's Military Way to the West, Origins and Nature of Russian Military Power 1700–1800* (Routledge & Kegan Paul, London, Boston and Henley, 1981)

(–) *The Military Life of Frederick the Great* (Atheneum, New York, 1986)

(–) *Siege Warfare: The Fortress in the Early Modern World 1494–1660* (Barnes and Noble Books, New York, 1996)

Dupuy, R.E. and T.N. Dupuy, *The Encyclopedia of Military History, from 3500 BC to the Present* (Harper & Row Publishers, New York, 1977)

Dupuy, T.N., *The Military Life of Gustavus Adolphus, Father of Modern War* (Franklin Watts, Inc., New York, 1969)

Elting, J.R., *Swords Around a Throne: Napoleon's Grande Armée* (The Free Press, New York, 1988)

Ergang, R., *The Potsdam Führer: Frederick William I, Father of Prussian Militarism* (Columbia University Press, New York, 1941)

Erlanger, P., *Louis XIV* (Praeger Publishers, New York and Washington, 1970)

Fischer, T.A., *The Scots in Sweden* (Otto Schulze & Co., Edinburgh, 1907)

Francis, D., *The First Peninsular War 1702–1713* (St Martin's Press, New York, 1975)

Frey, L. and M. Frey, *The Treaties on the War of the Spanish Succession, An Historical and Critical Dictionary* (Greenwood Press, Westport, CT. and London, 1995)

Gallaher, J.G., *Napoleon's Irish Legion* (Carbondale and Edwardsville, Southern Illinois University Press, 1993)

Gaydon

Gilbert, J.T., *A Jacobite Narrative of the War in Ireland 1688–1691* (Barnes & Noble Inc., New York, 1971)

Grehan, I., *The Dictionary of Irish Family Names* (Roberts Rinehart Publishers, Boulder, CO, 1997)

Guerrini, M., *Napoleon and Paris, Thirty Years of History* (Cassell, London, 1970)

Hall, J.R., *The Bourbon Restoration* (Alston Rivers, Ltd, London, 1909)

Hamilton, Count A., *Memoirs of Count Gramont* (David McKay, Publisher, Philadelphia, n.d.)

Hanotaux, G., *Contemporary France*, 4 volumes (Archibald Constable & Co. Ltd, London, 1909)

Hart, J. R., *The Bourbon Restoration* (Alston Rivers, Ltd, London, 1909)

Hayes, R., *Irish Swordsmen of France* (M.H. Gill and Son Ltd, Dublin, 1934)

(–) *Biographical Dictionary of Irishmen in France* (M.H. Gill & Son, Dublin, 1949)

Henderson, N., *Prince Eugen of Savoy, a biography* (Weidenfeld and Nicholson, London, 1964)

Hennessy, M., *The Wild Geese: The Irish Soldier in Exile* (Sidgwick & Jackson, London, 1973)

Henry, G., *The Irish Military Community in Spanish Flanders, 1586–1621* (Irish Academic Press, Dublin, 1992)

Hill, J.M., *Celtic Warfare 1595–1763* (Gregg Revivals, Aldershot, UK, 1993)

Hochedlinger, M., *Austria's Wars of Emergence 1683–1797* (Longman, London, UK, 2003)

Hogan, E. (editor), *The History of the War of Ireland from 1641 to 1653, By a British Officer, of the Regiment of Sir John Clottworthy* (McGlashan & Gill, Dublin, 1873)

Holmes, J.D.L., *Honour and Fidelity, The Louisiana Infantry Regiment and the Louisiana Militia Companies, 1766–1821* (private printing, Birmingham, AL, 1965)

Holmes, R., *The Road to Sedan, The French Army 1866–70* (Royal Historical Society and Humanities Press Inc., London and New Jersey, 1984)

Holt, E., *The Carlist Wars in Spain* (Dufour Editions, Chester Springs, PA, 1967)

(–) *Plon–Plon, The Life of Prince Napoleon [1822–1891]* (Michael Joseph, London, 1973)

Hutton, R., *Charles the Second, King of England, Scotland, and Ireland* (Clarendon Press, Oxford, 1989)

Jennings, B., *Wild Geese in Spanish Flanders 1582–1700* (Irish Manuscripts Commission, Dublin, 1964)

Johnstone, C. de., *A Memoir of the 'Forty-five'* (The Folio Society, London, 1958)

Kamen, H., *The War of the Spanish Succession 1700–15* (Indiana University Press, Bloomington, 1969)

Kann, R. A., *A History of the Habsburg Empire 1526–1918* (University of California Press, Berkeley/Los Angeles/London, 1977)

Kaplan, H., *Russia and the Outbreak of the Seven Years' War* (University of California Press, Berkeley and Los Angeles, 1968)

Kennett, L., *The French Armies in the Seven Years' War: A study in military organisation and administration* (Duke University Press, Durham, NC, 1967)

Kenyon, J. and J. Ohlmeyer (editors), *The Civil Wars: A Military History of England, Scotland and Ireland 1638–1660* (Oxford University Press, New York, 1998)

Kiernan, V. G., *The Revolution of 1854 in Spanish History* (The Clarendon Press, Oxford, 1966)

Klarwill, V. von (editor), translated by L. S. R. Byrne, *Fugger's Newsletters 1568–1605,* Second series (London, n.d.)

Kornauth, F. von., *Das Heer Maria Theresias* (Edition Tusch, Wien, 1973)

Kotasek, E., *Feldmarschall Graf Lacy: Ein Leben für Österreichs Heer* (Ferdinand Berger, Horn, Austria, 1956)

Lachouque, H., adapted from the French by A.S.K. Brown, *The Anatomy of Glory: Napoleon and his Guard* (Brown University, Providence and London, 1961)

Lackey, S.W., *The Rebirth of the Hapsburg Army, Friedrich Beck and the rise of the General Staff* (Westport, Connecticut & London, 1995)

Langer, W.L. (ed.), *An Encyclopedia of World History* (Houghton Mifflin, Company, Boston, 1968)

Latimer, E.W., *Spain in the Nineteenth Century* (A.C. McClurg and Company, Chicago, 1897)

Lisk, J., *The Struggle for Supremacy in the Baltic, 1600–1725* (Minerva Press, London, 1968)

Longworth, P., *The Three Empresses: Catherine I, Anne and Elizabeth of Russia* (Holt, Rinehart and Winston, New York, 1972)

Luvaas, J., *Napoleon on the Art of War* (The Free Press, New York, 1999)

Lynch, J., *Borubon Spain, 1700–1808* (Basil Blackwell, Oxford, 1989)

MacLysaght, E., *Irish Families, Their Names, Arms and Origins* (Crown Publishers, New York, 1972)

Manstein, C.H. von., *Contemporary Memoirs of Russia, from the year 1727 to 1744*, revised from 1770 London Edition (Longman, Brown, Green and Longmans, London, 1856)

McDermot, J.F. (ed.), *The Spanish in the Mississippi Valley 1762–1804* (University of Illinois Press, Urbana, 1974)

McDonnell, H., *The Wild Geese of the Antrim MacDonnells* (Irish Academic Press, Dublin, 1996)

McEntee, Girard L., *Military History of the World War* (Scribner's and Sons, New York, 1937)

McGee, J.A., *Sketches of Irish Soldiers in Every Land* (J.A. McGee, Publisher, New York, 1873)

McKay, D., *Prince Eugene of Savoy* (Thames and Hudson, London, 1977)

Meehan, C.P., *The Confederation of Kilkenny* (James Duffy, Dublin, 1860)

Meehan-Waters, B., *Autocracy & Aristocracy: The Russian Service Elite of 1730* (Rutgers University Press, New Brunswick, NJ, 1982)

Miller, P., *James (III)* (St Martin's Press, NY, 1971)

Mitchell, A., *Victors and Vanquished: The German Influence on Army and Church in France after 1870* (The University of North Carolina Press, Chapel Hill and London, 1984)

Moffat, M.M., *Maria Theresa* (E. P. Dutton and Company, New York, 1911)

Monro, Robert (edited by W.S. Monro jr), *Monro, His Expedition with the Worthy Scots Regiment called Mac-Keys* (Praeger Pubishers, Connecticut and London, 1999)

Murphy, J.A., *Justin MacCarthy, Lord Mountcashel Commander of the First Irish Brigade in France* (Cork University Press, Cork, 1959)

Nosworthy, B., *The Anatomy of Victory: Battle Tactics 1689–1763* (Hippocrene Books, New York, 1990)

O'Callaghan, J.C., *History of the Irish Brigades in the Service of France* (Glasgow, 1870)

O'Connell, M.J., *The Last Colonel of the Irish Brigade, Count O'Connell and Old Irish Life at Home and Abroad 1745–1833*, 2 volumes (in one) (Tower Books, Cork, 1977)

O'Connor, M., *Air Aces of the Austro–Hungarian Empire, 1914–1918* (Flying Machines Press, Mountain View, CA, 1986)

O'Conor, M., *Military History of the Irish Nation Comprising a Memoir of the Irish Brigade in the Service of France, etc.* (Hodges and Smith, Dublin, 1845)

O'Hart, J., *The Irish and Anglo–Irish Landed Gentry When Cromwell Came to Ireland* (Barnes & Noble Inc., New York, 1969, reprint of 1884 edition)

O'Kelly, C., edited by J. C. O'Callaghan, *Macariæ Excidium, or The Destruction of Cyprus being a secret history of the War of the Revolution in Ireland* (The Irish Archæological Society, Dublin, 1850)

Ohlmeyer, J.H., *Civil War and Restoration in the Three Stuart Kingdoms, The Career of Randal MacDonnell, Marquis of Antrim, 1609–1683* (Cambridge University Press, Cambridge, 1993)

Parker, G., *The Army of Flanders and the Spanish Road 1567–1659: The Logistics of Spanish Victory and Defeat in the Low Countries' Wars* (Cambridge University Press, Cambridge, 1972)

Parker, G. and L. M. Smith (editors), *The General Crisis of the Seventeenth Century* (Routledge & Kegan Paul, London, 1978)

Parkes, V. (ed.), *Siege! Spain and Britain, Battle of Pensacola March 9–May 8, 1781* (Pensacola Historical Society, Pensacola, 1981)

Petrie, C., *The Jacobite Movement: The First Phase 1688–1716* (Eyre & Spottiswode, London, 1948)

(–) *The Jacobite Movement: The Last Phase 1716–1807* (Eyre & Spottiswode, London, 1950)

(–) *The Marshal Duke of Berwick: The Picture of an Age* (Eyre & Spottiswode, London, 1953)

(–) *King Charles III of Spain: An Enlightened Despot* (Constable & Company, Ltd, London, 1971)

(–) *The Great Tyrconnel, A Chapter in Anglo–Irish Relations* (The Mercier Press, Cork and Dublin, 1972)

Polontsov, A.A., *Russian Biographical Dictionary*, Vol. 10 (St Petersburg, 1914)

Porch, D., *The French Foreign Legion: A complete history of the legendry fighting force* (HarperCollins Publishers, New York, 1991)

Prendergast, J.P., *The Cromwellian Settlement of Ireland* (Longman, Green, Longman, Roberts, & Green, London, 1865)

Rice, T.T., *Elizabeth, Empress of Russia* (Praeger Publishers, New York, Washington, 1970)

Roberts, M., *Essays in Swedish History* (University of Minnesota Press, Minneapolis, 1967)

Rothenberg, G., *The Army of Francis Joseph* (Perdue University Press, West Lafayette, 1998)

Schevill, F., *The Great Elector* (The University of Chicago Press, Chicago, 1947)

Schom, A., *Napoleon Bonaparte* (Harper Collins Publishers, New York, 1997)

Schreiber, G., *Des Kaisers Reiterei: Österreichische Kavallerie in vier Jahrhunderten* (F. Speidel-Verlag, Wein, 1967)

Seaton, A., *The Austro–Hungarian Army of the Seven Years' War* (Osprey Men-at-Arms, Reading, 1973)

Simms, J.G., *Jacobite Ireland 1685–91* (Routledge & Kegan Paul and University of Toronto Press, London and Toronto, 1969)

Smith, C.R., *Marines in the Revolution: A History of the Continental Marines in the American Revolution 1775–1783* (History and Museums Division, Headquarters, US Marine Corps, Washington, DC, 1975)

Soloviev, S.M., *Istoriia Rossii s drevnei-shikh vremen* (Moscow, 1959–1966)

Stenger, G., *The Return of Louis XVIII* (William Heinemann, London, 1909)

Stradling, R.A., *The Spanish Monarchy and Irish Mercenaries: The Wild Geese in Spain, 1618–68* (Irish Academic Press, Dublin, 1994)

Stuart, J., translated by A. Lytton Sells, *James II, The Memoirs of, his campaigns as Duke of York 1652–1660* (Indiana University Press, Bloomington, Indiana, 1962)

Sturgill, C.C., *Marshal Villars and the War of the Spanish Succession* (University of Kentucky Press, Lexington, 1965)

Szabo, F.A.J., *Kaunitz and Enlightened Absolutism 1753–1780* (Cambridge University Press, NY, 1994)

Tapié, V-L., *The Rise and Fall of the Habsburg Monarchy* (Praeger Publishers, New York, 1971)

Tate, L. (ed.), *Analecta Hibernica No. 21, Franco-Irish Correspondence December 1688–1691* (Stationary Office for the Irish Manuscripts Commission, Dublin, 1959)

Tranie, J. and J.-C. Carmigniani from the notes and manuscripts of Commandant H. Lachouque, *Napoleon's War in Spain, The French Peninsular Campaigns, 1807–1814* (Arms and Armour Press, London, Harrisburg, 1982)

Trevelyn, G.M., *England Under the Stuarts, Volume V, History of England* (Methuen & Co. Ltd, London, 1961)

(–) *Ramillies and the Union with Scotland: England under Queen Anne*, Vol. II (Longmans, Green and Co., London, New York, Toronto, 1932)

Tulard, J., *Dictionnaire du Second Empire* (Librarie Arthème Fayard, 1995)

Walsh, M.K., *Spanish Knights of Irish Origin: Documents from Continental Archives*, Volumes I, II and IV (Irish Manuscripts Commission, Dublin, 1960, 1965 and 1978)

(–) *The O'Neills in Spain* (The National University, Dublin, c. 1957)

(–) *The MacDonnells of Antrim on the Continent* (The National University, Dublin, c. 1960)

Warner, O., *The Sea and the Sword: The Baltic 1630–1945* (William Morrow and Company, New York, 1965)

Wauchop, P., *Patrick Sarsfield and the Williamite War* (Irish Academic Press, Dublin, 1992)

Weygand, M., *Turenne, Marshal of France* (Houghton Mifflin Company, Boston, 1930)

White, J.M., *Marshal of France: The Life and Times of Maurice de Saxe* (Rand McNally & Company, Chicago, 1962)

Wieczynski, J.L. (ed.), *The Modern Encyclopedia of Russian and Soviet History*, Vol. 19. (Academic International Press, 1981)

Williams, R.L., *Napoleon III and the Stoeffel Affair* (High Plains Publishing Company, Inc., Worland, WY, 1993)

Windrow, M. and F.K. Mason, *A Concise Dictionary of Military Biography* (Windrow and Greene Ltd, London, 1990)

Wormeley, K.P. (ed.), *The Prince De Ligne: His memoirs, letters, and miscellaneous papers*, 2 volumes (Hardy, Pratt & Company, Boston, 1902)

Journals

Casway, J., 'Henry O'Neill and the formation of the Irish regiment in the Netherlands, 1605', *Irish Historical Studies*, Vol. XVIII, No. 72, September 1973

Bjork, David K. (ed.), 'Documents relating to Alexandro O'Reilly and the expedition sent out by him from New Orleans to Natchioches, 1769-1770', *Louisiana Historical Quarterly* VII, No. 1 (January 1924), pp. 20–39.

Henning, J., 'Irish Soldiers in the Thirty Years' war', *The Journal of the Royal Society of Antiquaries of Ireland*, Vol. LXXXII, Part I, 1952, pp. 28–36

Jordon, J., 'Wild Geese in the North; (1) Denmark and Norway', *An Cosantóir, The Irish Defence Journal*, Vol. XIV, No. 2, February

1954, pp. 77–82

(–) 'Wild Geese in the North; (2) Sweden', *An Cosantóir, The Irish Defence Journal,* Vol. XIV, No. 3, March 1954, pp. 147–150

(–) 'The Wild Geese in the North; (3) Russia', *An Cosantóir, The Irish Defence Journal,* Vol. XIV, No. 4, April 1954, pp. 192–196

(–) 'The Generalship of Peter Lacy; Part I.—The Crimean Campaigns, 1737 and 1738', *An Cosantóir, The Irish Defence Journal,* Vol. XV, No. 5, May 1955, pp. 208–213

(–) 'The Generalship of Peter Lacy; Part II. —The Campaign of Willmanstrand, 1741', *An Cosantóir, The Irish Defence Journal,* Vol. XV, No. 6, June 1955, pp. 256–263

Ostwald, J., 'The "Decisive" Battle of Ramillies, 1706, Prerequisites for Decisiveness in Early Modern Warfare', *The Journal of Military History,* Vol. 64, No. 3, July 2000, pp. 649–677

The Irish Sword, Vol. I, No. 1 to Vol. XXVI No. 105, articles, notes, replies, including:

Alymer, R. J., 'The Imperial Service of William Alymer, 1800–14', Vol. XX, No. 81, Summer 1997, pp. 207–216

Beerman, E., 'Alexander O'Reilly, an Irish soldier in the service of Spain', Vol. XV, No. 59, Winter 1982, pp. 101–104

Bruns, J. Edgar., 'Captain Owen Sheridan and the "15"', Vol. III, No. 11, Winter 1957, pp. 126–127

(–) 'The Early Years and Diplomatic Missions of Sir Thomas Sheridan (1684–1746)', Vol. III, No. 13, Winter 1958, pp. 256–259

Carney, D., Jr., 'Notes. [General Count Daniel O'Mahoney, Hero of Cremona]', Vol. XIV, No. 54, Summer 1980, pp. 95–98

Carroll, F., 'Replies [Three Irish Soldiers, Query No. 45, Vol. II, p. 238 and Reply No. 27, Vol. II, p. 378]', Vol. III, No. 10, Summer 1957, pp. 71–72

Clark, G. B., 'Notes [Napoleon's Opinion of General Kilmaine]', Vol. VI, No. 24, Summer 1964, pp. 216

de Courcy Ireland, J.E., 'Baron Gottfried von Banfield (The last surviving Irish-descended officer of the Hapsburg navy)', Vol. XI, No. 44, Summer 1974, pp. 180–184

de Courcy Ireland, J., 'Notes [Banfield]' Vol. XI, No. 45, Winter 1974, pp. 249–250

de Courcy Ireland, J., 'Notes [Field Marshal Count Laval Nugent]', Vol. V, No. 18, Summer 1961, p. 62

de Courcy Ireland, J., 'Notes [The Ultonia Regiment at Oran]', Vol. XII, No. 48, Summer 1976, pp. 246–247

de Courcy Ireland, J., 'Henry MacDonnell, teniente general in the Spanish Navy', Vol. XV, No. 58, Summer 1982, pp. 23–29

de Courcy Ireland, J. 'Notes [Alexander O'Reilly]. Vol. XV, No. 60, Summer 1983, pp. 201–202

Duffy, C. J., 'The Irish in the Imperial Service, Some Observations', Vol. V, No. 19, Winter 1961, pp. 69–74

(–) 'The Irish at Hochkirch, 14 October 1758', Vol. XII, No. 48, Summer 1976, pp. 212–220

(–) 'More light on the Irish in the service of Imperial Austria', Vol. XV, No. 61, Winter 1983, pp. 267–270

Editor, 'A Trooper of FitzJames's Regiment, Irish Brigade, circa 1740', Vol. 1, No. 1, 1949–1950, p. 1, colour plate by P. White

Editor, 'Notes [The Hon. Captain Plunket's Hussars in Spain, 1706]', Vol. II, No. 9, Winter 1956, pp. 358–360

Editor, 'Notes [The Mac Mahon Sword]', Vol. 5, No. 18, Summer 1961, p. 63

Editor [with Patrick Logan], 'Some Irishmen in the Imperial Service', Vol. 5, No. 19, Winter 1961, pp. 75–80

Editor, 'Notes [Feldzeugmeister Thomas Baron Brady, 1752–1827]', Vol. VI. No. 26, Winter 1964, pp. 288–289

Editor, 'Notes [Banfield]' Vol. XVI, No. 65, Winter 1986, pp. 333–334

Fitzsimon, R.D., 'Irish Swordsmen in the Imperial Service in the 30 Years' War', Vol. IX, No. 34, Summer 1969, pp. 22–31

Gallwey, H.D., 'Notes [Captain General Juan Sherlock]', Vol. XV, No. 58, Summer 1982, pp. 59–60

Garland, J.L., 'Notes [Regiment of Clare–captured flags]', Vol. II, No. 6, Summer 1955, pp. 138–139

Garland, J.L., 'Replies [Irish Units in the Imperial Service]', Vol. II, No. 8, Summer 1956, p. 302

Garland, J. L., 'Notes [Some more Irish officers in Imperial service.]' Vol. XVI, No. 63, 1985, pp. 123–124

Giblin, C., 'Roger O'Connor, an Irishman in the French and Papal Service', Vol. II, No. 9, Winter 1956, pp. 309–314

Graham, D.L., 'Replies [Colonel Taaf]',Vol. XII, No. 48, Summer 1976, p. 258

(–) 'Replies [Colonel Taaf],' Vol. XIII, No. 53, Winter 1979, p. 383

Griffin, W.D., 'Irish generals and Spanish politics under Fernando VII', Vol. X, No. 38, Summer 1971, pp. 1–9

Grosjean, A. and S. Murdoch., 'Irish soldiers in Swedish service 1609–1613', Vol. XXIV, No. 96, Winter 2004, pp. 161–163

Hayes, R.J., 'Notes [Some Irish officers in the Spanish Service, 1778]', Vol. 1, No. 3, 1951–1952, pp. 229–230

(–) 'Reflections of an Irish Brigade officer', Vol. I, No. 2, 1950–1951, pp. 68–74

(–) 'General Thomas Arthur Count Lally', Vol. I, No. 3, 1951–1952, p. 197

(–) 'Irish Casualties in the French Military Service', Vol. I, No. 3, 1951–1952, pp. 198–201

(–) 'Notes [A Notable Irish Soldier–Thomas O'Meara]', Vol. I, No. 4, 1952–1953, p. 335

Holmes, J.D.L., 'Some Irish officers in Spanish Louisiana', Vol. VI, No. 25, Winter 1964, pp. 234–247

Jordon, J., 'John Delap: An Irish seaman in Russia', *The Irish Sword*, Vol. II, No. 5, 1954, pp. 54–61. Lambert, E.T.D., 'Notes [Irish generals and Spanish politics under Fernando VII]', Vol. X, No. 39, Winter 1971, pp. 171–172

McCarthy, D.J., 'The Kalabalik', *History Today*, June 1965, pp. 391–399

MacCauley, J.A., 'Lally-Tollendal in India, 1758–1761', Vol. V, No. 19, Winter 1961, pp. 81–87

Melvin, P., 'Notes [The Irish and the Vaudois]', Vol. XII, No. 49, Winter 1976, pp. 306–310

Millett, B., 'Notes [Hamilton's Regiment]', Vol. IV, No. 17, Winter 1960, pp. 269–270

Mullen, T.J. Jr., 'Campo Santo–The Darkling Plain, 1743', Vol. XI, No. 45, Winter 1974, pp. 222–225

Murphy, W.S., 'The Irish Brigade of France at the Siege of Savannah, 1779', Vol. II, No. 6, Summer 1955, pp. 95–102

Murphy, W.S., 'Replies [Irish Units in the Imperial Service]', Vol. III, No. 10, Summer 1957, pp. 74–75

Murtagh, H., 'Two Irish officers and the campaign to relieve Vienna, 1683', Vol. XV, No. 61, Winter 1983, pp. 255–257

(–) 'The assassination of Wallenstein, 1634', Vol. XVI, No. 62, 1984, p. 48

O'Briain, L. (ed.), 'The Chevalier Gaydon's Memoir of the Regiment of Dillon, 1738', From Vol. III, Nos. 11–17, 19–24

O'Carroll, D., 'Marshal Saxe', Vol. XIX, No. 78, Winter 1995, pp. 249–252

O'Cochlain, R.S., 'Count O'Donell and the Austrian Emperor', Vol. II, No. 8, Summer 1956, pp. 267–269

(–) 'The O'Donnells in Austria', Vol. V, No. 21, Winter 1962, pp. 197–206

(–) 'Leopold O'Donnell and the Spanish-Moroccan Campaign, 1859–60', Vol. VII, No. 28, Summer 1966, pp. 181–195

O'Doneven, 'Coote and Lally–Two Irish Personalities at War', Vol. VII, No. 28, Summer 1966, pp. 231–233

O'Hannracháin, E., 'An analysis of the Fitzjames Cavalry Regiment, 1737', Vol. XIX, No. 78, Winter 1995, pp. 253–276

O'Malley, K.J., 'Notes [Francis Patrick O'Neillan Baron Laimpruch zu Epurz]', Vol. XXI, No. 84, Winter 1998, pp. 220–221

O'Neill, J. and F.G. Thompson, 'Field Marshal Francis Maurice Lacy (1725–1801)', Vol. XVII, No. 66, Summer 1987, pp. 1–3

O'Neill, J., 'Conflicting loyalties, Irish regiments in the imperial service 1689–1710', Vol. XVII, No. 67, Winter 1987/Summer 1988, pp. 116–119

O'Ryan, W.D., 'Lieutenant-General Tomás O'Ryan y Vazquez', Vol. VI, No. 23, Winter 1963, pp. 81–87

Petrie, C., 'The Irish Brigade at Fontenoy', Vol. 1, No. 3, 1951–1952, pp. 166–172

(–) 'The Battle of Almansa', Vol. II, No. 5, 1954, pp. 6–11

(–) 'Irishmen in the Forty-five', Vol. II, No. 8, Summer 1956, pp. 275–282

Pierre G., 'Mercenaries Irlandais au Service de la France (1635–1664)', Vol. XII, No. 26, Summer 1965, pp. 58–75

Pyne, P., 'Irish Soldiers in Barcelona, 1653–4', Vol. XIX, No. 78, Winter 1995, pp. 277–289

Steele, R.V., 'FitzJames's Regiment of Horse of the Irish Brigade in the French Service', Vol. II, No. 7, Winter 1955, pp. 188–194

(–) 'The Regiment of Dillon of the Irish Brigade in the French Service', Vol. III, No. 11, Winter 1957, pp. 93–97

Thompson, F.G. and H. Murtagh, 'A Portrait of Lieutenant Field Marshal William O'Kelly (1703–67)', Vol. XV, No. 61, Winter 1983, p. 217

Van Brock, F.W., 'Lieutenant-General Robert Dillon, 1754–1831', Vol. XIV, No. 55, Winter 1980, pp. 172–187

Walsh, M., 'Lieutenant-General Ricardo Wall (1694–1778)', Vol. II, No. 6, Summer 1955, pp. 88–94

(–) 'From Overseas Archives [Regiment of Limerick. First of November, 1718]', Vol. III, No. 13, Winter 1958, pp. 261–262

(–) 'From Overseas Archives [Colonel's commission for the second Duke of Liria]', Vol. III, No. 13, Winter 1958, pp. 265–266

(–) 'From Overseas Archives [Colonel Thomas Barry]', Vol. III, No. 13, Winter 1958, pp. 267–268

(–) 'From Overseas Archives [O'Mahoney, from Luzzara, 26 September 1702]', Vol. III, No. 13, Winter 1958, pp. 268–271

(–) 'From Overseas Archives [Colonel Bourck, from Cremona, 9 February, 1702]', Vol. III, No. 13, Winter 1958, pp. 271–272

(–) 'Notes towards a biographical dictionary of the Irish in Spain', Vol. IV, No. 14, Summer 1959, pp. 5–15

(–) 'Further Notes on some Irishmen in the Imperial Service', Vol. 6, No. 22, Summer 1963, pp. 46–51

(–) continued from above. 'Further Notes on some Irishmen in the Imperial Service', Vol. VI, No. 23, Winter 1963, pp. 70–75

(–) continued from above. 'Further Notes on some Irishmen in the Imperial Service', Vol. VI, No. 24, Summer 1964, pp. 166–170

(–) 'Notes. [Dr. Don Thadeo Clery, Head Chaplain of the Regiment of Tyrconnell in Spanish Service]', Vol. XVII, No. 67, Winter 1987/Summer 1988, pp. 131–132

(–) ' Letters from Fontenoy', Vol. XIX, No. 78, Winter 1995 237–248

Walsh, P.V., 'Notes [Alexander O'Reilly]', Vol. XVII, No. 68, 1989, pp. 215–216

INDEX

Y

Z